GRACE ENOUGH FOR THREE

BY DON CLIFFORD

*Losing Three Children
but Finding God's All-Sufficient Grace*

GRACE ENOUGH FOR THREE

CONTENTS

Page

v

PART TWO

PREFACE

My desire in writing this book is to be obedient to what I feel God has directed me to do by sharing our family's testimony of God's all-sufficient grace. God promised us in his Word that while he wouldn't always spare us trials, His grace would always be sufficient to keep us through those trials. As we struggled with the deep emotional and spiritual issues surrounding the deaths of three of our children, my wife Karen, my two daughters Vicki and Rebecca, and I myself fought to keep our faith intact. Through the experiences of losing Michael, Rachel and Beth, we suffered great pain and were at times distressed, confused, bewildered and dismayed by what was happening to our family.

We are not theologians, nor are we psychologists, but we are life-long Christians who had never found God to come up short in the area of Grace bestowed upon his children. As God's confused children, we sought comfort and guidance through those dark valleys from the Holy Spirit and the Word of God. The observations and conclusions we share are simply testimonies of how God has dealt with us, shaped us, and perhaps even spoken to us through our experiences. They are hopefully validated to some degree by the survival of our faith and our resultant walk with God.

While the primary aim of the book is to glorify God, we hope that along the way it will meet a variety of needs. We wish to encourage and sustain those of you who are currently in sorrow over the loss of a loved one and I hope to show you how we survived and to provide some help for you during your grief process. I know from experience that someone who has just lost a loved one is not usually interested in reading about someone else's grief. However,

I have shared portions of Part 2 with family and friends who have had recent losses and they said it was helpful to them. As a result, my wife, Karen, and I have published a companion book entitled "Heavenly Grief," with the subtitle, "A Christian Guide to Spiritual and Emotional Healing." Maybe Part 2 is where you want to begin if that is what brought you to our story. We want to encourage you to know that there is life and happiness after the deepest sorrow. Hopefully, we can help you avoid the morass of self pity and depression that so easily ensnares all of us during periods of personal loss and the accompanying grief.

We also hope all Christians will be encouraged and inspired to see and realize that God provides for his children in the most tragic of circumstances, and even brings life abundantly out of the ashes. Our story tells how God ultimately brought us into a glorious and intimate relationship with himself in and through our losses. Most importantly, we have learned that God is completely in control of his universe; his will is unerringly perfect and his grace is completely sufficient. How God brought us to this understanding is a testimony we feel compelled to share.

Finally, we dare to hope we can be of some assistance to chaplains, pastors and other counselors, whether professional or personal, in understanding the needs of individuals and families who are going through grief situations.

I would like to express appreciation and thanks to several individuals who have assisted in the preparation of this book. Writing coach Mike Fak has added much to the story through his encouragements and suggestions. Most importantly, I want to acknowledge my wife Karen, and my daughters Vicki and Rebecca, who reviewed, reminded and rebuked as required, to ensure an accurate rendering of the details of our experiences. While it is I who wrote these words, the story we are about to share with you is our family's collective testimony.

I am assured in my spirit that this book is divinely motivated (I didn't say inspired) and I hope that we have been sufficiently tuned in to the Holy Spirit to allow us to claim his help and guidance in its preparation. Our prayer is that God will be glorified through our testimony and that it will encourage people everywhere to know God's grace is indeed sufficient for every situation.

PART 1

PROLOGUE

November, 1956

"A furious squall came up and the waves broke over the boat so that it was nearly swamped." Mark 4: 37

Heavy overcast skies and choppy seas greeted our sleek man of war as we slipped past the breakwater of the bustling Kaohsiung harbor. Chinese junks and rusty merchant ships plied the murky waters of the busy port, making way as the U.S.S. Samuel N. Moore cruised by. A noisy flock of sea gulls flying alongside kept us company as our small group of sailors manned our departure duty station on the fantail. A light rain began to pelt our faces as we huddled against the twin five-inch gun mount for protection from the rain and the cold north Pacific wind. The gray skies were reflected in the roiling water churned up by the twin screws beneath our feet as our ship began to pick up speed, but couldn't gain on the persistent sea gulls flying alongside. We were steaming towards the Formosa Straits, the narrow channel of water separating Mainland China from the island nation of Formosa, soon to become known as Taiwan.

A stocky, balding old salt nicknamed Marty grumbled in our small huddle "Boys, we're in for a stormy patrol. Seems like there's always a monster gale blowin' in these straits." Marty's resemblance to the actor Ernest Borgnine earned him his nickname, but the threatening clouds and brisk wind gave credence to his words. A couple of other veterans grunted their agreement. We all pulled our foul weather jackets a little tighter around our necks as we steamed toward the stormy channel. It wouldn't be long before we would agree with Marty's assessment of what we were in for.

This would be my first patrol through the dangerous and stormy Formosa Straits. I had reported aboard the Moore, designated as DD747, in Long Beach California a few months before, as an eighteen year old graduate of the Navy's Gun Fire Control School. I was still drying behind the ears when I joined the Navy as a 17-year old kid fresh out of high school. After boot camp I spent a year getting trained in electronics and gun fire control at the Great Lakes Naval Training Center, just north of Chicago. After being assigned to the Moore I learned that the nickname of the ship was the Rammin' Sammy Moore. That nickname resulted from an earlier incident when the Moore rammed a Japanese fishing boat in the fog off of Honshu, killing eight fishermen aboard.

Our ship was now beginning its annual 6-month tour of WesPac, meaning in Navy-talk the western Pacific region, including Japan, the Philippines, Taiwan, and as far south as Guam. We spent much of the time training at sea, usually pulling carrier escort duty. However, there would be no carriers to guard on this patrol. The next two weeks in the Formosa Straits would be the most difficult work of the six-month tour. Because of the perpetual gale in the straits, it was the most dreaded duty in the Pacific.

Eight years and a war in Korea hadn't lessened the atmosphere of hostility between the Communists on the mainland and Chiang Kai-Shek's exiled army on the island. Our destroyer was a warship built for speed and agility, carrying three twin five-inch gun turrets, several 40-millimeter anti-aircraft cannons and a supply of depth charges and torpedoes. Three hundred men called the USS Moore home, crammed like sardines into the cramped crew spaces below decks.

The Moore was steaming into the channel to provide a US presence in the region and to help discourage Mao's army from invading the island, a move that the Chinese on Formosa were expecting at any time. As we huddled by the gun mount, Charlie, a tall bespectacled buddy of mine from Boston, offered, "Well, if the weather is too rough, at least we shouldn't have any trouble from the Reds.

They wouldn't want to fight in this weather any more than we would." We weren't really expecting any show of armed force from the Mainland Chinese. There hadn't been any saber rattling since the Reds had lobbed a few artillery shells at the small offshore islands of Qeumoy and Matsu a few months before. Marty grumbled back, "I'd rather have a little excitement from the Chinese than what we're in for." Marty usually knew what he was talking about, so we weren't looking forward to the reception awaiting us in the channel.

We had barely cleared the wake of Formosa before the ship began to rock and roll and we knew we were in for two gut-wrenching weeks at sea. We quickly stashed our gear and battened down the hatches in preparation for rough seas. By nightfall our ship was on station, battling to maintain a heading into the howling gale winds and moun-tainous seas; seas that seemed to be waiting to show us what nature is capable of and to remind us who is in charge out there.

I was bunking in the aft crew quarters right above the twin screws that drove the 300-foot long sliver of steel through the water. I learned what countless other seamen have learned over the centu-ries. The sea is boss. If you are going to invade its territory, you do it on the sea's terms. At night we strapped ourselves into our bunks to keep from being rolled out onto the steel deck as the ship rolled up to 30 degrees from side to side. Fortunately, my fairly solid 5'10" frame fit nicely into the bunk, unlike the much taller Boston Charlie whose feet dangled off the end of his.

Each time our ship crested a swell it would then nose down into the next cavernous trough. The stern would rise out of the sea so high that the propellers would break free of their watery restric-tion. With no resistance the propeller shafts beneath our deck would scream as they revved up to several times their normal rpm. Then as the nose of the ship came up out of the watery depths, the tortured screws would dig into the water again and shudder as they found their normal resistance and slowed to a more normal rotation. The rolling of the ship and the intermittent screaming of the screws made sleep difficult to find, but the snoring of a veteran seaman in the bunk below mine reassured me that we weren't in any great danger. As his snores helped me relax and become drowsy, the pure exhaus-tion from battling the sea finally brought fitful slumber.

Despite the storm and the heaving motion of the vessel, life aboard ship went on, following a modified routine. At 0630 the boson's whistle sounded over the PA and the call of "Reveille, reveille, all hands heave to and trice up" sounded throughout the ship. I unstrapped and sleepily heaved myself out of my third level bunk. After retrieving a set of dungarees from my footlocker, I dressed and triced my suspended bunk up to the bulkhead, an action made more difficult by the crowd of grumbling sailors trying to keep their balance while getting dressed. With all of the bunks triced up, the passageway was opened so the men could move about more easily in the area, always holding onto a nearby support.

After a trip to the crowded head to clean up, the sailors found it was a challenge just to make their way from the aft crew's quarters through the long narrow internal passageways to the forward mess hall. We would at one moment be pressed against the port bulkhead, and moments later, as the ship rocked to starboard, we would find ourselves with one foot on the starboard bulkhead and the other on the deck. Forward motion was possible only as the ship rolled slowly though the vertical angle and dove into another wave.

After breakfast, I made my way up the steep internal ladders to the bridge deck where the Officer of the Day and the bridge crew were working to keep the ship headed into the huge waves. The view from the bridge was frightening as the ship plunged into the mountainous waves, washing tons of water up over the front gun mount, then the second mount, and right on up to the windshield of the bridge. I waited by an external hatch at the rear of the bridge compartment for the ship to right itself for a moment, and then dashed across the open deck to the closed hatch at the base of the gun director. I held onto the hatch handle as the ship lurched again and a wave washed spray up over the bridge, splashing me with salt water. I wiped the spray out of my eyes just as the ship righted itself again, then quickly opened the hatch and jumped inside. I barely had time to close the hatch behind me and dog it down before the ship dove into the next wave.

My job aboard the Moore was to operate and maintain the 5-inch (caliber) gun fire control system, which included the Mark 25 Radar system and the equipment in the gun director. The highest manned station on every man of war is the gun director, a steel cubicle about eight feet on a side, equipped with radar and optical equipment. On a destroyer, the gun director sits on an 8-foot high cylindrical base located behind the bridge, so the director is some six stories above the water line. The gun director is mounted on bearings so it can rotate on the cylindrical base to follow the targets. The ship's big 5-inch guns are slaved to the director so they aim where the director points. The Mark 25 radar or the optical range finder computes the distance to the target.

During General Quarters when the ship is called to battle stations, the Gunnery Officer sits in the front section of the director. Our Gunnery Officer was a tall thin man named Lt. Collins. The lieutenant had to be a contortionist to work his way up through the hatch and over to his station on the left side of the director. The top front edge of the director is beveled off at 45 degrees with a hatch on the left side through which the Gunnery Officer can view the battle scene. During battle drills, two enlisted men sit to his right with tele-scopes and radar screens controlling the horizontal and vertical aim of the big guns. These two sailors are usually simple seamen whom the somewhat elitist fire control techs called "deck apes." I knew the deck crew had even more colorful terms for the technicians. I sat in the back of the director controlling the radar and optical ranging system.

On this stormy morning I made my way up the ladder through the trap door into the forward control station. From there I could crack the gunnery officer's hatch a few inches and look out into the raging sea. The rain, mixed with salty sea spray, blew in my face blurring my vision. As I kept wiping my eyes on my dungaree sleeves, I could see that the waves were easily fifty to sixty feet high, from trough to peak, arranged in rows like the surf on a beach. I could judge the height of the waves from my vantage point high atop the ship, because the tops of the nearby waves were above my eye level and I was standing at least six stories above the waterline of the destroyer.

As the nose of the ship dove into the base of the next wave I watched the entire front of the ship disappear into the sea, giving the appearance that the entire ship was going to be completely submerged. But then the buoyancy of the ship would bring us out on the backside of the wave and the ship would pitch up in preparation for its next dive. The ride up there atop the ship was like a slow motion bucking bronco; diving—then pitching up while rolling from side to side, shuddering to pull up out of the waves, and then cresting a swell and diving again. Only the water-tight buoyancy of the ship with its deep keel, the power of the propellers, and the rudder holding our heading into the waves kept us upright and afloat in that stormy sea.

As I watched the fierce seas and the pitching of the ship, I dreaded to think what would happen if we experienced a mechanical problem. I thought, "If we lose either power or steering, the wind and waves will quickly turn the ship parallel to the line of waves and we will be capsized for sure." That has happened throughout history to countless ships that now lie scattered on the ocean's floor. I learned later that even two destroyers, similar to the Moore, had gone down in a typhoon during WW2 because of rudder or power malfunctions. But in my case that day, ignorance was bliss because I thought to myself, "Not in today's Navy.' I found myself feeling grateful that the designers and the builders of our ship were experts in their craft. They knew that a seafaring ship would eventually encounter great storms at sea. If the ship was to survive, *it would have to function in that environment.*

The billowing waves hammered and tossed us about like a toy, but each time we submerged into a wave, we unfailingly emerged on the other side, drenched and shuddering perhaps, but intact. The vessel and its crew were under a great strain and we were taking a beating, but we were certain that we had a sound ship, designed and built to withstand the worst storms we would ever encounter. We knew that we would ride out the storm. This ship had done it before, as had countless others. Our vessel was built to function in this environment and it was doing its job. We would survive. I was confident that all would be well.

I didn't realize at that time I was being taught an important lesson about life that would help me later, long after I was out of the Navy. I later came to realize that the three same principles that govern the safety and survival of an ocean going vessel govern our human survival as we struggle through the storms of life. The ship must first of all be seaworthy. It must have a reliable power source for propulsion, then a strong rudder to keep it directed into the storm. In life, we must also be designed and constructed to be seaworthy, or "lifeworthy," is a term I like to use. We must have a strong power source to provide the propulsion through life's storms, and finally we must have a strong rudder to keep us directed into the face of the storms. I didn't realize it at the time, but I was living a metaphor that would describe my future life after the Navy.

The following decades of my life would take me and my family through many storms... more than I would have ever imagined as I watched the tempest raging outside my secure compartment that day aboard the destroyer. We would find ourfselves searching for answers as we suffered the loss of three of our dear children. As we battled through these tragedies we were compelled to confront the hard questions of life. Has God created us to be lifeworthy? Has he provided us with the power and direction we will need to survive life's tests? Will he be there to help us survive such devastating storms? Are his provisions sufficient? Just as the ocean floors are strewn with the wreckage of ships that didn't survive, many lives have failed to survive the extreme tests of life, ending in brokenness, despair, depression and unending grief; and sometimes, even death. What remained to be seen in my life was whether God's provision for us would be sufficient for me and my future family as we battled the storms to come.

CHAPTER 1

THE ULTIMATE STORM
February, 1981

"The Lord is close to the brokenhearted and saves those who are crushed in spirit" Psalms 34:18

The ringing of the telephone beside my bed awakened me out of a fitful sleep on that Friday, February 13. I reached for the telephone before I was fully awake, noting the digital clock read 2:53 a.m. Dr. Kennedy's words came out of the darkness in a calm and quiet voice. He said, "Mr. Clifford, I'm sorry to call you at this hour. Beth's heart rate and blood pressure are dropping rapidly. It may be just a matter of minutes." Our five-year old daughter had been in a coma for three days since her accident. Now, our precious blue eyed, daughter was slipping away from us.

My wife, Karen, and I lay in bed with heavy hearts as we discussed the situation quietly. Should we even go down to the hospital? Karen, always the practical one, said, "What purpose will it serve? Maybe it would be better to just let it happen and avoid the pain of seeing her lifeless body." But, we realized we must go.

Beth had experienced severe brain damage from a drowning accident and we had essentially given her up the evening before. The Chief Neurologist had told us that except for the unfortunate fact that she was breathing on her own, her body and mind were essentially gone. He had recommended she not be put on life support equipment. Our remaining hope finally plummeted with that news and after discussing it between ourselves, we agreed. Only a miracle could save her life and make her the beautiful daughter we had come to know and love for the past five years. The presence or absence of life support equipment wouldn't make any difference. Not for Beth. Not for us.

Looking at the time, I woefully determined that it had been precisely 79 hours since 13-year old Becky had found her sister floating in the bathtub, apparently taken by a seizure before she could get out of the shallow tub.

Karen and I dressed quietly, trying not to awaken our two teenage daughters. The heavy snow that had fallen steadily for the past three days while Beth fought for her life had stopped as if to signal the end of her battle. We took interstate Highway 70 from our suburban home to downtown St. Louis, then exiting onto Grand Avenue we drove through miles of dark desolate streets that we usuallly avoided. Karen always made sure the car doors were locked as we drove through the inner city neighborhoods, but now the streets were deserted and banked high on both sides by towering piles of dirty snow pushed into heaps by the city plow trucks..

We finally came to Childrens Hospital, nestled amidst the huge array of great hospitals in central St. Louis. We parked on the deserted street in front of the hospital entrance and made our way upstairs through the long quiet corridors to the ICU ward. Dr. Kennedy, a kindly young resident doctor with compassionate eyes wearing a white lab coat, met us and took us into the room where Beth had struggled for her life over the past three days. There we found her thin, naked and lifeless body on the bed, covered from her waist down by a sheet. We held each other and Karen cried into my shoulder as I tried to be strong for her.

A metal apparatus known as a "Thompson Shunt" was protruding from the side of her head. It was the remnant of an unsuccessful attempt to relieve pressure on her brain and possibly restore her brain function before she died. It was grotesque and made us wish we hadn't seen her like that.

There was nothing more for us to do there. Karen and I knew the doctors and nurses had worked valiantly to save Beth after the accident. Karen thanked them through her tears for their care and compassion. Then, after agreeing on arrangements, we walked back down the stairs, and outside to our car. We sat in the car for a few minutes and held each other tight, but no words were spoken. We made the return trip home through those same desolate streets, silently, lost in our thoughts, dreading the days and weeks to come without Beth.

We finally returned to what now seemed an empty and lifeless house. It wasn't of course. Eighteen year-old Vicki, practical like her mother, always organized and usually talkative, would probably worry more about her Mom than about herself. And sweet, compassionate Becky, so vulnerable and so innocent, was carrying the guilt of Beth's accident. I dreaded having to tell her about Beth. But, they were there, asleep in their beds, unaware of what had just transpired. Karen and I went back to our bed and just lay there in the dark talking quietly about what we needed to do, now that she was gone.

When it began to get light outside, I went into Vicki's room and gently woke her. She asked, "What's wrong, Dad?" I just said to her, "Beth didn't make it honey." Then I sat on the edge of her bed and held her close for a moment as she sobbed quietly in my arms. I sent her to our bedroom to be with her mom, then went reluctantly on to Becky's room to wake her with the terrible but expected news. When I woke her, she knew immediately why I was there and I didn't have to say anything. She didn't come to me for comfort as she struggled with her emotions alone. I brought her back to our bedroom also, and there on the big bed the four of us huddled together. There was no hysterical crying or even loud sobbing. We just held on to each other and quietly shared our growing pain. It may seem unusual that we behaved in such a way, but you see we were experienced in grief and we knew what we were facing in the days and months ahead. This would be the third time we have suffered through the death of one of our family.

As I looked at the faces of each of my girls, I thought "Oh Lord, can we survive this again? Vicki and Becky have already been through so much. How can Becky possibly survive the terrible guilt she must feel because of Beth's accident while in her care? And my beautiful, sweet Karen – she is so strong, but it seems she has known nothing but pain and tragedy ever since she met me. How can she survive this loss? In many ways it's the worst of the three. Mothers have slipped into depression and even taken their own lives over lesser tragedies than this. And for myself, I had always been the easy going, compliant one in my family of six boys. As the second oldest I lived in the shadow of my strong and aggressive older brother who always stepped in to fight my battles for me. He won't be able to help me this time though. I pleaded, Lord, please help us. We can't do this on our own. We need help.

As we clutched each other in that pitiful little huddle, I began again to ask myself, Why? Why does this have to happen to me and my family? What had we done to deserve such painful and tragic losses? Was all of this grief meant to be punishment for the sins in my life? I had tried to live a good moral life. I had surely failed at times... there was no question about that. I knew the answer to my question was "No." By now I had learned enough about grief to know that my feelings of guilt were a normal part of the process. But why should my family be singled out for all this suffering? I could identify with the Jewish farmer Tibya in "Fiddler on the Roof" when he prayed "Lord, I know we are your chosen people, but could you choose someone else for a while?"

So, in this vein of apprehension and questioning, I began going back over the path of all that had happened since Karen and I first met, and even before we had met. I needed to go back and see if I could discern where God was leading us and why he was taking us through all this pain. First the loss of our son, Mike, at age two and a half in California after I graduated from college. He smothered in his blankets during a seizure in the night.

Then, a few years later, the loss of Rachel to spinal meningitis induced brain damage at age three and a half here in Missouri. And, now, Beth at the age of five and a half. Can God really expect us to just "suck it up" and go through the motions of accepting these tragedies as his will? Again? Can we even survive another terrible loss of this magnitude?

Because of our past experiences, I knew that it wasn't just up to us. God would have to be there to care for us and to see us through this process. We couldn't do it alone. There would be pain, no question about that. There would be sorrow and grief. But I knew that God promised never to leave us nor forsake us. If he truly was going to help us through this, he would have to provide the resources we needed to get through this latest tragedy to befall our family. He had already brought us through much, but now he would need to do it again, and in an even bigger way.

As I began to see again in my mind all that had gone before, I believe the Spirit of God began asking me again, "Can you trust me now? Can my grace be sufficient for this also?" "I don't know" I said. "Can it? Can there really be grace enough for three?"

CHAPTER 2

POWER AND DIRECTION

January, 1957

"When the wind did not allow is us to hold our course, we sailed to the lee of Crete, ...to a place called Fair Haven ."
Acts 27:8

The late winter sun was setting across the hazy fields and mountains of the Taiwanese countryside as I watched through the dirty window of the rickety train winding its way northward. I had boarded the train in the southern port city of Kao-hsiung to visit my aunt who lived in the interior city of Chaiyi (pronounced Jaw-ee). In her letter my aunt said she and the other missionaries in her compound would be thrilled to have a visitor from the States, even if it was just a young sailor whose ship was in port for a few days. She said she would meet me at the train, but that I should be sure to find someone on the train who could tell me when we were coming into Chaiyi since I wouldn't be able to read the signs.

Ella Ruth Hutson had gone to China as a young Quaker missionary in 1947. When Chiang Kai Sheck's army was driven from the mainland by Mao in 1949, Ella Ruth and the other Christian missionaries were expelled by the Communist regime. She didn't let that forced move stop her mission in life however, moving across the straits to the island that was then called Formosa to continue her work with the Chinese people.

When my ship put into Kao-hsiung in 1957 I was an adventurous young man eager to get away from the waterfront dives that captured most of the sailors on liberty in foreign ports. I was more interested in seeing the sights and exploring the island, so having a relative up in the mountains gave me the opportunity I needed. The Captain was hesitant to let me off the ship over the weekend in such an exotic port, but when I showed him the letter from my aunt inviting me to spend the weekend, he agreed to let me go. Now I was beginning to have second thoughts while looking out the dirty windows of the train as the darkness deepened into night and the surroundings began to take on a sinister character.

As the train began to slow, the conductor walked through the car calling out "Jaw-ee, Jaw-ee" and I knew my stop was coming up. It was completely dark when we finally pulled into the Chaiyi station. The train stopped just long enough for me to grab my overnight bag and step out onto the platform. A single naked light bulb on the front of the depot building provided the only light and revealed that I was the only passenger to disembark from the old train. More important to me than who else got off the train was who wasn't there to meet me. A quick look around the deserted station was sufficient to reveal that I was there alone; there was no one there to meet me.

As the train pulled out of the station, leaving me alone on the platform, I felt a sharp twinge of anxiety. I really hadn't thought this through. What would I do if there was no one there to meet me? It began to dawn on me that I was in a difficult situation. Where was Ella Ruth? I knew no Chinese words and couldn't read the signs which were all in Chinese characters. I couldn't even be positive that I was in Chaiyi, although I thought that was what the conductor was saying. You may have heard that English is spoken everywhere, but that's not true, and certainly not in the interior of Taiwan in 1957.

After standing there on the platform for several minutes, the cold night air began to penetrate my pea coat and I shivered as I pulled the collar up tight around my neck. While wondering how I was going to get out of this predicament, out of the darkness came a little Chinese man pedaling a bicycle-driven rickshaw called a pedicab. In those days it was the Taiwanese version of a taxi. Fortunately, I had Ella Ruth's letter and the return address was written in Chinese on the envelope. I showed it to the pedicab driver and he studied the address carefully in the dim light. Then he motioned me aboard his pedicab and we pedalled off into the darkness.

As I rode through those dark streets filled with exotic sights and smells, especially smells of food because it was dinner time, I kept asking myself, "What am I doing here? This is crazy. This guy may be taking me to some opium den where I could be robbed and who knows what else? Why am I even in the Navy? I don't even like the sea." Actually, I knew why I was there. I had frittered away much of my time in high school taking easy classes like drama and music and trying to avoid the more difficult technical subjects like math and science. I was surprised when the aptitude tests I took before graduation told me I should be pursuing a technical vocation. That's not what I expected or wanted to hear.

After graduation my two closest buddies, Dennis Williams and James Briscoe, came by the house and announced that they were joining the Navy. Neither of them did great in High School and I knew they really had no plans for the future. The Navy was probably a good decision for them. But I was fortunate to have been given a good brain as well as a good upbringing, so it wasn't such an easy decision for me. I had been a good student and was usually on the honor roll, even though I didn't take the most difficult classes. I had lined up a partial scholarship at a local liberal arts college but when the aptitude test results came in, I was in a quandary and I wasn't sure what I wanted to do.

So, in a state of confusion and without any other direction, I thought I might as well go into the service also. I had always dreamed of being a paratrooper, so I went down to the courthouse with my buddies and we stopped by the Army recruiting office. I was quickly turned down for the Airborne because of a previously broken leg, so I decided to go ahead and join the Navy with Dennis and James. We were told we would be together through boot camp, and maybe even beyond that. But, first I would have to get my parent's permission since I was still just seventeen. When I told Mom what I had in mind, she surprisingly agreed, saying, "Well, at least there's no war going on right now, so maybe that's not a bad idea." The Korean war was in its final days and Vietnam was still unheard of. My Dad wasn't so easy to convince but after I assured him that I could get a full year's training in electronics after boot camp, he reluctantly agreed to sign the papers.

Once I was in, the Navy quickly determined through a 3-day battery of tests that I was indeed best suited for a technical job after I completed my boot camp training. As a result I stayed at the Great Lakes Naval Training Center, simply moving across the base after boot camp to the fleet training center. I was in for an intense 52 week course of study in electronics, radar and gun fire control. After the year of study at the training center, I selected the assignment aboard the USS Moore, mainly because it was based out of Long Beach, California. I could imagine myself hanging out with movie stars and surfing with the Beach Boys in sunny California.

So, that is how I came to be in Taiwan that night, shivering in the cold night air, as much from the predicament as from the cold. The pedicab continued to meander slowly through the seemingly endless maze of dark streets and alleys of Chaiyi.

After what seemed like hours, the pedicab turned a corner and I came to attention as I spotted a building down the street with a bare light hanging above a white sign lettered in English and Chinese. As we drew nearer I could see that the sign was declaring that this building was the Chaiyi Friends Church. It was a small non-descript store front building with a couple of dark windows and a locked door, but at least it was a start. My hopes waned again, though, as I began to consider the prospect of spending the long winter night there on the street in front of the mission, waiting for someone to show up who could help me.

Fortunately, my pedicab driver was not easily discouraged. He rousted a neighbor lady and a spirited discussion followed that involved a lot of fast talking, hand waving and pointing. The driver finally seemed satisfied and motioned me back into the carriage and away we went again; through more dark streets which were surely full of opium dens and oriental gangsters. After a few more minutes, we arrived at a Western-style church building with an attached parsonage. Several sharp knocks on the door of the parsonage by my driver brought a distinguished looking man to the door. He was a middle-aged, portly Chinese man, dressed in a robe and slippers and wearing reading glasses. The gentleman listened politely to the driver's tale and examined my envelope. Then he looked at me and smiled, and said in perfect English, "Welcome Don, we've been waiting for you. We thought you were coming yesterday." (I learned later that Reverend Jong had graduated from Harvard University with a doctorate in theology.) The look on my face must have showed the relief I felt because he gave me a big bear hug and ushered me into his home where he called my aunt to come and collect me.

I had a delightful time visiting with Ella Ruth and the other missionaries in the community. Ella Ruth looked and talked the way you would expect a missionary to look and talk. She was a first cousin of my Dad's, but later in life when my grandmother's sister (Ella Ruth's mother) died, my grandma married her brother in law so Ella Ruth and my Dad became step siblings. Anyway, I called her aunt because she seemed like an aunt to me. She had her light colored hair in a bun on the back of her head and she wore metal rim glasses and heavy walking shoes under her long shapeless skirts.

Ella Ruth shared a comfortable Taiwanese home with an older missionary couple named Duval. Dr. Duval was a famous botanist and taught part time at the national university in Taipei. Howard Moore and his wife were also coworkers in the mission station. They were younger than Ella Ruth and the Duvals and had two small children. Howard was an enthusiastic extroverted man who wouldn't take no for an answer. He took me under his wing right away and by Sunday morning he had me singing a duet with him in a couple of their four Sunday church services.

The services tended to be somwhat lengthy because at least two interpreters were necessary. There were usually two or more Chinese dialects in attendance, in addition to the native Taiwanese language. Needless to say, no English was spoken but Ella Ruth would occasionally lean over and whisper to me what was being preached. But, the hymns were familiar and the people were all warm and loving. I thought, "How neat. You can go clear around the world and find a warm welcoming family, even though we'd never met before and we don't speak the same language. We were all members of the same family. The family of God."

The missionaries were all thrilled to have an American visitor, and especially a dark haired young sailor. I did bring my civies along and I was more comfortable wearing them about town than my uniform. I felt self conscious enough being a "Big Nose." Ella Ruth told me not to take it personally, but children would sometimes run along side us and pull on their noses, laughing and chattrering about my appearance. She said they always do that when they saw a Caucasian person because the Westerners all had bigger noses than the Chinese, and my nose was longer than most.

The missionaries gave me the royal treatment and involved me immediately in all of the activities of the missionary community. I felt right at home. I even participated in the morning hymn singing and prayer time with the missionaries and church leaders each day. After the hymn singing, we knelt in a circle, praying for the work there, and they prayed for me as I left to rejoin my ship. The weekend passed quickly and I left vowing to return if the opportunity presented itself.

I was comfortable in the missionary setting because I had been raised in a Christian home and I had been attending the Baptist church all of my life. I considered myself a fairly strong Christian, although I was naïve and inexperienced in my faith. Nevertheless, I found myself feeling much more comfortable with the missionaries than I was aboard the ship where I was considered to be a little peculiar. I didn't drink and I tried to avoid picking up the navy language sailors are known for. Anyone who has been in the service knows that is no easy task. My buddies didn't mind having me around though because they knew whenever we went ashore in the States that they always had a designated driver available to be sure they got back to the ship safely.

Almost a full year later, on our next tour to the Far East, our ship put into Kao-hsiung again, this time over the Christmas holidays. Happily, I was able to spend the entire Christmas week in Chaiyi. Ella Ruth introduced me to the Chinese young people in the churches, and even though we didn't speak each other's language, the church youth invited me to join them for Christmas carolling. I said, "Sure, I'm game for anything." Then I discovered that they went carolling at 4 a.m. on Christmas morning!

I had to ride a bicycle alone across the city in the middle of the night to join the group. It should have been scary, but I thought it was great fun. There were probably a dozen or more Chinese youth in the group, but of course, none of them could speak a word of English. Nevertheless, I thoroughly enjoyed myself, singing English to the familiar carols while the rest of the young people sang in two or three different dialects of Chinese. The recipients of our serenades didn't seem to mind being awakened in the middle of the night. One young family came to the door in their night clothes and expressed their appreciation by handing out Chinese snacks, most of which I declined. I was a little suspicious of their unknown content and origin. I truly enjoyed the Chinese people but their fare at the dinner table was not always what this American would consider palatable.

Taiwan is a lovely island. In fact it's older name, Formosa, means "Beautiful Island" in Portugese. The tropical mountainous island is about 245 miles long from north to south, and 89 miles across at its widest point. Chaiyi is a little north of the midpoint of the island and a few miles inland from the west coast. A range of mountains with many peaks over 10,000 feet runs the length of the island giving it the appearance of a tailless prehistoric dinosaur. There is a narrow but drivable road across the middle of the island, following the crests of the mountains. The road begins at the breathtaking Toroko Gorge near the sea on the east coast and eventually makes its way up the forested slopes to the highest mountains in Taiwan. There, high above the clouds, is a summer resort hotel at a breathtaking place called Lisan, where I was to visit with Ella Ruth years later on a return trip to Taiwan.

But for now, Ella Ruth took me aound the island by train, stopping to see various sites of interest. She took me to a religious shrine called (phonetically) Kwa-Jalein where fire and water came out together from a hole in the side of a hill. She took me to many Buddhist shrines and explained the various prayer wheels and pairs of wooden ears that were used by worshippers to learn the will of Buddha. We saw a funeral parade led by men carrying ornate golden statues of Buddha and other deities. I began to understand what the missionaries were up against as they sought to bring Christianity to the Taiwanese people.

As we travelled together Ella Ruth taught me much about a missionary's heart. When I asked her when she was going to go home, she replied surprisingly, "But Don, this is my home. God has placed me here and has given me these people to be my family. I don't ever plan to leave; I'll die here." That statement shocked me and caused me to think deeply about who and what these missionaries were. The dedication and commitment of those Quaker missionaries stirred something in me that would stay with me for the rest of my life. It included an appreciation for all missionary work and a desire to know their kind of love and dedication. Their God was so relevant to them and the needs of the Chinese people were so real to them, they saw their own lives as insignificant in comparison.

At the end of my shore leave and back at sea aboard ship, I lay in my bunk and reflected on my experiences at sea and in Taiwan. I began to be amazed and moved at how the missionaries were so happy in their work in such difficult circumstances. They were all highly educated and trained for their missionary assignments. Ella Ruth was even busy translating the Bible into various Chinese and Taiwanese dialects. But even with their support from home, they were still facing hardships and deprivation. There, in the back country of remote Taiwan, I saw godly people braving the difficulties of culture and religious differences, far from home and families. They were there to accomplish a God-goal that drove their lives. That singular goal was to bring the message of God's salvation to a remote and backward people who knew nothing of the true God.

Ella Ruth had shared with me some of the difficulties they encountered, including opposition, ridicule and even threats to their safety. She told of Chinese converts who were being disowned by their families and blacklisted at their jobs. But despite all these obstacles, the missionaries went about their work with joy in their hearts and overflowing love for the Chinese people. They had already planted several thriving churches and even founded a seminary for the national leaders.

Then, as though the Spirit of God was guiding my thoughts, another piece of life's puzzle fell into place. I thought back to those storms at sea and the similarities of a ship struggling through the tempestuous waters on the one hand, and those missionaries battling the storms they faced on the mission field. I saw that the same three principles were at work in the missionary situation. Their ship had to be seaworthy to allow them to face the hardships and difficulties they faced in their work. They obviously had an unusual energy source to keep them striving toward their goal, bringing the Chinese people to an understanding of who God is and how he sent his son, Jesus, to die for their sins. And their rudder was true, directing them and showing them the way through their confusing and foreign culture.

As a Navy-trained technician, and later as an engineer and scientist, it became clear that we humans have a super engineer as the designer of our bodies and souls. He has created us to be "life-worthy" in such a way that we can cope with the inevitable storms of life without capsizing. But there in Taiwan I was allowed to see where the propulsion and the rudder come into work in our human existence. These missionaries had a strong drive in their hearts and souls, and a sure direction in their lives and ministries. Their power and direction weren't humanly generated. God was at work in their lives, powering them, and empowering them to accomplish his purpose in the world. They held steadfastly on the course to meet the goal that God had given them. I could see that both their direction and their power came from their daily, continuous and intimate relationship with their Creator God. Their extended times of prayer and study of God's Word channeled God's power and direction into their work with the people they came to serve.

So, I was discovering that the Creator who designed and built us all is also the source of our power and direction. He also wants to be our rudder and our propulsion source if we will let him. What wonderful confidence that gave me! I was warmed and excited about the prospects of a life ahead with God as my designer, my rudder and my power. "Life should be a breeze" I thought in my youthful exuberance. But, what I hadn't fully realized was how much sacrifice and suffering those missionaries had to experience to come to the place where they could face their battles with faith and confidence. I had many lessons to learn about battling the storms of life before I could face it with the same confidence they did. At that moment though, I couldn't see the furies that were just beyond the horizon in my own life.

My time with the missionaries in Taiwan helped in a profound way to prepare me for those storms that surely lay ahead. Ella Ruth, the Duvals and the Moores inspired me and gave me a spiritual stability that helped carry me through the rest of my navy days and beyond. That was my first introduction to life on the mission field and one that has helped me understand and care about the dedicated people who give their lives, or their loved ones, to God's work around the world. And, I hadn't seen the last of Ella Ruth Hutson. She was to play an important role in our lives during a severe lifestorm many years later.

The missionary adventure was one of three significant events that occurred during my short naval career which was to have a lasting impact on my life. The second was my 'intellectual awakening.' The year of study at the naval training center ignited a strong appetite within me for technical study. Consequently, during the many long weeks and months my ship was at sea I took the opportunity to begin preparing seriously for college when my naval obligation was over. I became determined to make up for all the time I had frittered away in high school. I began reading everything technical I could get my hands on, even including math books. The most helpful book I had was given to me by my dad who had been a self-taught Ham radio operator. It was titled something like "Mathematics for Radio and Electronics." It, along with my navy training, really taught me all I needed to know to be ready for college.

Having no teacher at hand and no other shipmates interested in such studies, I had to learn on my own. I once tried going up to the officer's wardroom for help. After all, I thought, "These people are all college graduates so they should be able to help me." But no, most of them hadn't had as much math as I was already working through by myself. I did get encouragement from Lt. Collins, the Gunnery Officer, who encouraged me to keep working, and I did. By the time my discharge came around I felt that I was well prepared to tackle whatever the university could throw at me.

A third significant event in the navy was to affect my later decisions in a different way. It was really more of a process than an event. Many of those nights at sea I lay awake in my bunk and thought about my future. I knew I was not the kind of guy who would stay in the navy. I was designed to be a family man. I wanted a large family, so I wouldn't stay single very long.

Crammed into that compartment with all those other sailors, I was lonesome. I felt as though I could love and care for a wife and family and I dreamed of finding that wife after my discharge. I even prayed regularly about the girl I was to marry, and I clearly remember feeling God was telling me he had my future wife all picked out and she would be perfect for me. Our backgrounds and interests would be compatible and she would be beautiful. So I had the girl of my dreams pretty well defined in my mind by the time I got out of the Navy. Furthermore, I knew God had picked her out and that she would be waiting for me. All I had to do was find her.

CHAPTER 3

Preparing For The Next Voyage

April, 1958

"Jacob was in love with Rachel and said (to Laban), "I'll work for you seven years in return for your younger daughter.."
Genesis 29:18

When I was discharged from the Navy I felt as if I had been released from prison. I was happy to trade the stormy seas for the endless seas of wheat in the terra firma of Kansas. After almost four years in the Navy, the day before my twenty-first birthday in April of 1958, I checked out of the processing center in Long Beach and hitchhiked back to Kansas

I was anxious to get back into civilian life with my parents and five brothers in Wichita, and then to start college at Kansas University in the fall. Mom and Pop were good solid working-class citizens and good church-going people (my brothers and I all called our father Pop). In addition to being a long-standing deacon in the church, Pop was the superintendent of the Garvey Grain elevator, the largest grain elevator in the world, just south of Wichita. Pop only stood about five foot, eight inches tall, but he was solid as a rock. I must have gotten my beefy shoulders and chest from him. As long as I knew him he always combed his dark hair straight back on his head, except when he wore a crew cut. His stout solid build came from his cowboy father, but was strengthened from growing up on a farm in the Oklahoma panhandle during the dust bowl years where he pulled broom corn and plowed wheat fields from the time he was 12. He took up flying later in his life; in fact, shortly after I returned home from the Navy. He spent a lot of his spare time flying small planes around Kansas, earning his instructors and commercial licenses. Mom and Pop eventually invested in a flying business in Wichita but couldn't make a go of it financially.

Mom was an attractive woman with wavy brown hair and she was just as tall as Pop. She had her hands full raising six wild boys. My older brother, Les, was born when she was only 17. My youngest brother, Roger, was only four years old when I got out of the Navy 23 years later, You can see she had already been through a lot of testing, but still had plenty of work ahead of her. She flew with Pop frequently and while soaring above the wheat fields, Mom began to wonder what would happen if something happened to Pop. He could get sick and pass out, or even have a heart attack while she was flying with him. So, she took up flying lessons and quickly soloed herself. When Roger and Glenn came home from school they might find a message on the table telling them she was out flying but would be home in time to fix supper.

As the second oldest of the six boys in my family, I was the first to serve in the military and would be the first to go to college. My brother Jim, (brother number 4) joined the Air Force soon after I returned home, and after he was discharged he went to Bible College and became a preacher. Glenn and Roger, brothers 5 and 6, attended college years later and both went into the ministry for a time. But, that's another story.

One of the first things I did when I got home was to use my savings to purchase the car of my dreams, a 1954 Mercury, painted light blue. After getting my car and still having some Navy money left, I enjoyed exploring the old haunts from my high school days, driving through the familiar streets in my very own Mercury. It was good to be home.

Wichita is the largest city in Kansas, but that's not saying much. It was and is a typical mid-size city in the midwest, population around 400,000. They call themselves proudly "The Air Capital of the World." That's because of the Boeing, Beech, Cessna and Lear Jet plants as well as McConnell Air Force base that are all located there. In fact, it was Boeing that brought our family to Wichita during World War 2 when Pop was the radio operator on a B-29 test flight crew. As I mentioned earlier, Pop was a self-taught Ham radio operator and since he already had three boys when the war started, he was sent to South Dakota to teach radio to the new army recruits. Then in 1944 when the war effort was winding down, we moved to Wichita so he could take the job at Boeing. Then when the war ended and they shut down the B-29 line, Pop went back into the grain business.

Wichita is also a rail center and is the home of several huge terminal grain elevators, collecting and storing grain from the vast wheat fields in Western Kansas, Oklahoma and Nebraska. Most of my brothers and I worked in the grain elevators after high school and I worked there during summers while attending college. In fact, soon after returning home from the Navy, Pop put me to work on the construction crew at his elevator. The main elevator structure was already the largest in the country, a full half mile long. But more wheat kept coming in and they needed more storage capacity. When I arrived on the scene a construction crew was in the process of erecting several huge sheds extending out from the elevator structure like so many baby pigs feeding on a mother sow. The sheds were huge structures in themselves, with concrete walls about three stories high and metal roofs running the full 100-yard length of the sheds. Later, during my summers off from the university, I had to work in those sheds, usually fumigating the grain in temperatures that reached 140 degrees. But, that first summer I was put to work tying steel rebar and pouring the foundations on several of the sheds.

The Garvey Grain elevator had what was then a modern piece of technology for unloading the wheat from the boxcars. They had a gigantic robotic device which would pick up a boxcar full of grain and rotate it over on its side and shake it to get all the grain out. However, most of the older elevators still used manpower to unload their boxcars. So, when the grain rush began in earnest in late June, I went to work at the old Pillsbury elevator across town and spent about six weeks shovelling grain from the endless strings of boxcars coming in from the west. The pay was more than on the construction crew, but it was hot, hard, gruelling work. The temperature inside the sun-baked cars was over 140 degrees on a hot sunny day, and the hard work melted away any fat on my body that had accumulated during my years aboard ship. Eating three square meals a day with no exercise does tend to soften you up.

To empty a boxcar of wheat, first the wooden grain doors were pried off of the door of the car allowing grain to begin pouring out of the door into the grating below, where the wheat was carried into the elevator on big conveyor belts. After a couple of minutes, the grain would stop flowing out on its own, and that's when we went to work. Two men would work a car at the same time, one on each end. The power shovels we used were essentially thirty-inch square plates made of wood but covered with a thin layer of sheet metal on the front surface. The shovel had two protruding handles at the top and was attached to a chain drive with a steel cable attached to the center of the front surface. The cable ran to a constantly-running motor on the dock outside the car with a clutch which was disengaged while we reeled out the cable. Our job was to drag this power shovel up to the back end of the car, wading knee deep up the hill of grain and dragging the shovel behind us. To complicate matters, we had to wear a respirator mask to keep the thick grain dust out of our lungs. When we got to the back of the car, we would pull the shovel up and thrust it down into the grain against the back wall as far as we could. Then the chain drive would kick in and we would ride the shovel back to the door, pushing a huge wave of grain ahead of us. That process was repeated until we had emptied the car, which took two experienced men about 8 minutes. With four men on a crew, we would get a needed break by taking turns shovelling cars. Our work days during the wheat rush were 10 to 12 hours long leaving us exhausted and ready for a shower.

When I wasn't working that first summer back home, church was the center of my family's social life. I enjoyed getting back into the worship life of the church, but as a young man I especially enjoyed the social activities and sports. I tried out and won the position of pitcher on the church's fast-pitch softball team, and that's where I encountered another surprising change in the direction of my life.

I came home to Kansas not really expecting to find my dream girl until I got to college in the fall. Therefore, I wasn't really looking for her that summer. I was just enjoying being a civilian again, working, playing ball and continuing my preparation for college. It surprised me to find our ball team had a cheering section that was present at every game. I couldn't help noticing the leader of the fan club was a very cute brown-haired girl with big dimples which accentuated her beautiful smile. She was often dressed in black shorts and a polka dot blouse. I called it her Daisy Mae outfit (after the girl in the old comic strip, Li'l Abner.) Every time I pitched she cheered me on enthusiastically from the sidelines. It turned out she was Karen Atherton, the little girl I remembered seeing at some of my mother's Sunday School class gatherings at our house before I got out of the Navy. Karen had blossomed into a beautiful young lady, but I learned there was a lot more to her than her good looks. She was president of her Sunday School class, an alto in the church choir and an active leader of the church youth group. I also learned she was independent, knew what she wanted, and single-mindedly pursued her goals. Well, it turned out that I was one of her goals and that's a fact for which I will be eternally grateful.

Karen was just turning sixteen and even though I was attracted to her, she was so young it didn't occur to me that she might be the dream girl I had been praying for. However, it must have occurred to Karen because she saw to it that we continued to get acquainted. She frequently called my mother 'just to chat,' but didn't seem to want to hang up, at least if she knew I was home. So, Mom would hand the phone to me and say, "Here, you talk to her for a while. I've got things to do."

Karen and I always seemed to find a lot to talk about. She expressed great interest in my Navy experiences and my plans for college. Our conversations gradually became more personal and eventually led to our finding each other at various church and social events. Since I had a car she somehow usually ended up riding with my group to fellowships after church and to the monthly Sunday night singspirations.

All too quickly September rolled around and it was time for me to go away to the university in Lawrence. The week before I was to leave, Karen and I somehow found ourselves alone together in my car saying our good-byes. There is something magical about that first kiss... at least when it's the right person. I fell in love like the proverbial ton of bricks. I suddenly realized that this was the dream girl I had been praying for. She met all of the expectations I had in mind, except her age. (I hadn't thought to ask about that in my prayers.) But, I could wait that out. She wouldn't be too young forever.

Of course, as soon as I showed an interest in Karen, her parents understandably became concerned. After all, in their eyes I was a crusty old sailor and she was just an innocent child...and she really was. I respected their feelings and their wishes, but I couldn't deny my feelings for their daughter, nor hers for me. Karen's parents were long-time leaders and pillars in our church. I think her Dad was the Sunday School Superintendent and her mother played the organ or sung in the choir. Karen's Dad was very thin, about five-feet, eleven inches tall, and had been an industrial arts teacher in the high schools in Wichita for years. However, when television came along, he took a correspondence course and opened his own TV store.

The Athertons also came from Oklahoma, and both of them were acquainted with my Dad's family back in the panhandle. Karen's Mom, a short, dark haired lady with glasses, and Karen's Dad attended Panhandle State A&M college along with my Aunt Hazel and Uncle Bruce. Our parents had always been good friends and frequently socialized together while I was in the Navy. In fact, my dad went in to help Karen's dad for a short time to help get his TV store going. However, their socializing ended abruptly when I showed up and developed an interest in their daughter. Her parents guarded her closely when I was known to be around. They were greatly relieved when I packed my few belongings and moved to Lawrence to start college at KU.

But young love is not thwarted that easily. While I was away at college I managed to get home on weekends much more than I had originally intended. It was about a three hour drive from Lawrence to Wichita, so I could make it home on weekends if I was properly motivated, and I promise you I was very motivated. Karen and I weren't able to date when I was home, but we continued to talk by telephone and see each other at church. On rare occasions we managed to get next to each other in a crowded hallway at church and briefly hold hands. On occasion I would seek her out at a high school football or basketball game when I was able to get home for a Friday evening.

Despite the handicaps, our relationship continued to develop. Soon we began talking intimately as if we were already engaged.

I must admit, I never actually proposed, at least not formally. We just knew we were going to be married. We talked about how it would be after we were married and longed for the day to come. We both knew we were going to spend the rest of our lives together, even though we had never been alone together for more than a few minutes at a time.

Finally, after more than two years of this unusual courtship, Karen graduated from high school and we decided to announce our engagement. Our announcement surprised our families and friends in Wichita since most of them didn't even know Karen had a boyfriend. It was still difficult for her parents, but at least they had managed to get her through high school. When I went in to the TV store for a man-to-man talk with her dad, he said they still wanted to get her through college, then they would not stand in the way if we still wanted to be married. The thought of another four years didn't sit too well with either Karen or me, but at least the day after we announced our engagement, Karen's parents reluctuantly allowed us to go out on our first real date.

Since Karen's parents wanted very much for her to go to college (and it was her desire as well) she enrolled at Emporia State Teacher's college. Karen was an excellent student and had already laid the groundwork for an engineering degree. She finished her first year of calculus that semester at Emporia State. Emporia was fine with me because it was closer to Lawrence than to Wichita, situated approximately half way between the two. I spent many weekends in Emporia that semester, driving down after my Saturday morning physics classes and sleeping in my car most Saturday nights. Karen roomed with two of her friends in a boarding house near campus. That made it easier to see her on weekends, although her house parents kept a close watch on her.

My desire to hasten our marriage deepened when the snow began to fall. I found that it could get very cold in my old Mercury just before dawn with the car buried under 3 inches of snow. Our desire to be married was not just a matter of convenience, however. We knew our love for each other was for eternity and we belonged together.

That time was difficult for Karen, trying to keep her parents happy while dealing with my impatience. I was straining at the bit to get married but she knew her parents were still not ready to accept our marriage right then, and that our moving forward would cause a serious rift with her family. Karen was caught in a virtual tug of war. I was pulling on one arm and they were pulling on the other. The conditions were stormy for her, and she was having to find her way through the rough waters alone. She tried to negotiate a compromise with her parents, but it was impossible for them to accept losing their first-born at such a young age. Karen's two brothers, Terry and Craig, were several years younger so Karen was carrying the burden of being the oldest child and having to break new ground for every attempt to be herself and gain some independence.

Karen and I spent many hours talking over the options, looking for some solution that would not upset her parents, but would still bring us together. We finally decided that we would go ahead and get married, in spite of her parent's reluctance. So, as soon as that semester ended and Karen turned 18, we went to the City Hall in Wichita and got our Marriage License. Not wasting any more time, we went ahead with our wedding during the winter break between semesters.

We usually tell people we 'kind of eloped.' We had a quiet private wedding in our pastor's office with just my parents, my brother Bill (brother number 3) and his wife Brenda, and my buddy Dennis present. It was a cold January day but we were warmed at the prospect of finally being together. Karen's parents didn't come, but they did agree to allow our pastor, Dr. Reffner, to perform the ceremony, rather than push us into going to someone else. After the brief ceremony we stopped by their house to pick up some of her things, but her parents stayed in the bedroom until we left. Karen and I were both very hurt by this gesture but we prayed that her folks would come around quickly now that we were married. We would have to wait to take our honeymoon until the summer break.

We drove up to Lawrence that afternoon and spent our wedding night in the Top Hat Motel, just outside of town. My boss at Roberto's Pizzeria brought us a pizza for a wedding present. That was about it. Not much of a production compared with all that goes on in most weddings.

The next day Karen enrolled at the beautiful Mount Oread campus of Kansas University, and then we went apartment hunting. We moved into a sparsely furnished upstairs apartment adjacent to the campus. It had an outside stairway, a huge kitchen and a tiny bedroom barely large enough for a double bed. So, there on the scenic Mount Oread campus we began our lives together as one. We were very much in love and finally we were together.

And, yes, Karen's parents did come around. After a week or so, Karen's mom called and asked us to come to Wichita the next weekend because the ladies at church were throwing a wedding shower for Karen. We went of course, and it was a great shower with all of her friends and relatives present. I could hear the joy and laughter of the ladies from outside the building. That was a great healing time for Karen, and we were both very grateful that everything finally worked out. The gift from her folks was a portable black and white television from their store. That TV on a roll around stand saw us through the first several years of our marriage and was a great help, especially during the next phase of our lives when Karen was home alone. That old TV is an antique now, but we still have it stored in our garage. Her folks welcomed me into the family warmly after the shower and we have been as close as a family can be ever since.

Berthing Pains

"As soon as the sound of your greeting reached my ears, the baby in my womb leaped for joy" Luke 1:44

Surprisingly, Karen's assertive self confidence quickly faded after our marriage. I can't say why for sure, but possibly her young age and lack of experience in the world led her to drop that assertiveness and rely on me for everything. She became pregnant soon after our marriage and that condition, coupled with her isolation from her family and friends, forced her to lean entirely on me. In some ways she was almost a "clinging vine" wife, which I didn't mind.

I didn't help the situation because I was confident and opinionated enough for both of us. Karen learned quickly that she couldn't win an argument with me. It developed then that her only weapon against my forceful reasoning was the old silent treatment. That turned out to be a lethal weapon for her and I succumed quickly when she grew cold and distant. The problem was, I couldn't get her to talk about whatever was bothering her because she knew I would try to talk her out of it. So, I was forced to resort to the "20 Questions" game. I would begin reviewing aloud to her everything I could think of that might be bothering her. When I finally came to the thing she was upset about, she would let me know by just a shrug or brief humph. Then I could begin apologizing and trying to reconcile the situation. That happened occasionally for the first couple of years of our marriage until she began to come out of her shell and gained some new confidence.

Our first child came quickly – less than a year after our wedding. As I said before, I was ready to have a family. Karen's pregnancies would all be very difficult but her first was almost tragic. She quickly developed morning sickness that progressively worsened until it lasted all day and all night. She continued going to class as long as she could, but finally she couldn't make it up the long hill to Mt. Oread another day. Her doctor told her she had better give up going to class and go to bed. She continued to get sicker and sicker and eventually spent most of the first three months of her pregnancy sick in bed. Not surprisingly, her attempt to continue her college education came quickly to a halt.

Italian food has never been Karen's favorite. Unfortunately, I had a part time job at Roberto's Pizzeria delivering pizzas. I would come home to our tiny apartment late at night smelling of garlic and spices from the kitchen and she would head immediately for the bathroom to throw up. It finally got to where she would run for the bathroom when she heard me coming up the outside stairs and I would hear the stool flushing as I came in the door. I don't know if it was the baby, but something was jumping in her stomach. I can testify that it's very disconcerting for a young husband when he realizes he makes his bride sick every time he walks in the door. Many a night I was out scouring the food stores of Lawrence for something that Karen could eat, but always without success. At times she couldn't even keep a glass of water down.

On my birthday Karen worked valiantly to get up and get dressed so we could do something special. It was a sunny and warm April afternoon when I came home from class and saw her dressed for the first time in several weeks in something besides her loose fitting bed clothes. Her thin and frail appearance shocked me. It's not an exaggeration to say she looked like a refugee from a concentration camp. She was already thin when we were married and she had lost fifteen pounds by the third month of her pregnancy.

We walked down the hill into town and had just arrived on Main Street when she got dizzy and grabbed for me. I wrapped my arms around her and held her as tight as I could, but she fainted and slipped right through my arms onto the sidewalk. A crowd gathered quickly to see what had happened and when she came to they helped me get her into a shop where she could sit down and have a drink of water. But in a few minutes she fainted again so I quickly called a cab and got her back to our little apartment and back in her bed.

When I called her doctor and told her what had happened, she wanted me to bring her in immediately. The doctor took one look at my frail bride and immediately put her in the campus hospital. They put her on an I.V. at once to get some fluids into her badly dehydrated body. Once they got her fluid level up she was able to keep some broth down. After a few days in the hospital, she gradually began to regain her appetite. That medical treatment got her over the first trimester hump and the rest of the pregnancy was normal. We were able to take our honeymoon in the Ozarks at the end of the spring semester, with Karen 4 months pregnant. We seemed to be continuing our practice of doing things a little out of order.

When we returned to Lawrence for my last year of school, we found a somewhat nicer apartment in the basement of a new home a few blocks away from the campus. I liked it because they had a basketball goal on the concrete pavement in the back yard. Shooting hoops was a good way for me to relax after my intensive studies.

In the early morning hours on Halloween day our daughter Vicki Lynette Clifford was born. I had to wait outside and couldn't even go into the labor room. Hospitals were much more restrictive in those days than they are now. The labor went on for a few hours, but by daybreak Vicki was born, a chubby 8 pound baby, dark complected and feisty from birth. In a few days we were able to take her home and our parenting years had begun. I was very proud of our little girl. I remember taking her to a Kansas University basketball game in the Allen Field House when she was only a few weeks old. I carried her around and proudly showed her off to my classmates and instructors. I was determined that she would grow up to be a Jayhawk fan.

At Kansas, I majored in Engineering Physics which was essentially a degree in Physics but with most of the electives taken from the engineering field instead of the liberal arts. It was a challenging curriculum but one which I fully enjoyed. I had always been interested in the nuclear field so I took a minor in Nuclear Engineering. My service experience helped reduce the number of classes I had to take so I was able to graduate in four years while working summers back in Wichita in the grain elevator business.

Life as a university student with a wife and baby was challenging because Karen needed time with me, but at the same time my upperclass studies were the most difficult I had experienced up to that time. Vicki was a good baby but she taught me right away that my preconceived notions of how to raise a baby were hogwash. For example, I had decided that no baby of mine was going to suck on a pacifier. She changed that the first week. She cried incessantly for hours on end and nothing we could do seemed to make her happy. We changed her, fed her, rocked her, all to no avail. Finally, I went shopping for a pacifier late at night. I found one, took it home and stuck it in her mouth, and I immediately became a believer in pacifiers. She was happy. So were we.

We recently came across some old home movies taken at the home of Karen's parents in Wichita at the time of my graduation. We had Vicki on a blanket on the front lawn and she was about 6 months old. I showed her off by having her stand in my hand while holding her high in the air while I displayed my diploma in my other hand. Then we brought out a litter of kittens and put them on the blanket with her. We showed the film to her teenage children recently and they howled with laughter as she would grab a kitten in each hand

and try to put them in her mouth. Now we tease her about her appetite for kitty burgers.

Vicki was a model child by anyone's standards, although she did give us one good scare when she was a toddler. I arrived home one afternoon to find Karen waiting for me in the driveway. She was trying to be calm, but I could hear the concern in her voice as she said, "We have to get Vicki to the hospital right away. She's eaten a whole bottle of baby aspirin!" After eating the remaining Rolaids from a bottle in the kitchen, Vicki had climbed onto the sink in the bathroom and gotten the baby aspirin out of the medicine cabinet. Karen found her with the empty bottle and bits of the orange aspirin on her lips. She looked like the cat who ate the canary.

Karen thought there were only a few tablets in the Rolaids bottle but the baby aspirin was new. We rushed Vicki to the hospital where they gave her medicine to make her vomit and then pumped her stomach. They kept her in the hospital overnight, but she never seemed to show any symptoms of poisoning. Maybe the Rolaids saved the day since they counteracted the acid in the aspirin. We took her home the next morning and vowed to watch her and the accessibility of all medications more closely from then on.

Our Second Wedding

"Fourteen years ago I was taken up to heaven for a visit. Don't ask me whether my body was there or just my spirit, for I don't know: only God can answer that." 2 Corinthians 12:1-6

On our first anniversary, something very profound and very unusual happened to Karen and me. We've never discussed this experience with anyone because it was so personal and so "different." In fact, it is very difficult even now to describe or explain exactly what happened. However, I think it is essential to the telling of our story, and it may help others to understand how God prepares people for things to come in their lives. It also helps to see how we were able to maintain our marriage and sustain our faith through the violent storms which were to come.

We were in Wichita visiting our families during the break between my last two semesters at K.U. Vicki was just three months old and Karen's folks agreed to baby sit with her so we could go out to dinner on our first anniversary. We had a nice meal at our favorite restaurant, and then we did what we often did in those days. We drove to the airport and parked outside the fence to watch the planes land. We always found that to be an inexpensive and enjoyable way to be alone together. We talked and snuggled and were just enjoying our time alone together when it happened.

Before I tell you what happened that night, let me tell you about a passage from the Bible where the Apostle Paul related what may have been a similar experience in his life, though on a much grander scale. In Acts 14 Paul and Barnabus were on their first missionary journey when the Jewish leaders stirred up a mob against them at Lystra. They stoned Paul and dragged him to the edge of town, bleeding and unconscious, where they left him for dead. It was not this experience which reminded me of what happened with Karen and me, but what happened to Paul later. It is apparently this near-death experience that Paul refers to many years later when writing to the believers at Corinth about the trials and tribulations in his ministry.

Here's what Paul writes in 2 Corinthians 12:1-6 (The Living Bible Paraphrase). *"Fourteen years ago I was taken up to heaven for a visit. Don't ask me whether my body was there or just my spirit, for I don't know: only God can answer that. But anyway, there I was in paradise, and heard things so astounding that they are beyond a man's power to describe or put in words (and anyway I am not allowed to tell them to others)."*

While Karen and I were snuggled up there in my old Mercury on our first anniversary, God caught us up in some kind of out of body experience. I've never heard of this happening before, but this spiritual experience included both of us. It was like we were lifted up out of our bodies and out of the car. Together we were in God's presence. The feeling of oneness with each other and with God was overwhelming. No words were spoken, but the profound feeling of being wrapped together into one with each other and with God was unmistakable. It only lasted a short time; probably just seconds, but it was so real. When it was over, we looked at each other and we both said together, "What just happened?" Karen said, "I don't know, but it was spiritual and God was in it." I agreed and as we sat there in the car, we shared our thoughts and feelings about what had taken place. There was no question but that we had each experienced the same thing. We agreed that it was profound, it was spiritual and it was for both of us together. We had no way of knowing at that time what was in store for our lives and what role this spiritual experience would play in it.

In my mind, and in retrospect, what happened there that evening of our first anniversary, was that God blessed, sanctified and confirmed our marriage, and in the process bonded us together more tightly than we could have been otherwise. It was as if he validated our union when he performed another marriage ceremony in heaven, joining us together for life and for all eternity. I feel that our profound experience that night would see us through anything that might happen to us. It turned out the repeated blows we were to experience later were like a blacksmith's hammer serving only to drive us closer together, melding us into one being. God's work in our lives that night sealed our union forever.

In that same passage in 2 Corinthinians 12, Paul tells about his "Thorn in the Flesh." The reason for that thorn, Paul says, was to keep him from exalting himself because of his unique spiritual experiences. We also hesitate to share the experience we had for fear that we may be appearing to exalt ourselves. But, Paul's explanation of his heavenly experience helps us all to understand a little more why he was so convinced that his message was from God. In a sense, his testimony about that experience validates his instructions to the churches in his letters that are now part of Holy Scripture.

Paul prayed repeatedly for the thorn in his flesh to be removed, but God refused. Instead he told Paul *"My Grace is Sufficient for You."* The storms which were to come along shortly in Karen and my lives could be considered our thorn in the flesh, but regardless of whether they were or not, God's answer was the same for us as it was for Paul. "*My Grace is Sufficient for You.*" But, would God's grace really be sufficient for us? Would it be sufficient for repeated storms? Would his grace be enough for three?

CHAPTER 4

THE FIRST MAJOR STORM

Strangers In A Distant Land
June, 1962

"How can we sing the songs of the Lord while in a foreign land?" Psalm 137:4

By the time I graduated from Kansas University, Vicki was 7 months old and our second child was on the way. Needless to say, we weren't wasting any time building our family. With diploma and baby in hand, Karen and I packed our few belongings in the Mercury and headed for California and my first job as an engineer in the aerospace business. I was hired by a company known then as Atomics International, which was a division of North American Aviation. They were later folded into Rocketdyne and bought up by Rockwell, who later merged with Boeing. AI was engaged in developing nuclear power plants for space, which I thought would be very exciting work. The headquarters buildings were located in Canoga Park, a northern suburb of Los Angeles, although I would be working in a remote facility in the nearby Santa Susanna mountains. For our first home in California, we found a small 2-bedroom rental house in Granada Hills, across the San Fernando Valley from Canoga Park.

That is how Karen found herself at the ripe old age of 19, four months pregnant, stuck in a strange place, separated from home and family by 2000 miles, with a 7 month old baby to care for. It was the first time in our marriage that I had to go off to work and leave her alone all day. But with her baby and her black and white television, she got along. Regardless of those unsettled circumstances, we were very happy. We had each other and God blessed our marriage. We had faith to know that everything was proceeding roughly according to God's plan for our lives. He provided us with all of the support our young family really needed.

When we moved to California Karen and I were young adults, as well as being young spiritually in the sense that we were naive, trusting, and immature. We had what I now call "virgin psyches," never having been touched with real tragedy or grief. Karen and I were both brought up in strong Christian homes and had both professed at a young age our belief in Jesus Christ as the Son of God and our Savior. We both considered ourselves to be committed Christians. However, even though it took faith to work through our unusual courtship and marriage, as well as Karen's difficult pregnancy, our faith had never been severely tested. During my four years in the Navy my faith in God was never threatened and my time with the missionaries actually strengthened my faith. Then, with God's gracious intervention in our lives on that night of our first anniversary, we knew we were safe in his hands.

In California, we were like fish out of water. We didn't like the smog, the crowded highways, the high prices or the fast paced lifestyle. When I would drive home after a day's work at the test site up in the Santa Susanna hills, I would always cringe when I turned the corner at the top of the road to the valley below. What should have been a beautiful view of the valley below was instead a view of a thick blanket of smog filling the valley. It looked like a vast, dirty gray lake extending all the way across the valley to the San Gabriel mountians on the east side. I dreaded driving down into it, but my family was down there so I had to go. We lived in the valley for over a year before we realized there were mountains around us, the smog being so thick and pervasive that it usually reduced visibility to a mile or two. Only after a storm passed through did we have a day or two of good visibility where we could see the mountains around us. California has managed to reduce the smog since then, but that was what greeted us when we moved there in 1962.

We had a difficult time fitting in socially, even in the churches we visited. The smog-effect seemed to penetrate our social life as well. We had no friends or family there except for the sister of my missionary aunt, Ella Ruth, who lived with her family across the valley. Imogene had already been living in California and had frequently invited me over to their home in Compton while I was stationed at Long Beach in the Navy. She now lived out in the valley and while we didn't see her often, it was good to know that we had some family around during our time in California.

Our first house in Granada Hills was in what I called a "low rent district." Our small two bedroom house was one of four facing each other across a rectangular asphalt court. There were no basements or back yards. Two women occupied the house next to ours. One dressed in overalls and carried a lunch bucket to work. The other looked very feminine and stayed home. This was before gay lifestyles were lived openly and as conservative midwesterners, we tended to shy away from these two "unusual" women. We never managed to get acquainted with them and they seemed content to keep to themselves.

After a few months, we moved across the valley to Chatsworth where there were horse ranches and cowboys. Roy Rogers and Dale Evans even lived up above the town not far from us. I felt more comfortable in that community and I was 15 minutes closer to work. However, our housing situation was very similar. This time there were six small houses built around two asphalt courts, but with small yards. We did at least have a horse pasture with a pony behind our house. The families living in the development were friendly enough but we couldn't seem to find anyone in the neighborhood with whom we had anything in common. Consequently, we were not able to develop a close relationship with any of them.

I enjoyed my job at the remote nuclear test site in the Santa Susanna hills above Chatsworth. Hollywood filmed many westerns in those same hills. My company was developing the first (and as it turned out, the only) compact nuclear reactor power system to be launched into orbit by the U.S.A. There were rumors that the Soviets had orbited a nuclear reactor, but I never knew for sure. After the first several months, partly because of my service experience I'm sure, I was promoted to manager of a test facility used to check out the reactor fuel rods. In this "Critical Facility," we would load the actual fuel rods in a simulated flight reactor and take the core critical. However, while we kept the energy very low, we were still able to determine with certainty how the reactor would operate.

My company shared the test site with Rocketdyne, a sister company which operated several large static test stands for the Saturn rocket engines. Those were the days when we were racing Russia to put the first man on the moon and the huge rocket motors were being tested just across a narrow valley from our facility. We soon became accustomed to the loud roaring as the walls shook and frequently caused our test systems to shut down as the safety equipment mistakenly detected an earthquake.

As a working member of the nuclear industry, I had the opportunity to rub elbows with people who worked on the Manhattan Project at Los Alamos during World War II. Dr. Sid Harris had worked with Enrico Fermi at Los Alamos but had not been able to advance much in his career since. Dr. Sam Yee also worked with me in the critical facility as a design analyst. Both Sid and Sam were senior engineers but weren't interested in management, so after my first year there, they ended up reporting to me as the supervisor of the facility. The work and the professional atmosphere at my job were exciting and glamorous. However, I wasn't able to share much of my excitement with my young wife, nor was I able to develop a close friendship with any of my co-workers.

We actively sought out a church, but had a hard time finding one we liked. In our home church back in Kansas, we were a part of the family, but in California we felt like strangers. We visited a number of churches but they were either much smaller than we were accustomed to, or we just didn't feel comfortable. I guess we were looking for a church just like the one we grew up in, and that didn't exist; or at least we couldn't find it.

I'm sure our problems adapting to the Southern California scene were of our own making. There were cultural differences between Kansas and California we didn't understand, and that was a big part of our problem. Although we visited several churches, no one visited us or reached out to us in any way that I can remember.

Perhaps the reason had something to do with the fact that when we visited churches we were frequently greeted with the question, "Well, how do you guys like California?" When we didn't respond enthusiastically, the fervent, but usually transplanted, Californians were offended. The usual reply was, in so many words, "Well, if you don't like it why don't you go back where you came from?" I guess we should have at least tried to work up some enthusiasm for the area. We did agree it was probably a lovely place to live before there were so many people there.

The church we finally joined was a large "megachurch" 15 miles from our home across the San Fernando Valley; The First Baptist Church of Van Nuys. We only attended on Sunday mornings at first but then we joined the choir and tried to get active in the Young Married Bible Study Class. We weren't able to develop any personal friendships in the Bible Study group either, and after our son Mike was born, we dropped out of both that group and the choir. As a result, we spent our years in California in social isolation.

A Son – Welcome Aboard

"I prayed for this child and the Lord has granted me what I asked of Him. So, now I give him to the Lord" I Samuel 1:27-28

Our son Michael Allen was born a few months after we arrived in California. It was Almost a year to the day after Vicki was born. Vicki had been born on Halloween day, October 31st during my last year at the university, 1961. Mike was born a couple of weeks earlier than expected, arriving on October 21st in 1962. I was a little taken back when I first saw him in the hospital. He was smaller than Vicki when she was born; barely over 6 pounds. He had a fringe of dark hair and a wrinkled face that made him look like a little old man. Even so, I was thrilled to have a son. Like every dad, I looked forward to him growing up and getting involved in sports and all of the other things dads and sons do together.

Having two children so young was quite a handful for their Mom. As the children grew, Vicki, not even a full year older than

Mike, quickly took over the big sister role and took her little brother under her supervision. Mike quickly grew to be a fine handsome boy with sandy blond hair, brown eyes and a quiet, affectionate personality. He developed a sturdy build, not at all like the skinny baby he was when he was born. He was very bright, at least in the eyes of his proud parents, and he had a pleasant, "laid back" disposition. He loved to play and always had hugs and kisses for any member of the family who would receive them.

Mike loved to play with his little toy train, pushing it around the floor. I would often lie down on the living room floor to be with him, and when I did I knew that both Vicki and Mike would soon pile on for a game of rough house. Mike would always stick it out the longest. He would want me to roll over so he could get on my back and have a game of ride the horsey. He would get a little sparkle in those big brown eyes and a sly grin as he would yell "Horsey Daddy, horsey." I would walk around the floor on my hands and knees with him on my back, then he would move up on my shoulders and grab me around the neck and say "Piggy back, Daddy." So then I would struggle to my feet with him holding a choke hold around my neck, and we would go galloping around the small house. Mike would giggle and say "Run Daddy, run."

When Mike was about two, I remember pushing a shopping cart around the grocery store with him riding in the little seat facing me. Any time I would lean over to put something in the cart, he would wrap his arms around my neck and give me a big hug. One of my favorite pictures of Mike is a photo of him with his chubby cheeks, sitting inside a big cardboard box with one finger in his mouth, looking up with a questioning expression on his face as if he was saying, "How do I get out of here?" He was such a handsome little guy. He made me proud to be his daddy.

So, our young family was established, but since we hadn't been able to develop any close ties with neighbors or church members, there was no one to share it with. Our main source of entertainment was driving around the Southern California area. We would frequently use a tank of gas on a weekend driving to the mountains or down the coast. Sometimes we even visited Long Beach where I was stationed years before in the Navy. On a Friday night we would often pop up a big sack of popcorn, fix a bed in the back of our the F-85 station wagon for the kids, and go to a drive-in movie. Yes, my old Mercury finally bit the dust. But, it served us well to get us through college and out to California.

On one of our weekend trips, we visited a popular scenic lookout in the San Gabriel Mountains just north and east of Los Angeles. It turned out to be a long up hill walk from the parking lot to the lookout and we didn't have strollers for the kids. So, Karen and I took turns carrying them, or letting them walk. But, that was taking too long, so I scooped up both kids, and put one on each shoulder. I hadn't gone far when I began to get glaring looks from other dads who were walking slowly with their children. One young dad called out to me, "Hey man, you're setting a bad precedent. Knock it off." I thought, "Boy, you can't catch a break around here."

We had a real adventure with the two small ones when I was sent to a computer programming course in Las Vegas. The course was held in the old Thunderbird Hotel, right on the "Strip." We decided that Karen and the kids could come along since I would be driving and the company would be paying for the hotel. So, we packed up all the kid's stuff, including portable cribs for each of them, diaper bags, formula, suitcases etc. What we didn't know was that in order to get to the rooms at the hotel, you had to go through the casino to get to the reception area and the elevators to the rooms. We made quite a sight dragging all our paraphanalia and kids around between the crap tables, roulette wheels and slot machines to get to the elevators.

But, that wasn't the worst of it. Once in the room, Karen saw immediately that the room was barren of any entertainment; no TV, not even a radio. As I now recall I'm not even sure there were windows in the room. She was going to be stuck in the room all day with the kids while I was in class. In those days, at least, casinos were designed to keep the patrons in the gambling area as much as possible. The casinos had darkened windows, no clocks, and cocktail waitresses kept the gamblers furnished with free drinks while they gambled. The sleeping rooms were designed to make the patrons want to get out of the room and down to the casino. I'm sure the same philosophy holds today also.

Our technical sessions were having their own problems coping with the casino atmosphere. Halfway through each session, the band in the lounge just below our conference room would begin their floor show. The noise carried right through the floor and made it impossible to concentrate or be heard. The instructors finally began timing their breaks to coincide with the floor shows. As a result, about 30 young engineers would dump down into the lounge to watch the scantily clad dancers at each show. I used my break time the first day to run up to our room and try to entertain Karen and the kids for a few moments.

We decided the first day that this arrangement was not going to work. So, we piled into the station wagon after my afternoon class and scouted out a more appropriate venue for our family. Near the east end of the strip we found a motel where we could park right outside the room. It had a TV and a playground where Karen could take the kids. That evening, we dragged our kids and equipment back through the Thunderbird casino and relocated our camp to the motel.

Because we had two cribs for the babies, we had to rearrange the room by shoving the double bed over against the windows. That way we were able to put both cribs in the middle of the room where Karen could get to them easier in the night. I slept on the side of the bed against the windows.

We were startled at dawn the next morning by a loud banging on our door, followed by a loud gruff voice yelling "Open up, it's the Sheriff!" Struggling to rouse myself out of a sound sleep, I grumbled, "What in the world is going on." I crawled over Karen, pulled on a pair or pants, and opened the door. An officer was standing there looking very intense. He said, "Check your stuff. A cat burglar hit this place during the night." Then he said "They hit the rooms on either side of you, and the screens have been removed from your windows, so they probably got your stuff too." I quickly checked to see that all of our belongings were secure, then I told the officer "They couldn't have gotten in the window because I was sleeping there. Then I showed the officer how our bed was against the window. He said, "The burglar must have gotten the screen off and raised the window, then found you lying in his way. You lucked out. " Yeah,

I thought, the creep was standing there looking at me while I slept. I'm glad I didn't wake up." Later that day, we found Las Vegas had the highest crime rate in the country, especially for breaking and entering. Our guardian angel was looking out for us that night. We were glad to finally see Las Vegas in our rear view mirror as we headed back to California.

The Seizures - Storm Brewing

"I brought you my son who is possessed by a spirit... Whenever it seizes him, it throws him to the ground. He foams at the mouth, gnashes his teeth and becomes rigid. I asked your disciples to drive out the spirit, but they could not." Mark 9:17-18

Our first real family storm began to brew within a few months of our arrival in Southern California. The storm came gradually at first, but eventually developed into a full-blown tempest. Mike was only three months old when we took him to the doctor to get the new oral polio vaccine. That same evening we noticed his foot twitching as he slept on the living room couch. We had no idea what would cause something like that to happen and wondered if it had anything to do with the polio vaccine he had received that day. When it occurred again a few days later, we saw he wasn't asleep and his entire body was affected. His facial features were frozen in a twisted sort of way and his eyes stared blankly straight ahead. We were frightened and didn't know what it could mean. When we called the family doctor he told us to bring Mike in for an examination. The doctor could find nothing wrong with our boy so he decided to call in a pediatric neurologist who immediately put Mike into the hospital for tests. Meanwhile, Mike continued to have the seizures and they grew increasingly severe.

Mike went through a long series of very painful and difficult tests that went on for months while the seizures continued to increase in intensity. The worst test was the myelogram, a common test for neurological problems in the 60s before the days of CT scans and MRIs. A dye was injected into his spinal column and x-rays were taken of his brain. The injection obviously caused Mike to have a terrible headache and he couldn't turn his head for several days without crying.

The tests all came back negative. The diagnosis was 'idiopathic,' a medical "catch-all" word meaning no reason could be found for the problem. However, the young neurologist assigned to Mike's case frightened us unnecessarily by telling us over the telephone on a Friday that a degenerative condition might be indicated by the tests, but he couldn't meet with us to discuss it until the following Monday. That brief conversation upset us greatly. The term 'degenerative' frightened us and we needed to know exactly what that meant. We fretted all weekend wondering if Monday would ever come. We were at the hospital an hour early on Monday and had worked ourselves up to a fever pitch by the time the doctor showed up an hour late for our appointment. The young neurologist couldn't understand why we were upset when he finally drove up in his flashy sport car and seemed very flippant about the test results. Perhaps if someone told him he might have a degenerative problem, he would have had more empathy for Karen and me.

When we finally got to the subject of Mike's test, we found that the doctor was only speculating about some uncertainties he thought he detected in Mike's x-rays. He really couldn't tell us anything specific. That discussion might have been appropriate with his colleagues, but not with frightened young parents. Although we met many fine doctors over the ensuing years, that experience was not a good introduction for us to the field of specialty medicine.

The doctors prescribed a series of increasingly strong medications for Mike but none of them stopped the seizures. The heavy doses of medication caused him to look and act drugged at first, making it hard for him to function. When he was learning to walk it was not uncommon for him to fall and hit his head. Mike would frequently have several bumps and bruises showing on his forehead and face from his falls. But, he would gamely get up and keep trying. We tried wrapping his head and even investigated the possibility of getting him a crash helmet. However, Mike worked through that stage eventually, and the problem of falling into things took care of itself as he matured.

In most ways Mike developed as a normal child. He knew the alphabet at the age of two and a half and was able to do all of the things any two year old could do. But, his primary characteristic was his pleasant lovable personality. Although the medication probably enhanced his laid back disposition, he constantly filled our lives with laughter, love and joy.

Despite all of the medication, Mike begn having grand mal seizures frequently – two or three times a week not being unusual. The seizures were ugly, terrible ordeals for him and for us. We hated them. Time can never erase from our memories the distorted facial expressions, the drooling, and the rhythmic jerking of his body. There was nothing we could do during the seizures except to make sure his breathing path was clear and he didn't choke on his saliva. We learned to give him mouth to mouth resuscitation if he didn't appear to be breathing. Let me tell you, having to learn CPR because you believe you will need it to save your son's life is a traumatic experience in itself. Later, the nurses gave us a plastic breathing tube we could force down Mike's throat during a seizure to keep his breathing from being obstructed. Taking care of Mike during his seizures generated tremendous anxiety in Karen and me as we were brutally exposed us to the possibility that what we feared could become a reality.

The first seizures when Mike was very young were fairly brief passing episodes known as "petite mal" seizures. However, he soon progressed to "grand mal" seizures, which could last anywhere from one to three minutes and were characterized by tensed stiffened muscles and a rhythmic jerking. Sometimes the jerking was on just one side of the body, but other times it was over his entire body. In most cases, when the seizures had run their course, Mike would collapse, physically exhausted, and usually sleep for a short time. When he woke up, he went on about his business, not realizing what had happened. Then Karen and I could expect a day or two of respite before another seizure occurred.

We learned that seizures are believed to originate from a lesion in the brain, caused by some sort of trauma such as a blow to the head. The doctors had speculated in Mike's case that a moderately difficult birth delivery may have been the cause. However, we were never comfortable with their speculations. We were convinced that the doctors and medical staff at the hospital were truly mystified about the cause of Mike's seizures and were just throwing around medical jargon to hide the fact they knew no more about Mike's condition than we did. We were finding out first hand that the human neurological system was still a mystery to the medical profession. There is much about it that still cannot be explained, even today.

The Full Storm Hits

"I will fear no evil, for Thou art with me" Psalm 23:4 (KJV)

After almost three years in California, on Tuesday, April 13, 1965 we lost our son. The suddenness of it was terrible. I had gotten up early and slipped off to work while my family slept. When Karen got up, she found Mike dead in his bed, his face buried in the bedding. Apparently he had a seizure during the morning hours after I left for work. He had his face buried in the blankets and couldn't get his breath, essentially suffocating. Karen called me at my desk not long after I arrived at work. I'll never be able to forget my young wife's voice as she sobbed into the phone. "Honey, Mikie's dead! He's all purple!.."

It was normally a twenty-minute drive down the mountain road from the remote test area where I worked, down into the San Fernando Valley where we lived. As I sped dangerously down the mountainous road, I kept telling myself that this was just a night-mare and I would surely wake up soon. When I turned onto our street I saw the emergency vehicles with lights flashing in front of our little house and I knew this nightmare had crossed over into the realm of reality.

I ran into the house and saw Mike's discolored body lying on the living room couch, and a group of police officers and paramedics standing around talking. I ran to my wife who was still in her house-coat and held her sobbing body tight. I was not ready to admit Mike was really dead. I asked the medics, "Are you absolutely sure he's not just unconscious?." They assured me there was no doubt. Then I just held Karen and tried to comfort her. I kept saying, "Honey,

Mikie's all right now. He's in heaven and he's not going to have any more seizures. Honey, God knows best. We have to trust him." As I said all this to comfort Karen, in my own mind I was shocked, bewildered, hurt and shaken.

The medics called a funeral home for us and the attendants soon came and removed Mike's body. The police officer had already called our doctor and confirmed Mike was being treated for seizures and thus nothing unseemly was indicated. They had to rule out any possibility of child abuse being the cause of death and the doctor's explanation was enough to satifsy the officer. Later, we called the First Baptist Church in Van Nuys and they sent a staff minister over to visit us. I don't even remember his name. He appeared to be a pleasant and caring person, and he brought us a lovely book of poems, trying to give us some words of comfort. He seemed uncomfortable trying to minister to us when he didn't know us, but at least someone came. A few of our Chatsworth neighbors did express their sympathy, and my aunt and her husband from across the valley came over to be with us that first evening.

When Mike died, the trauma was excruciating. The grief and sorrow of his loss overwhelmed us and we wanted to get back to Kansas and be with our families as quickly as possible. We needed them and we wasted no time deciding to take Mike's body back home to Kansas for burial. I had already been looking for a job back in the Midwest so we were sure we wouldn't be staying much longer in California. We didn't want to have Mike's remains buried in a place we were planning to leave forever. We made the arrangements to have Mike's body flown to Kansas, then went to make travel arrangements to get our little family home.

Looking back now, when we compare that situation with the support we received years later from our church in Missouri, it makes us realize how important it is to belong to a community of believers. It was our own fault we hadn't gotten ourselves more involved with the church in California, but in our immaturity, we just couldn't find a place where we felt comfortable. We were also concerned that Mike's seizures would prevent us from leaving him in the nursery at church with people we didn't know.

So, while the church as an institution tried to minister to us through a sympathetic gesture, we realize now it is the people, not the institution, that ministers to people in emotional need. Comfort is ministered best through close personal relationships. People care about you when you are a part of their lives. We were not part of anyone's lives there in California when Mike died, and as a result we had only each other to lean on. We thank God that we were there for each other.

Following Mike's funeral in Kansas, I didn't have the strength or inclination to return to California and my job right away. We stayed in Kansas for a few days after the funeral, and in the state of mind I was in, I didn't care what happened with my job. It was so good to be surrounded by family and childhood friends as they comforted and affirmed us. I spent hours playing basketball in the driveway with Karen's two brothers, Terry and Craig and some of their friends. That was very therapeutic for me. Karen just needed to be with her Mom and Dad and the rest of her family. We slept at their house, but would often go across town to my parents house to spend time with them also.

One day I took my two youngest brothers, Glenn and Roger out rabbit hunting with our 22s in the country near my Dad's grain elevator. It was good to be with them having a "living" experience with family I loved to help take away for a moment the "death" exerience that was too frequently on my mind.

As I mentioned before, we six brothers all called our father "Pop." He wanted to spend some time with me also, so Pop took me flying in his club's Cessna 172. As we were flying over the flat Kansas countryside, he gave me some good advice. I had said that I guess we needed to go home and get back into our routine, but he replied, "No, you need to establish a new routine that doesn't always remind you of Mike."

Then, to lighten things up I said, "Hey, Pop. Let's peel off like the fighter planes do in the movies." He replied, "I don't think you want to do that. Aren't you the one who gets motion sickness?" I said, "Yeah, but I can handle it." So he said, "Okay, tighten your seat belt. Here we go." As he banked over into a steep dive, I immediately regretted the move as my stomach tried to make it's way up out of my throat. "Enough, enough, I cried." "I didn't think so," Pop chuckled as he leveled off and headed for the landing strip.

While we were in Kansas, I didn't even call in to my office to let them know I needed a few more days off. But, I knew we needed to get back or I would lose my job, so Karen and I finally gathered our composure and flew back to California. I reported in to my office to find that they had indeed begun termination proceedings on me, assuming I wasn't coming back. My supervisor was able to get me reinstated after much pleading, and I got my job back. However, I immediately began searching for a position back in the Midwest where we could be closer to family and, hopefully, a more compatible cultural environment.

I mentioned that we lived in a low rent district in Chatsworth. There was an odd couple who lived in the house behind us. Buck and Pansy were country folks from somewhere deep in the South. Buck was a burly redneck, coarse of language and manner. Pansy was a tall, thin and simple woman with a good heart. Buck and Pansy's marital squabbles were common knowledge around the neighborhood. It was hard not to be aware of them on nights when they would come home drunk at one o'clock in the morning. He would sometimes chase her down the street yelling profanities at the top of his lungs and threatening to kill her. Pansy's piercing screams would wake everyone within a mile radius.

When Mike died, Pansy wanted to help. While we were away in Kansas she didn't know what else to do, so she ordered some cut flowers brought to our house. She didn't know we would be gone for several days, so when we returned the flowers were on the front porch waiting for us. By then they were completely wilted and brown. Somehow, those pathetic lifeless flowers symbolized for us the three years we had spent in California. We arrived like fresh cut flowers, but were set out in a lonely barren place with no social nourishment or water to keep us blooming. With Mike gone, we felt like the flowers looked.

When we returned to California, we were essentially on our own again. Typically, after the funeral, the survivors are left alone to work through their grief and we had no choice but to experience that same dilemma. We had no one to lean on except each other. With my work schedule, Karen was alone at home with 3-year old Vicki during the day, and no friends she could even call on the telephone for support. She was so young, so vulnerable and I hated having to be at work and not being there for her. We had to do something to help her. It was a difficult time for both of us and a time when we needed love and comfort that was not there. We decided after a few days that Karen needed to take Vicki and fly back to Kansas to be with her family for a couple more weeks. I would be working and could take care of myself alone. So, I took them to the airport and put them on a plane back to Wichita to be with family and friends.

When they came back to me a couple of weeks later, Karen was better able to handle the time alone, but it was still a very hard time for her. Only a mother can know the grief of losing a child whom you had carried in your body for nine months, and then loved and nurtured constantly, as a full-time stay-at-home mom. She amazed me then, and she still amazes me today with her strength and her faith.

Have you ever had something happen that kind of scares you and makes the hair on your neck stand up? Sometime during those early weeks after Mike's death I was baby sitting with Vicki one evening while Karen was out. I was sitting in the easy chair reading while Vicki played on the floor with her toys. I saw that little Vicki was pretending to talk to her brother in heaven on the yellow toy telephone Mike had enjoyed so much. She suddenly stopped and said, "Daddy, it's Mikie. He wants to talk to you." As she was handing me the toy phone, the real telephone rang on the table beside my chair. I picked up the phone and said "Hello." There was only silence on the line. A chill ran down my spine as I said again, "Hello...Hello. Is anybody there?" Still no response. I was shivering as I hung up the phone wondering if my son had just called to let me know that he was there watching us. Intellectually, I thought "Nah, no way." I knew better. It was just a weird coincidence. However, in the frame of mind we were in during those days of mourning, we didn't know what to think. To this day I don't have the answer to what really happened that night.

Waves Of Grief

"As he approached the town gate, a dead (child) was being carried out — the only son of his mother... When the Lord saw her, his heart went out to her and he said, "Don't cry." Luke 7:12-13

The emotions we experienced when our son died were deep and painful. For me, the pain of grief when we lost Mike was harder to bear than any physical pain I had ever experienced. The tears flowed for weeks before the wound began to heal enough that we were able to go for a significant length of time without having our minds occupied only with thoughts of him.

While we were back in Kansas for the funeral, family and friends would try to divert our attention from our grief by talking about other things. But it was hard to think of anything else. I remember one time several of us were sitting in the living room talking. I was lost in my thoughts about Mike when Karen's dad broke into my conciousness, saying "Don, Don, did you hear what I was saying?" I think it would have been better if they had encouraged us to talk about our son, or about what we were feeling, rather than avoiding the subject. It would have been helpful for us to ventilate those feelings of grief and sorrow, rather than try to pretend they weren't there. So, during those days, the emotional storm was in its full fury, tossing our frail souls about like a cork in the ocean.

Shifting the analogy a bit, I would say that as the healing progressed, we experienced grief like a slowly receding tide on the shore. The waves of sorrow continued to roll in, but the period between waves increased, ever so gradually, and each wave wasn't quite as big as the one before. Then the tide would come in again and it seemed as if the tragedy had happened just yesterday. But, then again, the waves would recede a little, maybe more quickly this time.

Waves of grief would be triggered in Karen and me without warning by some subtle reminder of Mike. Just shopping in the super market could suddenly trigger emotions of grief as we came around an aisle and remembered Mike riding in the shopping cart and reaching for something in that very place. Later, we learned to call these surprises "ambushes." We would be unexpectedly plunged again beneath the waves of grief, which sometimes seemed to overwhelm us. The waves would always recede, however, and we would not drown beneath them. We were learning that we were indeed life-worthy, and that we were able to weather the storm of grief.

Then, as time wore on, the waves began to recede further until we gained some sense of equilibrium. That took several months after Mike died, but as the months turned into years, the waves came less frequently, until finally, after maybe a year or two, the sorrow receded to a remote corner of our consciousness. Today, decades after Mike's death, small waves still wash up over our feet on occasion and remind us of what we have lost.

You might be asking, "How were we doing spiritually during this time?" Did we turn against God in bitterness for taking our child from us? Did we blame him for what happened, or did we begin to wonder if God was even up there? Did we question his love for us, and even his goodness? Did we ask "Why?"

We didn't blame God, but of course we asked why. We certainly didn't understand what was happening to us. We were just kids and we were hurting, not understanding why this tragedy had to happen to us. We wondered if God was punishing us for something we had done, or had failed to do. We felt overpowering guilt as we told ourselves, "If only we had watched him closer." Or, "If only we had gone to another doctor, maybe they could have prescribed a different medication." There were a hundred other "if only" thoughts that crowded our minds. I believe the ministry of God's comforting Spirit finally convinced us that we couldn't allow ourselves to think that way. We couldn't keep blaming ourselves. Perhaps we could have done something different, but what was done was done and no one could do anything about it. We finally realized that we had to trust God and his perfect will. There was no other way.

Karen had felt all along that God was going to heal Mike of his seizures. One Sunday morning during a worship service she felt the Lord was speaking to her through the worship experience, giving her assurance that he was there and in control of Mike's situation. So Mike's death left Karen spiritually confused as well as hurt. Though we were both confused, it never occurred to us to doubt God. The faith our upbringing instilled in us and God's previous work in our lives kept us from doubting God's existence and his ways. We knew he was there and we had to believe God knew best.

I told Karen that I was convinced that Mike wouldn't have gotten better if he hadn't had the fatal seizure. We finally came to realize and accept the fact that death is a form of healing. You can't believe that unless you know in your heart that Heaven is real and that it is a perfect place. Mike is in the very arms of Jesus now, happy and secure, bubbling with that little laugh of his. But death and going to God wasn't the kind of healing we were praying for. We may pray for death to spare a painfully ill grandparent, but not a cute little boy, even if he did have seizures. I believe that God showed us his grace by allowing us to see and know that for Mike, death was a permanent healing and the most gracious answer to prayer God in his wisdom could give us.

As I reflect back on those days now, I can see that God was indeed in control. He knew the storm was coming and he had made us and prepared us to be lifeworthy in this terrible tempest. I can see now that he was there, providing power and direction to keep us headed into the storm, and eventually, through it. He wouldn't let us collapse and give in to the tempest. Like the popular poem about footsteps in the sand, he was keeping us afloat in his tender care, comforting us and helping us every step of the way.

The Shunnamite Woman

Elisha to the Shunnamite woman - "Is it well with you? Is it well with the child?" The Shunnamite woman- "It is well." 2 Kings 4:26 (KJV)

There is a tender and touching story in the Old Testament that helped us spiritually to understand and know that faith in God would see us through, even when the world seemed to be falling in. It is the Old Testament story of a simple woman with no name and no accomplishments of note, but she is my favorite heroine in the Bible. She is simply known as "the Shunnamite woman." I love her story as told in the King James version of the Bible, 2 Kings Chapter 4. The prophet Elisha had ministered to this woman and her aging husband after they had befriended him. He prayed for the childless couple to be blessed with a baby. The baby was born and grew to be a young boy. While visiting in the field with his father, the boy became ill. They brought him to his mother, where she held him in her arms until he died.

Without giving a reason to her husband, she saddled her donkey and rode off to find her pastor, Elisha the prophet. When Elisha saw her approaching from a distance, he sent his servant to meet her, and to ask her, *"Is it well with you? Is it well with the child?"* The Shunnamite woman amazingly sent back the answer, *"It is well."* How could she give such an answer? It certainly was not well! It was horrible. Her child had died in her arms.

When the Shunnamite woman came to Elisha, he knew immediately something was terribly wrong. He said, *"She is in bitter distress, but the Lord has hidden it from me and has not told me why"*. Then the Shunnamite woman responded, *"Did I ask you for a son, my lord? Didn't I tell you, 'Don't raise my hopes?'"* Then Elisha realized the child had died. He responded quickly, rushed to the boy, and there he demonstrated the compassion of Almighty God. A great miracle was performed and recorded for all ages as the child was raised from the dead.

But why did the woman answer in the first place that *"It is well?"* Why didn't she tell the prophet immediately that her boy had died? I think the answer is that even in her deep distress, she knew God had miraculously given her the child and the boy belonged to the Lord. She could say *"it is well"* only if she had an unwavering faith in God's goodness and a deep assurance God was in control. Because her faith in God was deep, she knew no matter what the circumstances indicated, and no matter how she hurt inside, God was in control, and therefore it was well! Karen and I had to come to that same faith position. We knew Mike was a gift from God and we knew God was loving and kind. He had demonstrated that to us many times in our lives. So, even when Mike died, we needed to be able to say, it is well.

The Shunnamite woman obviously needed her pastor. She was distressed but she was in control of her emotions. She needed the prophet's reassurance God was in control. She needed spiritual counsel and ministry and Elisha provided it, but she received much more than support in her sorrow. Her great faith was rewarded beyond her expectations. I don't know if she even hoped Elisha would raise her son from the dead. Those things didn't happen in those days any more that they do now. She would have no reason to expect a miracle unless God had impressed her directly that it was to be so. But regardless of whether or not she had a word from God, she was faithful to trust him. She went to the prophet and then relied on God to do his perfect will. What an inspirational testimony of faith. The Shunnamite woman has helped us to understand that no matter what the circumstances, when you know God is in control, "*It is well.*"

Michael's Memorial

During the time Karen and Vicki were back in Kansas and I was alone, I wrote some simple verses about Mike and fixed up a memory book with photos of him interspersed with the verses. While the verses are not profound poetry, I share them here to illustrate the thoughts and feelings of a young father grieving for his lost son.

MICHAEL ALLEN CLIFFORD
October 26, 1962 to April 13, 1965

It's so sad to write, but it now must be done.
In April this year we lost our sweet son.
What can we say through our sorrows and tears,
but that we loved him completely through his few short years.
Life would have been hard, not all joy and fun
for our sweet, loving and most precious son.

Our little Mike was a joy to his dad;
he was chunky and handsome, such a strong little lad.
He would welcome me home at the end of the day
with a big hug and kiss and a yearning to play.
He filled my heart with abundance of love,
and oh how I miss him, my sweet precious dove.

Little Mikie loved his dear mommy so much.
With just a few words he would reach in and touch
her deepest well of love, and happiness too,
when he said simply, "Mommy, I wuv you."
She misses him still, and shall always in love,
till at last we're together in God's heaven above.

Little Mike lives in our hearts to this day,
and we know he's only a short prayer away.
Vicki says in her sweet prayers at night
that she loves her brother and knows he's all right.
Because he's with Jesus, all safe and secure,
and his love for us will forever endure.

Mike left as he came, without any fuss,
but he brought with him a lesson for us.
He showed us how deep is this feeling called love,
and as all good things, it must come from above.
This love is the sweetest emotion we'll know,
Our Father has ordained that it should be so.

We're born into life through no wish of our own,
but for those of us who rebel and moan,
God says in his wisdom, "Life worthwhile will be.
I'll provide you with love, the very essence of Me."
We hadn't rebelled, I think we can say,
but God still saw fit to show us the way.

Our Father showed us that the love we are given
is our own private, personal preview of heaven.
That the fullness of life is measured by love;
our lives were full, but our son from above
came to show us how much more life can mean
if someone else loves you and on you must lean.

We miss our sweet boy and the pain is severe,
but we're thankful he came and brought to us here
an even greater abundance of love to share;
to give us a reason to love and to care.
Yes, the Lord surely knows that we love our young son,
but first of all, most of all, God's will be done.

As I have mentioned before, soon after Mike's death we realized
we had to get back to the Midwest and closer to our families. We
seemed unable to develop relationships in Southern California and
we didn't want to cope with our grief and loneliness alone. Within a
few weeks I found a job back in the Midwest and in August we left
California behind. Many questions were still unanswered, but as far
as we were concerned God was in control and God's will had been
done. Our faith had been tested and shaken, but it still held firm.
However, our virgin psyches had been wounded, and as far as we
could tell, we would never be the same again, emotionally or spiritually. However, we still had much to learn about the grace of God.

CHAPTER 5

Rebuilding After The Storm

August, 1965

"But one thing I do: Forgetting what is behind and straining toward what is ahead, I press on toward the goal..."
Phillipians 3:13

I found my new job through advertisements in the Los Angeles papers for aerospace engineers at a firm called McDonnell Aircraft Company, located in St. Louis, Missouri. I knew nothing about the company except that their newspaper ads indicated they were building the Gemini space capsules as part of the U.S. space program. That was a big plus for me because I always wanted to be a part of the "race for space" that was enthralling the country at that time. When we checked the maps we found St. Louis was right between Arkansas where my parents were retiring, and Iowa and Illinois where two of my brothers (Les and Bill, brothers No. 1 and 3) were living. It is also about a six hour drive from our home town of Wichita where Karen's family still lived. I arranged by phone for an interview with the McDonnell recruiters at the L.A. International Airport where they had rented an office trailer to interview people from all over the Los Angeles area. They offered me a job on the spot and I accepted it on the spot. Three weeks later we left the sad memories of Mike's death 2,000 miles behind us.

The move was good for us. The intense activity associated with all the logistics of moving kept our minds and bodies occupied.

When we arrived in the St. Louis area, the new environment was very different from Southern California. We had expected a northeastern big city atmosphere, and there was some of that. Even so, we found a Midwestern Ozark flavor blended in which we found to be very acceptable. The new experiences that constantly bombarded our minds were unrelated in any way to our memories of Mike. The change helped us to get on with our lives and to begin building new memories.

Before we left California, I resolved that no matter what happened after we got relocated, we were going to get active in a church. I had formulated a plan for visiting churches and evaluating them so even if we couldn't find a church that perfectly satisfied us, we would join the best of the ones we could find within a 6 week period. I was determined that we would get active in Sunday School, choir, Wednesday night prayer meeting and whatever other opportunities were available. We would make it work.

Our first house was located in the suburbs on the west side of St. Louis, and near my new job at McDonnell Aircraft Company. We found our church on the third try and within a month we were members of historic Fee Fee Baptist Church in Bridgeton, Missouri. It's an odd name and they get their share of kidding, but Fee Fee church got its name from the early French settlers in the area and it is known as the "Oldest Baptist Church West of the Mississippi." For Karen and me it was the doorway to our spiritual maturity. We were ready to enter into our adult spiritual experience and we had found fertile soil where we could grow.

The church took us in warmly, knowing nothing of our recent grief experience. The first Sunday morning we attended an adult Bible study class as well as the worship service. The class happened to have a social activity scheduled for the next weekend and they insisted we attend. So we did. We felt at home immediately and joined the church the next Sunday, fitting in as if we had been there all of our lives. Unknown to us, God was preparing us for the next moving of His Spirit in our lives.

Troubled Waters

"You knit me together in my mother's womb...My frame was not hidden from you when I was made in the secret place. When I was woven together... your eyes saw my unformed body. All the days ordained for me were written in your book before one of them came to be." Psalm 139:13 - 16

After Mike's death, Karen and I talked about having more children. The possibility of losing another child scarcely entered our minds. Karen said, "Those things only happen to other people." So, we decided to try to have another baby right away instead of waiting a few years as we had originally planned before Mike died. Karen became pregnant right away, but miscarried at 9 weeks into the pregnancy. She began spotting early and the doctor confined her to bed where she stayed until she finally miscarried. Karen caught the fetus and saved the inch-long baby for the doctor to examine. We blamed the miscarriage on a case of influenza that Karen had a few weeks after she got pregnant.

Several months later Karen was pregnant again, and again began having problems early in her pregnancy. The doctor ordered her off her feet when she was just a couple of months along and she spent the next ten weeks confined to bed. Ten weeks is an eternity for a healthy young mother to lie in bed when she feels fine. It's also a long time for her husband who has to take care of all the household needs and a four-year old while holding down a full time job. Karen continued to spot and her doctor wouldn't allow her to get up except to go to the bathroom. Those weeks were very difficult for all three of us. The seas were rough with lots of whitecaps, but still they were navigable. During both pregnancies, with me at work and Karen confined to bed, four year old Vicki had to fend for herself much of the time. She was actually a big help to her mom while I was away from home.

Some new friends from church came over and helped clean and cook on a couple of occasions, but most of the time Vicki and I did what had to be done. I didn't realize so much dirt could accumulate inside a house until I had to sweep the floors regularly. To complicate matters even further during those pregnancies, I was working overtime and going to night school working on my Master's Degree. Karen says that I somehow found time to play softball with the church team. I don't remember that but she's probably right.

I was glad we had 24-hour grocery stores because I did most of our food shopping late at night. Those were long difficult days for a young family, and with my work and school I wasn't there as much as I should have been. Looking back now, I realize I should have at least dropped out of my night classes (and softball) and stayed home to help my family when they needed me.

When Karen miscarried the second time she was four and a half months along. I was with her when she delivered the fetus in the bathroom. When she realized what was happening she yelled at me, "Honey, I think the baby is coming now!" I rushed into the bathroom and managed to catch the tiny baby. It was small enough that I could cup it in my two hands. How can I describe the emotions as I held that living baby in the palms of my hands? I knew that at less than five months the baby had no chance of living, even if Karen had been in the hospital at the time. I cut the umbilical cord with a pair of scissors, and in our panic, I didn't think to tie or clamp the cord to the placenta. I found a plastic ice cream carton and put the baby in it, then I wrapped Karen up in a blanket and we headed for the hospital in downtown St. Louis.

Karen's obstetrician met us at the emergency room entrance since I had called ahead and told him what was happening. I gave him the container with the baby in it and waited in the corridor while he examined Karen. When he came out his only words to me were, "That baby hasn't been dead very long. It's a shame we couldn't have held on a few more weeks. We might have been able to save it." Then the doctor left orders for Karen to be taken upstairs to the operating room for a D&C. At the time the baby came so suddenly, I couldn't think of anything except getting Karen to the hospital. But, later as I sat in the waiting room, I had time to reflect on what had happened. I thought to myself, I was actually holding a living child with its heart beating right there in my hands. As I reflected on that moment, I realized I had been holding all the hopes and dreams we had for this child right there in my two hands, and I had to acknowledge to myself that they were not going to happen. The little baby I held in my hands represented both the gift of life and the tragedy of loss we had already experienced before, and would experience again. We never learned whether the baby was a boy or a girl. Karen asked the doctor later and he said he never bothered to check. The baby was treated as a routine miscarriage and nothing more was done to acknowledge the birth and death of our third child.

At the time the doctor ordered Karen to be taken to OR, it happened to be lunch hour and no one came to pick her up for almost 20 minutes. As a result of my failure to tie the cord to the placenta, Karen lost an immense amount of blood, and I seriously endangered her life. The orderlies finally wheeled her out of the emergency waiting area and I didn't see her again until they delivered her to a private room a couple of hours later after the D&C procedure.

Shortly after getting settled into her room, Karen began complaining about feeling light headed as if she were going to faint. I tried to comfort her and convince her that she was all right. I kept telling her, "Calm down. You'll feel better in a little while." She continued to complain however and finally said, "You'd better find a nurse. Something's badly wrong."

I finally located a nurse and brought her to the room. She tried to take Karen's pulse, and then her blood pressure, but it wouldn't register. Suddenly all kinds of commotion broke out. Nurses were shouting, bells were ringing and lights were flashing. A young resident doctor finally came running into the room. The nurse shouted "Her blood pressure has dropped out of sight. I'm afraid she's going into shock." The doctor calmly started an I-V drip to bring up her blood pressure and fortunately Karen stabilized after a few anxious moments.

The multiple examinations and the operating room staff had failed to discern the serious amount of blood Karen had lost. The doctor ordered a blood transfusion and after the first unit of blood was administered Karen began feeling better. During the second unit she began to break out with a rash on her stomach. We summoned the young resident, who happened to be Asian. He must not have been in the States very long because he spoke only a little English. We were amused at his diagnosis. He said "Oh, maybe bed bugs."

"What kind of hospital had he come from" we wondered. After our reaction to that comment died down, he shrugged and said, "Well, if you get any more lash (rash), call me." Although we have told that story and laughed many times since, we were glad he was there when we needed him.

The miscarriages were difficult for us, but after recently losing a two and a half year old son, the grief was put into perspective for us. We could weather this storm. Up to that point in our lives, we didn't think of an early miscarriage as losing a child. However, after I held that little baby in my hands, I knew that it was indeed a living human being and I grieved that we had not been able to save it.

Our disappointment after the miscarriages included a feeling of discouragement after investing so much time and emotional energy in the problems of the pregnancies. The doctors didn't think there was anything genetic which could cause two consecutive failed pregnancies and they didn't try to discourage us from trying again. We made it through that difficult time and then we tried one more time to have a baby.

We never had a problem getting pregnant. To our relief, Karen's next pregnancy went smoothly with none of the problems of the previous miscarriages, and at 11:35 p.m. on April 17 in 1968 our daughter Rebecca Dawn was born. My birthday is on the 18th but she didn't want to wait another 25 minutes. Her mother and the doctor agreed and Becky came when she was ready. She was a perfect, beautiful and healthy baby girl.

I had told Karen years before that if we ever had a girl born in April, I wanted to name her April Dawn. Then when that actually happened, we chickened out. We decided that while it was a beautiful name, we were concerned about what her friends would call her when she grew older. They would no doubt call her "Ape." So we went with our second choice and named her Rebecca Dawn. Becky was a beautiful baby, with just a hint of red in her hair, and she was sweet and easy going even as a baby. She says now that she can still remember me rocking her to sleep and singing "Pretty Baby" to her.

Her delivery and subsequent health restored our confidence and we decided when the time was right, we could have at least one more child. But I'm getting ahead of myself. We will get to Rachel's story later.

Spiritual Growth

"Do your best to present yourself to God as one approved, a workman who does not need to be ashamed and who correctly handles the word of truth." 2 Timothy 2:15

During the years after we arrived in Missouri, the church became our focus. We grew rapidly in the rich spiritual soil and quickly became integrated into the work and fellowship of the church. We sang in the choir, served on committees and attended all of the meetings of the church. We especially enjoyed studying the Bible, soon graduating from sitting in an adult Bible Study class to teaching youth classes. A few years later we worked up to teaching young adults. We discovered what every teacher knows; teaching is the best way to learn. We couldn't get enough of the riches of God's Word and we soaked it up like sponges. After just a few years, the church elected me to serve as a deacon. After a few more years I was elected to the office of Chairman of Deacons. I was happy to serve anywhere the church asked me to.

I came to have a very high regard for the Scriptures as the inspired Word of God. I found the teachings of the Bible can be trusted to provide guidance and strength through every experience in life, no matter how difficult that experience may be. Time and time again God used the Scriptures to speak to our family and give us peace, comfort, assurance and strength through all of our trials. I was so impressed by the beauty, the meaningfulness, and the power of the Scriptures that I began an extensive Scripture memorization program. For nearly ten years I memorized a verse a day until I had much of the New Testament and many of the Psalms committed to memory. I memorized by chapter and book rather than individual verses, memorizing a new verse each morning and reviewing the previous two or three verses at the same time to lock them into my memory. I can't overstate the amount of strength and comfort that came from 'hiding the Word in my heart.' I couldn't recite all those passages ver batim today, but I have a pretty good idea what's in there and where to find whatever I'm looking for in the Bible.

I saw a cartoon recently that intrigued me. It said, "This life is a test. It is only a test. If it were a real life, you would have been given instructions on where to go and what to do." The writer apparently thought that was pretty amusing, but obviously he didn't realize we have actually been given those instructions. The Bible is the instruction book for the human life. It is the ultimate Owners' Manual. I like the "Message" paraphrase of the 119th Psalm, which is the longest chapter in the Bible and is dedicated to glorifying the Word of God. In particular, verses 9-12 have been an encouragement to my life. *"How can a young person live a clean life? By carefully reading the map of your Word. I'm single-minded in pursuit of you: don't let me miss the road signs you've posted."*

Of course, one cannot become immersed in the Word of God and not at the same time become a person of prayer. The Scriptures themselves are God speaking to us and prayer is but a two way conversation with God. As the words of the Bible are read and meditated upon, a conversation with God naturally ensues. The blessings and promises found in Scripture stimulate us to praise and thanksgiving. Moreover, the conviction of sin that inevitably comes from a serious reading of the Word drives us to our knees in repentance.

When a ship has survived storms at seas, the wear and tear on the vessel is often significant. Periodically, the ship goes into dry dock for repairs and refurbishing. The destroyer I served aboard in the Pacific was in dry dock in the Long Beach Naval Shipyard when I reported aboard. In that safe and stable environment, the repairs could be made and the ship's systems upgraded in preparation for the next cruise. I think of those years at Fee Fee as our dry dock experience. We were being fitted out for our next cruise and the storms that would be part of it. I'm sure we could not have survived what was to follow in our lives without the Spirit of God ministering to us through those fellowship times with him and through the fellowship of his church. God prepared us for the difficult times to come by strengthening our spiritual foundation and growing our faith. As we taught the Bible and became involved in various leadership positions in the church, we also became an integral part of a close-knit family of believers. That fellowship was to become a key element in the next chapter of our story.

CHAPTER 6

THE SECOND STORM

An Angel Unaware

July 1970

"Then God remembered Rachel" Genesis 30:22

It was two years after Becky was born that Rachel Dianne arrived on the scene. Rachel was a beautiful bright-eyed happy baby, immediately winning our hearts with her sweet bubbly personality. She had a round happy face with sparkling blue eyes; truly a beautiful baby. Within a few weeks she was smiling and gurgling, filling our hearts with joy. Vicki and Becky loved to play with her and altogether we were a blessed happy family.

Karen and I were so blessed with the joy that comes from healthy loving children. I mentioned earlier I had always wanted a large family. Our theory as a young couple was that love is the key to happiness, so the more love you have in your life, the happier you will be. Every family member brings additional love into our lives which increases our happiness. Logically therefore, in my mind a large family is a happy family, bringing joy to all.

I was learning, however, that love isn't the only thing children can bring. They can also be the source of great heartache and pain, at all ages. Still, the love our children brought to us far out shadowed the heartache caused by their illnesses and even by our losing them. We will always be grateful for the years we had with each of our five living children.

Rachel was three months old in October of 1970 when I had to take a business trip to Florida. I flew out on a Sunday afternoon. One of the workers in the Sunday School nursery that morning told us she thought Rachel was coming down with a cold because she had a little fever and didn't seem to feel well. We all assumed it was a cold coming on and it shouldn't interfere with my trip. Rachel was sicker than we realized, however.

I made the trip to Florida, checked into my hotel, and had a rest-less night's sleep, worrying about Rachel. The next morning, shortly after arriving at my meeting, someone interrupted to tell me I had a phone call. "They said it was an emergency." I felt a familiar sinking feeling in my stomach. Since our experience with Mike a few years before, I dreaded unexpected telephone calls. Now, five years later it was our pastor from St. Louis saying in a matter of fact tone, "Don, your baby is very sick. Karen called the doctor this morning as soon as she could get him. Then she called me and the ambulance, but before we could get there, Rachel stopped breathing. Karen gave her mouth to mouth respiration to keep her alive. We got her to the hospital as soon as we could. The doctor thinks it's spinal meningitis. Rachel is on a respirator machine now and the doctor doesn't know if she will make it or not." I remember saying, "We're going to lose her. I know we're going to lose her." I was remembering Mike and feeling that now God was going to take Rachel from us as well.

I rushed to the airport and was fortunately able to catch a flight home right away. Friends from church were waiting for me at the gate when I arrived in St. Louis and rushed me to the hospital in nearby St. Charles. Karen was waiting for me and quickly ushered me into the intensive care unit where Rachel was isolated behind a window in a closed room. The doctor said he was surprised she was still alive because the deadly Beta Strep germ that had somehow gotten into her nervous system was usually fatal within 24 hours. She was breathing on her own, but she was still in critical condition.

As we stared helplessly through the window at our little baby, Karen brought me up to date on what had happened. She said, "I stayed up with Rachel all night after you left. She was crying and feverish all night, and toward morning I really started to get worried. I called the pediatrician as soon as it was daylight. He told me to check the soft spot on the top of Rachel's head. When I did, it was swollen and bulging out. He said she probably had meningitis and I should get her to the hospital as quickly as possible."

Then Karen said, "I called Brother Jones to see if he could come and help me, but before he could get there, Rachel stopped breathing. I had to give her mouth to mouth resuscitation." My poor, brave wife had been a hero when I wasn't there to help. Later I learned that even after the pastor came and took Karen and Rachel to the police station nearby, Karen had to continue the mouth-to-mouth resuscitation in the presence of the police officers who didn't seem to know what to do. The doctors later remarked that Karen had done a fantastic job because there was no evidence of hypoxia (lack of oxygen) at all. If any brain damage occurred, it would be produced entirely by the bacterial infection and inflammation of the meninges (the membranes surrounding the brain).

Waiting Out The Storm

" David pleaded with God for the child. He fasted and went into his house and spent the nights lying on the ground."
2 Samuel 12:16

The next 3 or 4 days we waited and watched while the nurses and doctors worked to save our little baby Rachel's life. Five years after our son Mike died, the path of our spiritual pilgrimage turned back into that familiar but unwelcome valley of the shadow of death. As Rachel lay near death in the intensive care unit, I prayed, "Lord, please either heal her or take her, just don't leave her in a badly brain-damaged condition." During the long nights of vigil in the hospital corridors and on my knees beside the bed at home, I struggled with the possibility that neither of my options would be God's will.

During those few days God intervened in a very special way. Karen and I had taken a break from the hospital to do some grocery shopping for the girls at home. We were driving through the business district when we spotted a woman crossing the street whose appearance was unmistakable. She was the stereotype of a foreign missionary. A long grey dress, hair in a bun, metal-rim glasses, heavy walking shoes. It could only be Ella Ruth Hutson. How in the world could this dear saint whom I last saw in Taiwan 13 years ago, be walking down the sidewalk in Bridgeton, Missouri? We quickly turned the car around and pulled up beside her as she walked down the sidewalk. "Ella Ruth" I yelled. "Is that you?" It was indeed her. She turned around in surprise and exclaimed, "There you are. I went to your house but there was nobody home."

My dear missionary aunt from Taiwan was home on furlough and the Holy Spirit brought her to us at a critical time in our lives. When she had found no one home at our house, she went looking for a motel. That's what she was doing when the Lord led us to her on the street.

She didn't even know we had a sick baby when she arrived, but she quickly grasped the seriousness of our situation. She immediately began praying with us and then I shared with her my prayer that God would either heal Rachel or take her. Ella Ruth asked, "Don, are you trying to limit God? He might have something better in mind. Can't you just trust him? Will you accept his will whatever he chooses to do?" She encouraged us and helped us to see we must leave Rachel to God, and just pray for him to do his perfect will. Then she said, "Don't worry. God's grace will always be sufficient for you. No matter what happens, He will never leave you alone." So, again we were to forced to hope and rely on God's grace. But would it be enough?

As Rachel continued to live, the doctors began to feel she would not die, and our hopes were raised. However, before that news came, I had come through in my prayers to the acceptance of whatever God's will might be, even to leaving her brain damaged for life. However long that might be.

Rachel didn't die. Not then, anyway. When we were finally allowed to pick her up and hold her, we knew immediately that something was seriously wrong. I can't describe the feeling I had when I held her in my arms. She was cold, stiff and unresponsive. It wasn't like holding a baby at all. However, because she was so young, it was difficult to know just what her condition was. At three months of age, all she could do before she got sick was coo, grin and kick like any healthy baby. Now she was doing none of those things.

Her eyes were not clear and alert and she didn't try to make any kind of movement, unless it was writhing in pain.

We took her home after a few more days and anxiously watched for a sign of response to her surroundings. Eye movement, turning her head to follow sounds, any kind of voluntary movement. Anything. We looked and watched and waited for anything that would tell us our beloved Rachel was back with us. But, there was nothing. She didn't even react to loud noises. There was nothing to indicate consciousness except her eyes were open. She could barely suck a bottle and maintain her essential bodily functions. We did indeed have a badly brain-damaged baby.

Course Adjustment

"I have learned to be content, whatever the circumstances"
Philippians 4:11

As time went by, we began to realize the extent of Rachel's brain damage. Most people, not having the emotional investment of love in our child would say she was essentially a vegetable. As her condition became more apparent to us, so did the waves of grief. Our grief was real, and just as relentless as the grief we experienced when Mike died. We had lost the baby we had known. Yet, the grief this time was somehow different. It was experienced more gradually and mixed with it was a dread of what Rachel's condition might mean to her and to our family in the future. When death is sudden, the shock is acute and intense. Thoughts of the future are all about the loss, and the emptiness which will have to be dealt with. In Rachel's case, the future was fearsome and uncertain. We had lost our child, but we still had a grievous situation to deal with, and we didn't know what would be involved in handling Rachel's condition, nor for how long.

It was a difficult time, filled with heartache and weeping. But, with God's help, we gradually began to make the adjustment. That meant coming to an acceptance of the bleak prospect of no viable life for Rachel. That also meant facing the prospect of caring for Rachel in her brain-damaged state for who knows how long.

It may be surprising to some people, but we still loved our little girl. As Rachel continued to recover from the meningitis she was no longer cold and stiff as she was in the ICU ward at the hospital. She became warm and compliant in our arms. We could sense an invisible response of love from her physically unresponsive body. It was nothing that could be measured or recorded. It just seemed that when we held her and loved her she somehow responded. We needed that little something because through the next 3 years that Rachel lived, she required constant and careful attention and was in and out of hospitals frequently. During that time, Rachel nearly died several times. Over a dozen times we kept her alive by giving her mouth to mouth resuscitation. The training we had received to save Mike was now coming into play with another of our children.

Because of her brain damage, Rachel's body could not regulate the proper fluid level in her blood stream and she would dehydrate without warning. Many times we took her into a hospital emergency room and saw the young resident doctors get very alarmed at her condition. We would assure them that they only needed to get her on an I.V. immediately and then she would respond as well as she could in her condition. Once the hospital staff got some fluids in her, she would be all right. The specialists were eventually able to diagnose her dehydration problem and Karen and I learned to give her shots of a synthetic hormone called pitrussin in her abdomen a few times a week. The shots helped her kidneys regulate the fluid level in her body and that stopped the dehydration problem. However, after getting the shot she would swell up for a day or so, causing her to cry continuously for 24 hours. Then as the shot wore off, she would be all right for one day. Then she would begin to dehydrate again and we would start the cycle over again.

It was explained to us that Rachel's temperature would fluctuate because of damage to the hypothalamus region of her brain. She went through a period of having convulsions when she was still under a year old. They were not the same kind Mike had, but more of a rhythmic contracting of her whole body into a fetal position. The doctors diagnosed the convulsions as hyper-rhythmia, a type of convulsion that frequently precedes death. Then before Rachel was a year old they suddenly stopped.

Rachel was hospitalized several times over the next three years. During one of her stays in Children's Hospital in St. Louis, I was in the room with her trying to communicate with her in a way I had come to use frequently. Rachel could suck on a bottle, so at some primitive level her brain was still functioning. The fact that Rachel had feeling in her lips had led me to communicate with her by lip contact. I would hold Rachel and kiss her face and when I contacted her lips, she would respond, probably just like a baby does seeking food. But, it was a response, and the only response I could elicit from her. On this occasion, Rachel was lying in the small bed in her hospital room. I was leaning over the bed and was communicating with her by lip contact. A nurse happened to walk by, and seeing what I was doing, she assumed that Rachel was having trouble breathing and I was giving her mouth to mouth resusitation. She ran into the room all excited and tried to get to Rachel to see what her problem was. I said, "It's okay, she's fine. We were just talking."

Rachel's bowels could not move on their own and Karen was left with the unenviable task of massaging her abdomen every day and using a glass rectal thermometer to empty her colon.

The doctors who treated Rachel frequently advised us that we should not use heroic measures to prolong her life. When we told them we had given her mouth to mouth resuscitation to keep her breathing, they told us we shouldn't have done that. "That was a mistake" they said. "You're just prolonging her life and making things harder for yourselves." It is an extremely difficult thing to be told your child's life isn't worth preserving, either for her or for us. On one occasion a visiting doctor happened to be in the Emergency Room when we brought Rachel to the hospital in a particularly bad condition. The doctor, not knowing of her condition, saved her life by finding a vein in her foot to start an I.V. When he learned of her brain-damaged condition he apologized to us for saving her. He said, "If only I'd known I wouldn't have tried to save her." We assured him that as far as we were concerned, he had done the right thing.

Caring for Rachel was a full time job for Karen. As a young pre-teen, Vicki was now old enough to help care for her, and we sometimes found relief for a couple of hours by leaving her with her big sister. Also, the ladies at church who worked in the nursery were very compassionate and understanding and they were willing to watch Rachel during church activities. Their service allowed us to carry her to church and leave her in the nursery a few times a week and continue in our church responsibilities. Being far from our families, the church was our only support, and we did not take that blessing lightly. Karen felt if we stayed away from church because of Rachel, we would be opposing God's will and forfeiting the help and blessing He provided.

God's Provision: Living Above The Storm

"And God raised us up with Christ and seated us with him in the heavenly realms in Christ Jesus in order that ... he might show the incomparable riches of His grace..." Ephesians 2:6

As we look back now on those three and a half years we shared with Rachel, for all the burden and anxiety over her constant problems, they were still some of the happiest years we have ever experienced. God demonstrated His abundant grace and drew us closer to Him than we had ever been, or have ever been since. He gave us peace and joy in the midst of what should have been an overwhelming storm. We were as happy as any family could hope to be. I remember times when we would be in the home of friends who also had young children. As I watched their babies crawling on the floor, I sometimes found myself actually feeling sorry for the parents. I would think to myself, "They just have a regular baby, but we have such a special gift from God in our Rachel." God clearly demonstrated to us that we don't have to live under our circumstances. We are above our circumstances, seated in the heavenlies with Christ.

God taught us other things too during those days. We learned lessons that have helped us in other areas of our lives, and have allowed us to help others as we have shared with them in their problems. One of the most important lessons we learned is that we must not let the enemy of our souls gain victory by causing us to become anxious and worried about what might happen in the future. This is an extremely important point that I feel compelled to share with you. When prospects for the future are uncertain or bleak, it's very natural to worry. But, worry is a tool of Satan. He wants us to lose our joy by fretting about what might happen. A Christian neighbor often quoted a verse from the Sermon on the Mount that I never understood at the time. He always quoted the King James version that says, *"Sufficient unto the day is the evil thereof"* (Matt. 6:34). The NIV makes it a lot clearer when it says, *"Do not worry about tomorrow, for tomorrow will worry about itself. Each day has enough trouble of its own."*

That particular verse concludes a lengthy passage where Jesus expands on the futility of worrying about anything. In Jesus' days, people frequently didn't even know where their next meal was coming from, or where the money would come from to clothe and house their family. That's why Jesus drew such large crowds after he fed the thousands from just a few morsels of fish and bread. They were thinking, "Hey, here's a permanent meal ticket." But Jesus told them that God knows exactly what they need, and we must trust him to provide it. He said, *"Seek ye first the kindom of heaven and His righteousness, and all these things will be added unto you."*

As we carried Rachel to church and laid her in the nursery crib, thoughts would come into our minds about how difficult it would become in the future when she would grow too big to carry around. By the time she was three, she was almost too big for the cribs in the nursery. We found ourselves wrestling with our fears. Would we have to put her in an institution, or would we have to hire someone to help with her? Where would we get the money? What would we do? All of these questions would flood our minds, always starting with the words "What if?." But God's Holy Spirit, I'm sure, repeatedly impressed me with that wonderful verse. *"Do not worry about tomorrow, for tomorrow will worry about itself."*

When I prayed and shared my concens about the future, I sensed him asking me "Am I taking care of you right now? How are you doing today?" I would have to answer, "We're doing great today. Yes Lord, everything is fine right now. We're very happy despite the circumstances. But, what if...?" He would stop me there and ask me again... "Am I taking care of you right now?" I'd say "Yes, but what about when she...." He repeated, "Am I taking care of you right now?" My answer was finally, "Yes Lord, You are taking great care of us now, and I know you will take great care of us tomorrow, and the next day, and always, no matter what happens. Thank you Lord for teaching me that lesson."

After that, to a degree we were freed from the anxiety that worrying about the future always brings. Even though we knew intellectually that God had us in his care, we were still human and had to continue to work on living that truth. That's not to say that it isn't proper to look ahead and make provisions where that is reasonable and prudent. But when there's nothing one can do about the future, it does no good to worry and fret about it. Even today, we sometimes have to be reminded of that truth.

I think this principle also holds when a spouse or other loved one has passed away. In the midst of our grief, we worry about how we will do without them or how much it will hurt to be alone. Things are going to be different without them, that's true. But, even then, take comfort in knowing that God's grace will always be sufficient for the moment.

God gives us grace for the moment at hand. He gave his manna to the children of Israel during the forty years in the wilderness. However, he gave them just enough each day to meet their needs for that day. They couldn't collect extra manna and store it up for the future or it would spoil. They had to trust God to provide each day what would be required for that day. That's the lesson he wanted them to learn and it's the same lesson he wants us to learn. He always comes through. He provided for the children of Israel in the wilderness, and he will also provide for us in our wilderness, whatever that may be.

We finally learned that lesson during our time with Rachel. Just trust him, one day at a time… one minute at a time if necessary. But always, just trust him.

Rachel's Haven Of Rest

"What is your life? You are a mist that appears for a little while and then vanishes." James 4:14

God released Rachel from her damaged body in February 1974 when she was three and a half years old. Before he did, however, he gave us a wonderful sign. Rachel began to smile! We knew for her to smile was essentially impossible. We had no evidence she could even see to know what a smile was, let alone control the facial muscles required to do it. Her smiles were beautiful and not the contorted features caused by gas pains or some other explainable physiological reaction. Karen was able to photograph Rachel smiling one day and we excitedly showed the photos around to our friends. At first we took it as a sign that her physical condition was going to improve, but it was really her good-bye to us. Within a few weeks, she was completely healed; not physically in her body, but in heaven with Jesus where there is no more sickness or disease. She was made whole in Christ Jesus.

The circumstances of her death were coincidentally strange. For some reason, the Lord saw fit to have Karen alone with Rachel when our baby died, just as she was alone when Rachel was taken ill with the meningitis. Even more strangely, I was out of town on a trip to Florida when Rachel died, as I was in Florida when she contracted the meningitis. I seldom ever traveled to Florida in my business, but for some reason I had another trip scheduled there that February. Rachel had been having a rougher time than usual during those days. She had been in the hospital the week before my trip was scheduled, as she had been many times before. This time, I considered canceling my trip because she seemed to be getting weaker. The doctor released her from the hospital, however, and said she would be all right and there appeared to be no reason I should cancel my trip. So, I went ahead.

I called Karen after arriving at the hotel that night and she was concerned, but not alarmed about Rachel. I was troubled though, and I worried this might be the time when Rachel would leave us. What if Rachel died while I was gone? I couldn't bear to think of Karen being there alone if that happened. I prayed fervently in the night, "Lord, please protect Rachel, at least until I can get home." There was not a flight back to St. Louis until mid morning the next day or I would have gone back home that very evening. I prayed, "Please God, don't let anything happen to Rachel while I'm gone. Don't put that burden on Karen while she is alone. Please. Lord, you promised us in your Word you would give us the desires of our heart. This is truly my deepest desire. Please keep Rachel safe until I can get home."

I called again at daybreak and Karen was deeply concerned. She said, "Rachel is getting weaker and weaker. She's stopped breathing a couple of times and I've had to give her mouth to mouth to keep her alive." Since there was nothing I could do until the flight left later in the morning, I went on to my meeting. I wasn't able to concentrate on the business at hand and stepped out frequently to call home. After a couple of hours I called to find that Karen had taken Rachel back to the hospital and the doctors thought she was in grave condition. I left the meeting and went to the airport to wait for the flight. Just before I boarded the plane, I called again and reached our pastor at the hospital. He simply said, "Don, I'm sorry....Rachel just died a few minutes ago."

I choked back the lump in my throat and told our pastor, "Rachel has just gone on to heaven ahead of us. We will join her and Mike there later. Please take care of Karen until I can get there."

I boarded the plane and pulled my New Testament out of my pocket. I turned to that beautiful passage. The 14th Chapter of John. I re-read those comforting verses, then I put the testament away, laid back and closed my eyes and let the Holy Spirit minister to me through those comforting words. He soothed my spirit as He reminded me of the Savior's words, *"Let not your hearts be troubled. You believe in God, believe also in me."* And later in that chapter, *"Peace I leave with you; my peace I give to you...Do not let your hearts be troubled and do not be afraid... If you loved me, you would be glad that I am going to the Father." John 14:27-28.* I felt the Lord saying to me, "If you love Rachel, you should be glad she has gone to the Father." A few days later my pastor brother Jim conducted the graveside funeral service for Rachel. I was deeply touched by the Lord's presence as Jim began by telling us that the passage of Scripture the Lord had given him was John 14:27. It was the same passage God had used to comfort me the day of her death.

My pastor brother Jim was a few years younger than me as brother number 4. He actually grew up with Karen in the same youth group at church, but we became very close after I got out of the Navy and he surrendered to the ministry. Jim comforted us many times during our trials, including preaching that funeral service for Rachel. Jim had many interests and spent several years in England as a church planter and missionary. He was a spelunker, a coin collector, a rare bottle collector and loved to use his metal detector to find rare and unusual treasures around the world. But Jim was first and foremost a family man and an evangelist; a supremely effective one. I've watched him meet a stranger and within a few moments have that person weeping on his shoulder and asking him how he could get right with God. Jim and I were soul brothers in the Lord, as well as brothers in the flesh.

Jim was also a musician. He played a guitar and sang for youth groups and for his own enjoyment. Jim wrote and published only one song, as far as I know. It is entitled "My Grace Is Sufficient For Thee"[1] Here are the words he wrote, based loosely on 2 Corinthians 12, words and music that ministered to our souls.

My Grace Is Sufficient For Thee
By Jim Clifford
My grace is sufficient for Thee, my child
My grace is sufficient for thee.
For my strength is made perfect in weakness,
And my grace is sufficient for thee.

A thorn in the flesh I received one day,
A thorn in the flesh that would not go away.
And though I prayed with all of my might,
No answer came, the thorn remained, and I cried, Why?

My Grace is sufficient for thee, my child,
My grace is sufficient for thee.
For My strength is made perfect in weakness,
And My grace is sufficient for thee.

This thorn in my flesh gave such suffering.
I knew it was Satan's buffeting.
But as I prayed, the Lord said to me,
Your answer came, this thorn remains, it's good for thee.

My Grace is sufficient for thee, my child
My grace is sufficient for thee.
For My strength is made perfect in weakness,
And My grace is sufficient for thee.

Jim is no longer with us now. He died of a brain tumor a few years ago, leaving his wife, Sharon, and three grown daughters, plus a number of grandchildren. Jim sang his beautiful song at his own funeral! We played a tape recording, made years earlier, of him playing the guitar and singing that plaintive melody in his soft tenor voice. It ministered to us then and it has ministered to us before and since. Jim's love, his support, his counsel and his song will always be remembered, not only by me and our family, but by all the others he touched with his life. I look forward to singing it together with him in eternity as we praise God and thank him for his tender mercies during our lives on earth.

Despite my most fervent prayers, I wasn't there with Karen when our Rachel died. I've asked God why He couldn't have kept her alive just a few hours longer. But, that's not how it happened. The only answer I received was *"My grace is sufficient for thee, my child."* And it was sufficient, even for Karen in such terrible circumstances. His grace was sufficient, and it still is. The church had mobilized around Karen by the time Rachel died, and the Lord ministered to her through our pastor and his wife and other friends who surrounded her. Also, unseen by Karen, was a cloud of heavenly angels surrounding her, protecting and strengthening her. My wife, Karen, is a wonderfully strong person. With her heavenly reinforcements, she weathered the storm, and she weathered the storm without me there. Yes, his grace is indeed sufficient.

I still believe God accomplished His will in Rachel's life. The experiences with Mike and Rachel led us to a deeper understanding of his unfailing commitment to keep us in every circumstance. He prepared us until he knew we would suffer the loss for him and remain faithful. That knowledge allowed him to give us our next child to raise. Why God chose us for this mission, I don't know, but through his own sovereign will he did. We can do no less than praise him and give him thanks. We give thanksgiving for three years with Rachel that we will always remember as some of the happiest days of our lives. We are immeasurably richer because she was a part of our family for those few short years. The memories, the strength and the blessings we gained were precious gifts from God. I wouldn't take anything for the fellowship with the Father that we gained through our time with Rachel. We do indeed thank him for allowing us to participate in his sovereign plan.

After Rachel died, our family mourned, together and separately. Becky was very attached to Rachel and was in kindergarten when Rachel died. The teachers remarked that they thought Becky was having some emotional reaction to losing her sister, but nothing major. Vicki had spent many hours caring for Rachel and I know she grieved deeply in her heart. We recently came across a note written to us from a camp counselor shortly after Rachel's death when Vicki was 12. I would like to share some of it with you. It was from a girl named Elizabeth who went by the nickname "Lizard" at camp. She wrote,

"Hi, this is Lizard, the camp counselor of Vicki. I wanted to write to you about Vicki. I absolutely, without a doubt, will cherish her for eternity. She is a very special young lady. She told me about her sister and it was beautiful. Not many adults have that wonderful an outlook on death. The love of God shows through in a rainbow of beauty in her. She was a real inspiration to me at camp and I'll always love her. You are so blessed to have her. Sincerely, Elizabeth"

After Rachel died, we prayed long and hard about whether it was God's will that we have another child. Karen had exhibited some diabetic tendencies during her pregnancies, and we worried about potential problems after our experiences with Mike and Rachel. We were assured by the neurologists that both of the children's problems were caused by events after their births and they were not genetic problems. We also consulted the obstetrician who assured us there were no unusual risks with Karen's gestational diabetes. However, some members of our families weren't so sure we should have another child. They said "Enough is enough." But, our lives seemed so very empty with Rachel gone, and after much prayer we decided to go ahead and try to have another baby. As I mentioned before, getting pregnant was never a problem for us.

CHAPTER 7

THE LAST ANGEL

Our Cup Runneth Over
July 1976

"Thou preparest a table before me... Thou annointest my head with oil. My cup runneth over." Psalm 23:5 (KJV)

Beth Elaine Clifford came along with little delay and was born just a year after Rachel died. Beth was a beautiful baby. From birth she had bright blue eyes and golden yellow hair which didn't darken as she aged. God certainly answered our prayers for a baby to occupy our attention and be the center of our lives. Beth turned out to be just that. She was full of energy and full of life from the day she was born. We often told people we wanted a baby to fill the void in our lives after losing Rachel, but we didn't know that this child would fill it so full! She was a joy, but she was also a full time job. Karen often said if Beth had been our first child, she probably would have been our last.

We loved it. When she was born we were so emotionally starved after losing Rachel that we loved her incessantly. We spoiled her I'm sure, but every minute with her was a joy. We needed to be needed and Beth saw to it that we weren't disappointed. Beth brought us generous measures of heaven-sent joy. Vicki and Becky loved her too and we all felt that finally our family was complete. I was happy in my work, our church was experiencing revival and all was well with the world. We rejoiced in God's goodness to us.

The Fearsome Waves

"Let not your heart be troubled; neither let it be afraid"
John 14:27 (KJV)

We never lost the joy of having Beth in our family. However, that joy was soon tempered with concern. It all began when Beth was still a tiny baby and we visited Karen's family in Wichita while enroute to a vacation in New Mexico and Colorado. I was feeding Beth a bottle early one morning and there was no one else in the room with me to see what happened. As I was holding her I saw her facial features distort just slightly and freeze with a blank stare. It passed in a few seconds, but a cold chill went down my spine. The look on Beth's face was unmistakable. I had seen it too many times before. I flashed back ten years earlier to our son Mike and saw again the hated seizures distorting his features and torturing his poor little body. And I saw again his lifeless body lying on the living room couch, the victim of a seizure that ended his life. The look on Beth's face that morning was the same look we had seen so many times on Mike's face during his early seizures. I recognized it for what it was and fought back the feelings of panic and fear it evoked.

I couldn't bring myself to tell Karen what I had seen with Beth that morning. I even tried to convince myself that I hadn't really seen anything to be alarmed about. "I probably imagined it" I thought to myself. "Maybe it was just a gas pain that passed momentarily." A few days later, while we were in New Mexico on our vacation, I finally got up the nerve and carefully asked Karen, "Honey, have you noticed anything unusual going on with Beth?" Karen replied, "No, why? Have you?" I just shrugged and said, "No, not really," hoping I was telling the truth.

Then a few weeks later, it happened again, and I didn't have to tell her. Karen had carried Beth out to the car after church one Sunday evening. I was still inside talking to someone when a friend came running into the building shouting, "Don, Don, Karen is having trouble with Beth in the car. You'd better get out there fast!" I knew in my heart what it was. By the time I reached the car the seizure had passed and Beth was crying frantically.

Then the painful series of doctors, hospitals and tests began again as we faced that same recurring horror we had gone through with Mike ten years before in California. We knew before we began how it would turn out. No reason could be found for the seizures. Idiopathic was again the diagnosis. A scholarly term used by the medical profession to tell us they don't know what's wrong with a child, our child. We would have to try to control the seizures with medication. Maybe this time she will grow out of it. Maybe they have some new medicines now that can control seizures better. Maybe. Pray, pray, pray.

The experience with the doctors and hospitals seemed like a recurring nightmare. Now Beth was the third of our children to begin the exhausting and painful process of hospitalizations, tests and medications. The doctors were at a loss to explain how two children in the same family could have similar seizure disorders. Seizures are not hereditary. They couldn't blame Beth's seizures on a difficult pregnancy or on problems during delivery. Those conditions were fairly normal and Karen's pregnancy with Beth was probably the easiest of the seven for Karen. I know because I was in the delivery room witnessing her arrival. So, when Beth turned up with a seizure disorder exactly like her brother's, the doctors were mystified. As far as I know, they still have no explanation or understanding of any genetic connection.*

We never were able to control Beth's seizures. We went through a number of medications but nothing would stop them. They were identical to Mike's, including the frequency and intensity. It was hard to tell if the medications were doing any good at all and we toyed with the thought of taking her off of them altogether. However, the side effects from the drugs seemed minimal so we didn't take the chance. The seizures weren't affecting her development and she was a normal child in other respects. Maybe this time would be different. We would just have to watch her very closely. Very closely.

Beth grew to be a lovely and lovable child. Besides her silvery blond hair and blue eyes, she had a mischievous smile that would steal your heart. She grew more beautiful as she grew into a toddler and then a little girl. I could always spot her from a block away because of her bright blond hair. She was smart as a whip and perpetually happy. She loved to make people laugh, constantly keeping us in stitches. She was also mischievous and very busy. She would get into her sisters' things knowing it would make them angry, and then walk away from their scoldings with a smile on her face, having accomplished her purpose. Despite her mischievous shenanigans, she was a joy to everyone in the family and she was loved by everyone who knew her.

The seizures continued to come, however, never skipping more that two or three days at a time. They became a way of life for us, but they never became easy to accept. We hated them. We detested them. Our beautiful daughter, so happy and full of fun one moment, would suddenly become a slave to the seizure, twisted and tortured by this thing that controlled her. Every seizure was a battle for us, draining us emotionally as much as it did her physically. Only God's assurance that he was in control gave us peace to accept the situation. But even then, we had to watch her very carefully. We could never forget what had happened to Mike. We couldn't let that happen to Beth.

I prayed daily for God to protect and keep Beth. As the years went by, the seizures continued, but so did Beth's development. Beth started school, and aside from the seizures, her life was full and happy and so were ours. We began to hope that everything would work out all right for our little girl as she continued to mature. We thought "maybe she would outgrow the seizures." We continued to trust her to God. May his will be done.

Karen has wondered if the medications she took during her pregnancies could be involved. She began having severe abdominal pains during her pregnancy with Mike which were later diagnosed as gall bladder attacks. They only came when she was pregnant so she didn't pursue the problem after the babies came and she was no longer bothered by the attacks. The doctor in California prescribed a medication that Karen took during her pregnancy with Mike and during all of her subsequent pregnancies. That included her pregnancies with Becky, Rachel and Beth. Becky never had any evidence of a seizure problem and neither did Rachel in the months before her meningitis. The medication was called Chardonna. It included charcoal and phenobarbital.

Please, Not Our Beth
February, 1982

"Yea, though I walk through the valley of the shadow of death..." Psalms 23:4 (KJV)

Beth was five years old when Karen and I left her with Becky one evening while we went to church visitation. Beth had suffered a seizure at school that morning so we were comfortable leaving her with her sister for an hour or so. The seizures, although hateful, came every few days allowing us to relax just a bit after an episode. Beth had never had two big seizures in the same day. Vicki was working at her part time job at a local department store so Becky was alone with Beth when we left. As we were leaving home that night the heavy quiet snow that was to continue for the next three days began to fall.

We returned home that evening to find a plain clothes police officer waiting for us in the snow outside our home. When I got out of the car and approached him, He said, "Mr. Clifford?" I said, "Yes?", wondering who this person was, and why he was on our property. He identified himself as an officer of the Bridgeton Police Department, and then he said, "your daughter has had an accident. An ambulance took her to De Paul hospital." Karen and I both thought he meant Vicki, so I asked hesitantly, "What happened? Is she O.K.? Did she have an accident in the snow?" Then he said, "No, it's Beth, your five year old daughter. She had an accident in the bathtub. Your daughter Becky found her face down in the water and called 911 for emergency help." Then he repeated, "Beth has been taken to DePaul Hospital and they want you to get over there right away."

It didn't occur to me that it could be anything serious. Maybe just a bump on the head. Maybe she slipped and fell getting out of the tub, and had broken an arm. We went into the house and found two of our friends from church who were close neighbors sitting on the living room couch with Becky sitting between them. Becky sat quietly and didn't say a word to us. One of the neighbors said excitedly "We just heard from the hospital. They said that Beth has a heartbeat and a pulse." I still hadn't grasped the seriousness of what had happened. I thought, "Of course she has a heartbeat and a pulse." The gravity of what had happened still hadn't soaked in.

I thanked the neighbors for helping, then Karen and I hurried to the car and headed for the nearby hospital. The police officer brought Becky along in his car. On the way, I still couldn't believe it could be very serious, but Karen repeatedly prayed aloud, "Not my Beth Lord; please, not my Beth. Lord, you've already taken two of our children. You won't take another from us, will you? You promised us you wouldn't take Beth from us. Didn't you? Please, please, not my Beth."

We pulled up to the Emergency Room entrance and hurried inside where we found a nurse waiting for us. She said, "The police picked up Vicki from her job and brought her over because we needed someone from the family to sign the release papers. Our medical team had to do whatever was necessary until you arrived." Without stopping, she continued "The doctors are still evaluating Beth's condition, but I will take you in." The nurse ushered Karen and me into the examination room where Beth was lying unconscious on the examination table. When the doctors showed me that Beth's pupils weren't dilating when they shined a light in her eyes, I began to realize how grave her condition was.

Our Heroine's Plight

"Come unto me all ye that labor and are heavy laden, and I will give you rest.... ...You shall find rest for your souls"
Matthew 11:28-29 (KJV)

The doctors decided that they should transfer Beth to Children's Hospital in central St. Louis where specialized facilities and staff were available for pediatric care. Within a few minutes they had put Beth on a stretcher and transferred her to an awaiting ambulance. Karen rode in the ambulance with Beth while Becky and I followed behind in our car. Brother Jones, our pastor, arrived at the Bridgeton hospital as we were leaving so he brought Vicki in his car. During the 30 minute drive through the heavy snow, now falling steadily in large wet flakes, Becky was still unable to say anything to me. At one point I said to her, "I'm afraid we're going to lose her, Beck." Becky didn't respond, setting the painful pattern for our silent relationship for the remaining years that she lived with us.

When we arrived at Children's Hospital, Beth's pediatric neurologist, who had been in charge of her case from the beginning, was briefed on her condition and how the accident had happened. He examined Beth carefully while we waited out in the hall. When he came out he said, "Please come into my office. All of you." Then he took our family and pastor into his office. The first thing he said was, "Becky, you are a very brave and a very resourceful young lady. If it wasn't for your call to 911, Beth wouldn't still be alive." Then he said, "Unfortunately, it looks very bad for Beth. We will run some tests to see what we can determine about her brain condition, but I'm not sure what we can do." Then, turning again to our young daughter, he said, "Becky, there was nothing you or anyone else could have done. Beth apparently suffered a massive seizure and nothing you could have done would have made any difference. Your actions were truly heroic."

Karen and I both embraced Becky and reinforced the doctor's praise, trying to reassure her that we didn't blame her for the accident. Becky seemed to take some momentary strength from our collective encouragement. However, while she tried to convince herself that what we said was true, I know she blamed herself and she was probably destined to carry feelings of guilt for years to come.

Our family stood by as the doctors worked feverishly to save Beth but she remained in a coma. She never regained consciousness. We stayed by her bed day and night, praying and begging God to save her life. As long as there was any possibility she might regain consciousness we weren't going to leave her side. The doctors were very pessimistic, however, and we prepared ourselves as best we could for the worst. At one time we were encouraged briefly, when at the end of 48 hours, an electro-encephalograph showed some brain activity. That was the first ray of hope we had received. When the doctors told me the test results I excitedly ran to awaken Karen where she had been resting in the adjoining room. "Honey" I cried, "they see some brain activity. There may be some hope."

By the time we hurried back into Beth's room, the doctors were conferring about what the test meant. The senior neurologist decided there might be reason for heroic measures at this point. He ordered a Thompson brain shunt which was a metal tube inserted through the skull into the brain cavity to relieve pressure on the brain. I went to Beth's side and took her little hand in mine. While we were talking, I definitely felt Beth's hand squeeze my finger. I quickly called Karen over. She took Beth's hand and began talking to her, hoping our child could hear. Our hopes rose sharply and we redoubled our vigil of prayer by her bed.

The encouragement was short lived, however, because the shunt didn't improve Beth's condition and another encephalograph several hours later showed nothing to encourage the doctors. I objected to the doctor's pessimistic opinion, saying "But I felt her squeeze my finger." One of the resident doctors then told me the gripping of Beth's hand was only a reflex from the base of the brain caused by bending her hand at the wrist. He demonstrated by having me hold her hand while he bent her wrist repeatedly. Each time he would bend her wrist, I would feel the squeeze of her fingers. Our hopes plummeted then, and when later that evening the chief neurologist told us there was no reason to put her on life support equipment, we were forced to accept the apparently inevitable outcome.

When they took the equipment away, Beth was breathing on her own. However, we had no way of knowing how long she would remain as she was, unconscious, but alive. Would she remain in this condition and live in a coma for years to come? The thought reminded us of Rachel. We knew what that was like and we didn't want that for her. After some time passed, we decided it was time for us to go home and be with our other daughters and try to get some much needed rest. Beth was in God's hands. That was the same night the telephone awakened me to tell me the time had already come. So soon. God help us.

Notes From The Ship's Log

"I thank my God every time I remember you" Phillipians 1:3

I wrote the following words in my journal about one month after Beth died. I might write them differently today, but I want to share them with you as I wrote them in my journal at the time of my deepest grief. I think they accurately convey the feelings and thoughts of a young father mourning the loss of his daughter.

"As I write this, the wound is still fresh from losing Beth. The pain still feels as intense as the first day she left us. I know healing is taking place, but only because time is passing. Still, at the very thought of her, even now as I write, my heart seems to expand painfully in my chest, breathing becomes difficult, and I find myself sighing deeply as the familiar sadness and sorrow come over me.

Still, while it is painful, I know from our previous experiences that it is good to write down the dearest memories while they are fresh in our minds and hearts. The process itself is therapeutic and it captures the memories on paper for a time in the future when we will be able to take pleasure in remembering our Beth. So, please bear with me now while I reminisce about our little girl.

Beth was five years old and full of life. She was a beautiful girl with golden hair and bright blue eyes. She was bursting with personality. She was loving, active, and always wanting to help. She was often in trouble, usually for trying to help where help wasn't needed. She constantly demanded attention, never wanting to play alone. During my time at home before her bedtime, she was on my lap or in my arms as much of the time as I would allow her to be. Her response to discipline or scolding (which came frequently because of her tendency to hyperactivity and her persistent demands for attention) was always a reluctant withdrawal, always hoping for a sign of relenting that would allow her to get back into your sphere of attention and affection.

Beth learned early in her life that Daddy would lie down on the living room couch for a short nap soon after he got home from work. Always the helper, before I even thought of taking a nap, she would greet me at the door with a hug, then she would run to the living room and arrange the cushions on the couch for my nap. As soon as I lay down, she would lie down with me and snuggle up to me and announce that she was going to take a nap too, which was a laugh. She was too active to settle down long enough to get sleepy. After snuggling with me for a minute or two, she would get bored with the lack of activity. She would begin wrestling around or playing with something on the coffee table she wasn't supposed to touch. Finally, I would send her away so I could take my nap. Reluctantly she would go back to Sesame Street on the TV or off to the kitchen to bug her mom who was fixing supper. Her mom would soon be yelling for one of Beth's sisters to come and get her out of the kitchen and play with her for a while."

The "Beth-Isms"

"It is right for me to feel this way about... you, since I have you in my heart;" Phillipians 1:7

"And then there are the Beth-isms. Those personality traits and sayings that were particularly and uniquely Beth. No one could ever ask a "who wants to ...?" question without Beth's hand shooting up and her saying "I do, I do" before the question was even completed. She was a great volunteer. We always got a chuckle out of her raising her hand enthusiastically in church every time the pastor asked for visitors to identify themselves. She wanted to be in on everything.

A frequent response to questions was "I don't know either." If asked why something was the way it was, her alternate answer was "because it wants to." When scolded for misbehavior, she learned to answer "I'm sorry, I didn't mean to. I won't do it again." She spoke these words with a big eyed innocent look, and her arms extended out and down with palms spread wide. All the time, she was ready to go do it again.

At the dinner table Beth insisted on a prayer at every meal whether in public or at home. If one of her sisters started to eat before the prayer, she quickly pointed them out with an accusing finger and a loud "She's eating!." If I asked who would volunteer to say the prayer, as always, her hand would go up with a big "I will." She would too, though for years her prayers were unintelligible mumbles. Later, they began to sound more like the prayers she had heard others say (though many adult's prayers sound like mumbles too, come to think of it).

Karen and I often used to remark that when Beth came into the room, it was like the sun coming out from behind a cloud. She lit up our lives constantly and she loved the song by that title which was popular at that time. She would sing "You light up my life" and we would bask in the light of her happy smiling face; a face always singing and happy. She would often wake up in the early morning darkness and begin singing. She liked to get into Vicki and Becky's clothes. We would get a big laugh when she came into the room wearing their clothing. Sometimes her sisters would scold her for getting into their things, and she would respond by singing a song as if she hadn't heard them.

I can't count how many Saturday mornings I spent with Beth while the rest of the family slept in. She would come shuffling into our bedroom around 6:00 a.m. and climb in on my side of the bed and snuggle up for a while. Occasionally, she would take a short nap, but usually she insisted that I get up, and there was no rest until I did. "Come on Dad, let's go shave," she would whisper in my ear. Then we would go into the bathroom to supervise my morning ritual of scraping off the whiskers. It was always a battle keeping her out of things and off the sink where she wanted to sit while she supervised my shaving to make sure I didn't miss any spots.

Afterwards, we were off to the kitchen for some breakfast, and then she was ready for her game. Beth enjoyed playing "Match Game," a form of the game Concentration, where pairs of picture cards would be placed face down in a tray and the players would take turns turning over a pair and trying to get a match. She was good at it and she would play with anyone she could con into playing with her. Saturday mornings were my turn to get beaten at "Match Game." Oh, how I miss those times with her.

When Beth was about four, I took her to the local hardware store with me to do some Saturday morning shopping. While I was searching for what I needed, I suddenly realized that she wasn't with me. She had disappeared. I searched the store but she was nowhere to be found. I even looked out the front door to see if she was in the parking lot. Nothing there either. I finally asked Mrs. Telcher, who owned the store, if she had seen a little blond haired girl in the store. She replied, "Yes, I think I saw her following my husband into the storage room out back. I quickly made my way to the back room and there was Beth, watching with interest and asking questions as Mr. Telcher cut a screen for a window frame. When I saw her, I shouted with some emotion, "Beth Elaine Clifford, what are you doing back here? Her reaction was to spin around and fall down to the floor, holding her arms up as if she expected to be beaten. I swear, I never hit her once in her whole life. But, I'm sure Mr. Telcher thought I must be a child abuser. Anyway, she happily got to her feet and said calmly, "Ready to go Dad?"

Beth loved Sunday School and Church just as she loved anything where there was some action. I think our most lasting memories of Beth will be seeing her at church in the children's rooms playing with the toys and giving the teachers fits, or in the children's choir, or on Wednesday nights at church suppers, or sitting with us in big church in the evening worship service. Probably one of the saddest times for me now is the period of time after the Sunday morning worship services in the church parlor. Beth was usually instructed to sit quietly on a couch until we finished visiting with friends. There was always a crowd in the parlor after church, and several of the men in the church especially loved to stop and visit with her and get their hug, which she gave out freely. She always had plenty of company there until the crowd thinned out. Then she was impatient to be up and away since she knew we were usually the last ones out the door.

We usually ate out after church on Sundays and on one or two week nights. She was always a part of that experience in a big way. She was a part of everything in our lives, and that's the way Karen, the girls and I wanted it. That's the way Beth wanted it too. Remember, that's why we had her, to fill the void in our lives after the loss of Rachel. Now, the need is there again. Not for another baby, but for that beautiful little five year old who loved her sisters and her Mommy and Daddy."

School Days

"And the child grew and became strong... filled with wisdom, and the grace of God was upon Him." Luke 2:40

Continuing in my journal..."In addition to her seizure disorder which necessitated heavy medication, Beth had some learning disabilities. Those problems required her to attend Kindergarten at the Special School District and we had a difficult time deciding if that was in her best interest. We feared, unnecessarily so, that once in Special Schools it would be hard to get her out, even if she overcame her handicap. It was difficult to pin point what her disability was exactly. She was a beautiful girl, completely normal looking with bright alert eyes and an inquisitive mind. She was good at abstract problem solving and could read the letters of the alphabet by the age of three. However, she had difficulty assimilating verbal information or instructions and was so impulsive and distractible that she had a hard time staying on one task, particularly since she refused to do anything alone.

After an early childhood screening test, she was put in the learning disabled category that identified her as a candidate for the Special School District. We finally agreed that she should attend Special after she tried regular Kindergarten for one week and it didn't work for her at all. She was confused and frustrated and got very upset. Her teacher warned us that, based upon what she observed, Beth would have a very difficult time competing with the other children.

So, Beth started at the Special School, and she just loved it, and they loved her. Her teachers at school fell in love with her immediately as did everyone who met her. She was the only girl in the small class and the young lady teachers enjoyed her tremendously. Her lead teacher was "Mrs. Ann" and Beth loved her. Mrs. Ann was firm with Beth and Beth responded well in her school work. Each day Beth brought home her work and on the front was a daily report card in the form of happy, neutral or frowning faces. The subjects were listed down the sheet and next to each was a happy face if she had done well that day, which she usually did. Some days there would be a neutral face, and occasionally a sad face.

We enjoyed going over her report card with her and reviewing her work with her each day after school. When I would get to a problem solving exercise she enjoyed, she would run to find a pencil or crayon and rework the exercises with us. She also wanted to share her work with Vicki and Becky. If she got some praise from one of her sisters, she would skip away proudly, singing her favorite song of the day. Sharing her school work was one of her ways to get us to spend time with her. During the last few months she was with us, we spent much time doing problems, practicing writing letters and numbers, and other school work. For Christmas, we got her several problem solving books such as "connect-the-dot" puzzles. Oh, what wonderful days those were. She was such a source of joy to our lives.

The teachers were always disappointed if Beth couldn't participate in a field trip or party. Sometimes her daily grade cards would have brief notes included, like "wouldn't keep her hands off other people's trays at lunch," or "grouchy today — is she coming down with something?", or on one of her last days at school - "WOW!! Super Day!"

Karen tended to be concerned for Beth while she was away at school, fearing she might have a seizure, which she did several times. However, the teachers were marvelous and handled them with no problem at all. Apparently they were trained to work with handicapped children with such problems and the teachers handled Beth's seizures in a calm, matter of fact way. Since Beth enjoyed school so much, Karen was able to relax and let Beth go, knowing she would soon come bounding happily off the school bus, excitedly telling her latest news about what had happened that day.

I don't think Beth was conscious of her seizures until just before her death. They would come on her suddenly, last for two or three minutes, and then leave her exhausted. As with Mike, none of the medications seemed to help much. After a seizure she slept or rested for a while, then she was up and at it again as if nothing had happened. She seemed to have no memory of the seizures coming on her, and she was essentially unconscious during the entire time. It was tempting to start worrying that the seizures would be a problem for her when she grew older and became aware of the social implications of her disorder. However, we knew better than to worry because God was taking care of her moment by moment.

The day of her fatal accident she had suffered a seizure at school. When she came home, Karen asked her if she had a problem at school that day. She said "No, I didn't have a problem, I had a seizure." The teachers were apparently discussing her seizures with her as a matter of fact. I thought to myself, "Now the social awareness begins." Then, that evening, she had what would be her last seizure.

I asked Becky to write some words describing Beth's accident that night. Here is what she wrote. "When Beth had her seizure in the bath, I was playing the piano. She called to me that she wanted to get out and I said, ok, just let me finish this song. By the time I had finished and went to get her out, she was floating in the water unconscious. So I screamed and pulled her out and called 911. I didn't understand that there was a danger of her having a seizure in the bath and if she did what that would mean. I naturally felt responsible because if I had got her out when she called me, she would probably have been okay (although I don't ever remember looking after her when she had a seizure). I understand now that I was only 13 and was oblivious to any danger. It was a horrible accident. What got me through was the verse that says God works everything for good. I may have been interpreting it wrong, but it helped."

Several of Beth's teachers came to the memorial service and we were a little hurt when Mrs. Ann didn't stop to talk to us. Later, however, she wrote a beautiful letter, explaining how she couldn't speak to us because she was too upset emotionally. She shared in the letter how Beth "lit up" all the teacher's lives, just as she did ours when she came into the room. Her persistent happiness and love of life endeared her to all of them. Mrs. Ann said she would never forget Beth as long as she teaches. We will never forget Mrs. Ann either because she was so special to Beth and added so much joy to Beth's life at school.

Beth was always good about staying at home when we wanted to leave her with one of her sisters, even though she wanted to go along. I remember on that last night that Beth had somehow gotten the idea everyone was leaving except her and she tearfully asked "Do I have to stay home all by myself?" I said "No, of course not, honey. Becky is staying home too." "O.K.," she said. Then it was all right. Poor Beth, she thought we were going to leave her alone. I wonder now, did she somehow know something was going to happen that night?

Whenever we had to leave her home she would look so disappointed, but when it was clear she must stay home, then she wanted a big hug and kisses before escorting us to the door to the garage. After watching out the garage door until we were in the car, she would race to the living room windows to watch and wave until we drove out of sight. That's the way it was that last Monday night as the snow began to fall. That was the last time we saw her conscious."

Trust His Heart

"When Beth died, there was a brief graveside service, followed that Sunday evening by Beth's memorial service. The crowd filled the large church to capacity. It was a service of worship and celebration for Beth's release from her seizures and her new joy in God's paradise. The congregation sang hymns of praise and my brother Jim's song blessed us again, reminding us that "My Grace Is Sufficient For Thee, My Child." Darryl Pursley, our close friend and Minister of Music sang the song for us. Karen's pastor brother, Craig Atherton, spoke personal words for the family and Pastor Jones brought a message from the Bible and his own experiences with Beth. The service was positive and uplifting and ended with an altar call. One young girl came and gave her life to Jesus. Nothing could have been more fitting."

We will get back to the journal entries in a moment, but first I want to share something that ministered to us in a profound way then, and still does now. In those days our church choir often performed Easter and Christmas pageants. In one of those pageants, a special song was sung which spoke to our feelings and thoughts about God's goodness. Songwriters Eddie Carswell and Babbie Mason expressed the mystery of God's working in their beautiful Christmas song entitled, "Trust His Heart."

Trust His Heart [2]
By Eddie Carswell and Babbie Mason

Gabriel says to Mary:
  "God is too wise to be mistaken,
  God is too good to be unkind.
  So when you don't understand,
  when you can't see His plan,
  when you can't trace His hand,
  trust His heart."
Mary replies:
  "I'll trust that all things work for our good,
  though sometimes we can't see how they could.
  Struggles that break our hearts in two
  sometimes blind us to the truth.
  Our Father knows what's best for us,
  His ways are not our own.
  So when your pathway grows dim,
  and you just can't see Him,
  remember, you're never alone."
Joseph says:
  "He sees the master plan.
  He holds the future in his hands.
  So don't live as those who have no hope,
  for our hope is found in him.
  We see the present clearly,
  but he sees the first and the last,
  and like a tapestry,
  He's weaving you and me,
  to someday be just like him."
Mary and Joseph together sing:
  "God is too wise to be mistaken,
  God is too good to be unkind.
  So, when you don't understand,
  when you can't see His plan,
  when you can't trace His hand,
  Trust His Heart."

It is many years later now, and as we look back on all that happened with Beth, we can say "Thank you Lord for giving her to us for those few short years." The pain of losing her was intense, but it gradually lessened with time. However, the love and joy she brought into our lives will stay with us as long as we live. Our lives are richer and fuller for having had her with us for even those short five years. We now look forward to the time when we will see her again. What a joyous reunion that will be. The streets of gold and the gates of pearl will pale in comparison with the joy of seeing our sweet children again.

Michael Allen at 1 year

**Mike and Dad (Mike's head had been
shaved recently for medical tests)**

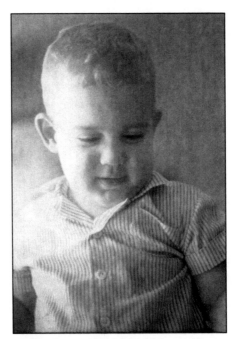

Mike just weeks before his accident

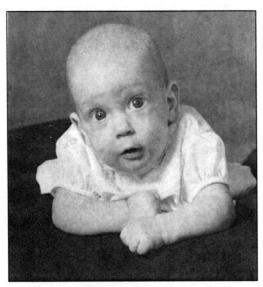

Rachel at 3 months,
just before contracting meningitis

**Karen with Rachel smiling
just before her homegoing**

Family portrait with brain-damaged Rachel

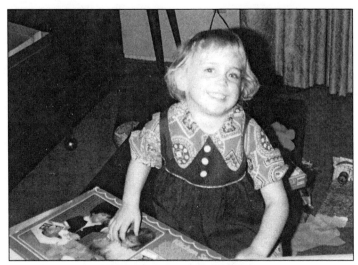

Beth Elaine at about age 3

Angelic Beth at age 5

Family portrait with Beth just weeks before her accident

PART TWO

CHAPTER 8

OUR GETHSEMANES

"Jesus went as usual to the Mount of Olives. He withdrew about a stone's throw from them, knelt down and prayed.."
Luke 22:39-40

In the Garden of Gethsemane, the night before his crucifixion, Jesus agonized for hours in prayer to his Heavenly Father about the impending crucifixion and death he faced. In reality, Jesus fought and won the faith battle there in the garden alone, while his closest friends slept nearby. In this case, Jesus fought the faith battle before the death event actually happened. By the time he finished his prayers, the battle was won and the following events were just a formality; painful and agonizing beyond our ability to comprehend, but nevertheless a formality. His first prayer in the garden was for the Father to spare him the agony to come if that could be possible. Jesus first prayed *"Father, if you are willing, take this cup from me."* How many times did our family pray that prayer? Many, many. But, inevitably, Jesus worked through his situation, remembering that he had been brought to this place for the very purpose of suffering and dying for all humanity. He finally surrendered his own human will when he prayed, *"Yet, not my will, but yours be done."*

Fighting The Faith Battle

"Now I know that none of you... will ever see me again. Keep watch over yourselves and all the flock of which the Holy Spirit has made you overseers." Acts 20:25,28

Our family spent our times in our Gardens of Gethsemane during the illness and death of each of our children who died, but it was after we lost Beth that we fought the most difficult battle for our faith. We didn't love her any more or less than we loved Mike and Rachel, but she was with us longer than they were, and we had more time with her and more memories of her as she was growing up. It was also a different experience from the others. In some ways, Mike's death was more traumatic for us because it was so sudden and we were so young and vulnerable. Rachel's was unique in a different way because for her and us her death was a release, even though we loved her dearly. Beth's death was profound and even though we were more experienced, the pain was deep and lasted longer.

When Beth died, we couldn't pray as Jesus did for 'this cup to pass from us if possible' because it had already been ours to drink. However, in order for us to come out of the experience with our faith intact, we had to find something in all of our confusion and distress to comfort and reassure us that our faith indeed had not been in vain.

More Notes From My Journal

Two months after Beth's funeral... "Now all we have left is a scrapbook full of pictures and memorabilia and hearts full of memories. Our lives now seem so empty. Especially Karen's. Of course we still have each other, and we still have Vicki and Becky. Both Karen and I treasure our two daughters dearly and are so thankful we've had them through these difficulties. Becky and Vicki also suffered the painful loss of their sister and they too have had to go through the grieving process. However, we all cope with grief in our own ways, and one person's grief is not always compatible with the others. Vicki has her own life now and is able to fill her hours with college, work and friends. Becky struggled mightily to cope with her sister's death. She had the added burden of knowing that Beth's accident happened while in her charge. She began to withdraw from the rest of the family and she became a bit of a recluse when she was home. She hibernated in her room with her music and a book, leaving the rest of the house very quiet when Vicki was gone. Of course, I have my work and my tendency is to bury myself in it. However, Beth *was* Karen's work. Now Karen has nothing else to occupy her time and that makes her grief even more difficult to deal with. I need to resist my tendency to lose myself in my work and spend as much time with her as I can. Karen is going to have to make a big adjustment in her lifestyle.

When Beth died, Vicki was eighteen years old. That meant Karen had been busy being a mom to little ones for over half of her life. Now there are just hours and days of loneliness and quiet. After the rush of the funeral, our extended family and friends went back to their own lives, leaving Karen home alone. The emptiness seemed unbearable at times. That's when Karen turned to God's Word for comfort and understanding. I am so thankful God's Holy Spirit lifted us all from that miry clay of pain and self pity and proved to us that he is there and he will see us through. I felt so helpless myself to help Karen, but we could feel God's love enveloping us and sustaining us, easing the pain, giving hope and assurance, holding us close day by day. If everyone else abandons us, we know our God is always there and his grace is sufficient." That's what the balance of this book is all about.

So ends the entry in my journal, written a few weeks after Beth's death. I needed to write about the feelings and thoughts we were going through because just the process of writing it all down was helpful. It might not work for everyone, but it helped me release some of the emotions and longings in my heart. Just expressing the thoughts on the surface of the consciousness uncovers the deeper thoughts and allows them to the brought out and expressed. As the process continues, the suppressed thoughts and feelings can be surfaced and dealt with. It is all part of the process that promotes healing and helps bring peace and comfort to the soul.

Wrestling With God

"Abba Father... everything is possible for you. Take this cup from me. Yet not what I will but what you will." Mark 14:36

As I have related the stories of the children we have lost, I'm sure you have discerned some of the spiritual questioning we went through as we tried to cope with our losses. It was not until some time after we lost Beth that both Karen and I came to essentially the same position in our respective faith struggles, though we arrived there by different paths. Before I share with you about the answers that finally came, however, I would like to talk about some of the emotional issues and questions that framed and shaped our spiritual battles. The bombardment of emotional traumas took their toll and played a role in the spiritual struggles that followed.

One of the emotions often cited in the grief process is anger. Many times people experience anger with God when a loved one dies. I don't remember either of us expressing anger during any of our three losses. However, we certainly felt a sense of betrayal or abandonment. Perhaps we were angry with God and didn't want to admit it. After Beth's death we talked about our feelings of resentment, which are at least closely related to anger. But I think rather than feeling anger towards God, we felt hurt and deserted by him.

We had to deal with a terrible amount of guilt in the losses of all three of our children. When a child dies, the normal feelings of guilt are greatly magnified. After all, the safety and well being of our children is our first responsibility as parents. We thought after Mike died in his sleep, "How could we ever forgive ourselves for letting our child die? Why weren't we there watching over him? His death was unnecessary and it was our fault." With Rachel, we thought if we had not waited to get her to the doctor, they might have been able to catch the meningitis in time. I couldn't get it out of my mind that I had gone off on a business trip and left her moaning in her crib. While people told us it was normal to have such thoughts, these self-imposed admonitions were still devastating. The terrible guilt feelings that plague us during such times are some of the personal demons we have to deal with in our sorrow. I think Satan, the great accuser, uses feelings of guilt to rob us of God's comfort in our time of grief. Even if we were somehow negligent, we have to accept God's forgiveness and immerse ourselves in His love, mercy and grace.

After we lost our third child we had very strong feelings of paranoia. Feelings that we were being singled out for emotional abuse. What had happened to us didn't seem fair. Why did we have to go through this again and again? There was a feeling of utter discouragement and a great tendency to wallow in that dreaded Satanic pool of self pity. However, we were certain in our minds that God was there and in his time he would help us to understand.

The emotional wounds produced by the deaths of our children took their toll on our psyches. After our three losses we were never quite the same again, inside. The emotional wounds healed with time, but they left behind scars; invisible, but nevertheless real. As with physical scar tissue, we found there is a kind of numbness in the soul produced by emotional traumas that prevents us from experiencing sharply felt emotions again, whether good or bad. For many years it was difficult to feel much emotion in our souls, just as one does not experience sharp pain in physical scar tissue.

By the time we lost Beth, the pain reached much deeper in our souls, reaching below the point of crying, down to the deepest depths of our beings. And it was there in the dark pit of that valley we each had to face our personal spiritual battles and learn once and for all whether our faith was real.

The Wife Of Noble Character

"Her children arise and call her blessed; her husband also, and he praises her" Proverbs 31:2

Karen's faith battle was hers to fight, just as Vicki, Becky and I each had our own. But as a mother, Karen had the heaviest load to carry. So now, let me tell you about my wife Karen, a most remarkable woman.

Karen has never ceased to amaze me with her strength and resilience. She has come through our repeated losses and sorrows as a true hero. In my mind she can take her place with the heroes of the faith listed in Hebrews 11, where the author rehearses the lives and sacrifices of faithful servants of God over the ages. Many people I know have been hardened and embittered by grief. I've read of mothers who have committed suicide after losing a child. Karen, however, is characterized by her love of life, her great sense of humor and her concern for her family. The experiences through which she has passed have molded her more and more to the image of Christ. She has been through the "Refiner's Fire" repeatedly and has come out as a 24 carat spiritual saint.

Although the emotional scars are there, she still cares deeply. When we lost our children, there were tears, freely flowing, expressing grief, cleansing the soul and bringing healing over time. Each time, however, after the tears she picked herself up and went on in a healthy process of healing, adjustment and recovery. God wouldn't allow her to slip into depression and self pity.

The young girl who began our married life as a dependent clinging vine had quickly grown out of her dependency and had regained her confidence, and her assertiveness. That early behavior and the process of growing out of it had been a normal part of the adjustments which most marriages must pass through. Karen became an able and proficient wife, mother and church leader. A couple of years after losing Beth, Karen began studying for a career in the travel business. Her years as a professional travel agent gave her an opportunity to prove to herself and others that she was capable of being an effective business woman. The experiences with our children served to strengthen her and mold her more to the likeness of Jesus. She responded to the Master Potter's hands and became a vessel of honor, glorifying the Father who made her.

In the book of 2nd Timothy, the apostle Paul realizes he is nearing the end of his ministry, and indeed, his life. He writes to his young protégé, Timothy, who is probably pastoring the church at Ephesus at that time. His words are encouraging and full of pathos. His words have inspired Christian workers and all believers over the centuries. He writes, *"For I am already being poured out like a drink offering, and the time has come for my departure. I have fought the good fight. I have finished the race. I have kept the faith. Now there is in*

store for me the crown of righteousness, which the Lord, the right-
teous judge, will award to me on that day – and not only to me, but
also to all who have longed for his appearing." 2 Timothy:6-8

While Paul wrote these words near the end of his life, I think
they apply, at least in part, to Karen. She may have many years to
go before the final end of her race, but she has certainly run this lap
of the race well. She fought the good fight, and most importantly,
she has kept the faith. I worried about her faith when we lost Mike. I
wasn't sure how she would be able to handle the loss. I didn't know
if she would blame God and fall away from her faith. But, while she
had plenty of questions for God, she never wavered in her faith.

In Luke, Chapter 22, Jesus was spending his last night with his
disciples. As he told them what to expect that evening, Peter declared
that he would follow Jesus to the end, no matter what happened. The
Jews were about to confront and capture Jesus, and he knew what
would happen to Peter. He would fail the test and deny the Lord three
times. Jesus said to Peter, *"Simon, Simon. Satan has asked to sift*
you as wheat. But I have prayed for you, Simon, that your faith may
not fail. And when you have turned back, strengthen your brothers."
Luke 22:31-32. Jesus did not pray that Peter would be spared the
temptation and trial, but he prayed that Peter's faith would not fail.
Isn't that interesting? Peter was indeed sifted by Satan; he failed the
test which he was so sure he would be able to handle. But, afterwards, he repented and rushed to the feet of Jesus when the chance
presented itself. His faith survived and ultimately did not fail.

In the same way, I'm sure that Jesus prayed with me for Karen
that her faith wouldn't fail. Certainly he allowed her to be sifted
as wheat by Satan. But her faith did not fail. I think we can extend
this principle to other believers in times of trial and temptation. I'm
sure that anytime his dear children are tested severely, Jesus is there
at that time praying for them that their faith may not fail. Karen's
faith has held fast. And, once she had come through that test, the
Lord directed her with the last part of that Scripture passage to use
her experience to help strengthen her brothers and sisters in Christ.
Karen has done that. She has counseled weeping mothers and shared
her wisdom with others as they question God's care for them and
their work. She has been faithful to freely share with any who could

benefit from her testimony. There may be other fights and races ahead, but Karen has done well through this series of trials and her faith has not failed. Indeed, it has grown stronger and more vibrant with time.

I don't personally know of any other woman who has experienced such deep and repeated trauma as my wife has. Karen has not only lost three living children, she also suffered two miscarriages. Seven times she has been pregnant, but only two children have survived to adulthood. I've seen people devastated by one miscarriage, and I know their pain is real. Our pain was certainly real when Karen miscarried those two times before Becky was born. However, the pain from the miscarriages was nothing like the pain of losing the children whom we had known and loved for years.

Besides the losses, Karen spent her young adult life caring for children with exceptional problems. From our marriage in 1961 until 1982 when Beth died, Karen seldom had a period of time when she wasn't challenged by the needs of her children or by difficulties with her pregnancies. First it was our troubling courtship followed by her difficult pregnancy with Vicki. Then the real problems began with Mike's seizures and death, followed by the two miscarriages which kept her in bed for months on end. Then Karen was challenged with brain-damaged Rachel and her constant requirement for care. After Rachel, she cared for Beth with her seizure disorder and learning disabilities for five years. Although Karen had her times of discouragement and even dismay, I never once heard her complain about her own situation. She was always faithful to her family and felt it was her duty to care for all of our needs. She always did it with love and she did it well.

People often tell Karen, "I don't know how you can go on," or "I couldn't take what you've gone through." Karen's response is that you do what you have to do and lean on the Lord and those close to you to help you through it. She had to experience even more pain because some of her friends didn't know what to say, so they didn't say anything. Like Beth's teacher, Mrs. Ann, some of those friends actually avoided her after Beth died because they could not face her. I'm not sure why some people avoided Karen, and I suppose there are many different reasons, each as individual as the people who stayed away during those sad times. Maybe like Mrs. Ann, they felt they couldn't do anything but cry if they tried to talk to her. Perhaps they couldn't bear to be reminded that the possibility existed that their children could be taken from them. Karen's pain was unnecessarily exacerbated by the apparent rejection of friends when she needed them most.

Through it all, Karen has always exhibited an amazing inner strength. I'm sure the experiences with Mike and his seizures strengthened her and prepared her for what was to come with Rachel. That experience in turn helped her handle Beth's death. Maybe the strength that developed in those experiences is why she never panics in times of stress. She is usually the one who is most in control in emergencies.

For example, one night when Vicki was a young teenager our daughter awakened us in the night screaming in her bedroom. Before I was fully awake Karen was in Vicki's room where she immediately saw that the electric blanket was on fire. By the time I got there Karen had unplugged the blanket, pulled it off Vicki, smothered the flames, and handed me the smoldering mess, saying "Hurry up and take this outside and throw it in the snow before it smokes up the rest of the house." Vicki and I hadn't yet figured out what was happening.

This young wife who at first wanted to rely on her husband and lean on him for everything, found herself alone when the most severe tests of her life came. She was alone when she found Mike dead in his crib. I wasn't even in the same state when Rachel's sickness hit, and later when her death came. Karen's faith and her strength allowed her to pass those tests, battered emotionally, but not beaten. But still, she needed assurance from her God that He was first of all there, and through all that was happening He had not forsaken her.

Karen's Answer

"I will rejoice in the Lord, I will be joyful in God my savior. The Sovereign Lord is my strength." Habbakuk 3:17

Karen's faith was tried to the maximum when Beth died. In addition to the cumulative effect of our previous losses, her life had been totally wrapped up in Beth. At that time our other daughters were teenagers and were involved with their own friends and activities. Karen had never worked outside the home. Her entire married life had been spent raising her children with their special problems. In the years before Beth began school, it was just Karen and Beth alone together during the day.

When Beth's seizure disorder became known, Karen felt the Lord gave her a promise from Isaiah 43:18-19 where it was written, *"Forget the former things; do not dwell on the past. See, I am doing a new thing!"* Karen interpreted this verse as a promise from the Lord that Beth wouldn't suffer the same fate as her brother Mike. She took strength from that verse and was encouraged that the Lord would protect Beth from harm.

Then, when Beth died, Karen was crushed. She thought God had promised her Beth would not die. Disillusionment and doubt were piled on top of the sorrow of her loss. She was confused. Had she just found a verse in the Bible that told her what she wanted to hear? Had God led her down the primrose path? The spiritual dilemma multiplied her pain.

It was to Karen's credit that she went back to God and his Word for the answer to her distress. She searched the Bible daily, reading and waiting for God to speak and tell her what he was doing and why this terrible thing had happened. She wanted and needed an answer. Then, finally, God spoke to her. However, it was not to answer all of her questions, but simply to give her a beautiful word of encouragement to just trust him. She found the words that satisfied her need in the inspired words of the prophet Habbakuk.

> *"Though the fig tree does not bud and there are no grapes on the vines, though the olive crop fails and the fields produce no food, though there are no sheep in the pen and no cattle in the stalls, Yet I will rejoice in the Lord, I will be joyful in God my savior. The Sovereign Lord is my strength."* *Habbakuk 3:17*

The prophet Habakkuk understood the character of God. He recognized God as perfectly holy and pure and one who can do no wrong, even though circumstances make it appear that he has deserted us. Our all-loving and holy God could never be the source of sin or error. Therefore, whatever God decides to do is the correct, perfect and proper course of action, even if it requires us to experience difficulties and temporary pain. Our tiny brains can never begin to comprehend the complexities of God's plans. We can't see beyond the present moment. On the other hand, God knows the future in the context of eternity.

The faith of Habakkuk did not require the circumstances be pleasant before he could trust God. Through his inspired words Karen came to that same position. Her trust and faith in God could not be based upon external circumstances, even if those circumstances included losing three of her children. She drew strength from the assurance in that passage that God is in control and his unbounded love for us will carry us through any and all disasters. She knew now she could and would love him and trust him, no matter what. And it wasn't just an intellectual answer. God's Holy Spirit used that verse to open her to the embrace of the Father. She was buoyed and comforted in her spirit through God's promise to her.

Both Karen and Habakkuk came to understand that no matter what calamity befalls us, we must trust God and rejoice in his goodness and his care for us. He has promised us, as a minimum, that tribulations will produce Godly character in us that he can use if we will perservere. He has also promised us our current sufferings are nothing compared with the glories awaiting us in heaven. Another precious verse in Romans 8 speaks of this reality. *"I consider that our present sufferings are not worth comparing with the glory that will be revealed in us.... But, we ourselves, who have the first fruits of the Spirit, groan inwardly as we wait eagerly for our adoption as sons, the redemption of our bodies." Romans 8:18,23*

During those trying days, it was helpful to both of us to remember our first wedding anniversary. That night when God showed us himself and his love for us, he gave us an anchor to hold on to when things got rough. It was a stake in the ground, marking with certainty our eternal relationship with God and with each other. Holding tight to the memory of that spiritual experience helped keep us from capsizing.

As Karen worked through her spiritual struggle, God brought healing and restoration to her, resulting in a beauty and calmness that belies the battles she has fought. She has met her challenges and has grown to unusual spiritual heights through those experiences that seemed so unbearable. I believe her restoration demonstrates an important spiritual principle. One which hasn't been discussed very much. The principle, simply stated, is this, *God rewards our faithfulness.* The Old Testament passage of 1 Samuel 26:23 says *"The Lord rewards every man for his righteousness and faithfulness."* This principle is illustrated clearly in the story of Job's restoration in Chapter 42 where God rewards Job's faithfulness by blessing the latter part of Job's life more than the first. Even though Job had complained and questioned God, he was still rewarded very generously by God. Not only were his material possessions multiplied but he and his wife were blessed with additional children. They had seven sons and three daughters. I sometimes wonder if Job's wife was as thrilled to have all those additional children at her advanced age. Perhaps she shouldn't have advised Job to curse God and die. Anyway, Job lived to see his grandchildren and great grandchildren and had a rich and rewarding life after his trials and testing.

If Karen had continued to dwell in her grief and had harbored resentment or bitterness in her heart, she may have never experienced the glorious restoration which she now exhibits. So many people who have undergone great traumas clearly show the effects. They may be bitter, withdrawn, angry, hardened or just chronically depressed.

Prolonged intense pain or suffering has a profound effect on the human psyche. I believe the only way a person can escape such lasting effects, is through faith in God, our Creator. Only by looking to God and wholly trusting him, and by accepting his will, can we find true healing. They must believe God is in charge and is working his perfect will in their life. Such faith is a joy to God and he will not let it go unrewarded. That is one of the primary reasons for this book. We want to help people avoid such a prolonged agony and despair by testifying that it is not necessary. You don't have to go through that. Karen is my proof of God's care for his children, even when it is his will for them to go through trials and tribulations for him and for the furtherence of his Kingdom. Karen is my inspiration and my joy. I thank God for blessing me so richly with a wife of such faith and character. She is the greatest blessing in my life.

Becky's Release

"Then you will know the truth and the truth will make you free" John 8:32

Becky's story is different, but it also has a happy ending. Becky was in kindergarten when Rachel died. The teachers remarked that they thought Becky was having some emotional reaction to losing her sister. She had become more withdrawn but still responded to her teacher's requests. Becky says she doesn't remember a lot about Rachel except that she was laying around on the couch all the time. After Beth's death, however, Becky had a rougher time. Of course, she was baby sitting with Beth when the accident occurred and we were concerned about Becky blaming herself. She never said anything that gave us any indication she was, but that in itself was strange. Knowing her sensitive nature, it was hard for us to believe she was not hurting tremendously inside.

Everyone has to cope with grief situations in their own way, but Becky's way was a problem for us. From our perspective, Becky withdrew from us and isolated herself emotionally from the rest of the family. Her memories of those days were not that negative, however. She doesn't think she withdrew any more than any other "introverted teenager." We didn't think of her as being introverted in those days, so we blamed some of her withdrawal on the accident and her emotional trauma that resulted from it. She did become her normal bubbly self again with her friends, but we were never sure it wasn't a facade. She certainly didn't let on outwardly that she was having a problem coping with her sister's death. We feared, however, she was not letting herself grieve and was in denial.

One thing was certain. She seemed unable to relate to her family. However, at the time Karen and I didn't understand her actions. We were confused and hurt because it seemed when we needed her the most, she withdrew from us. She spent almost all of her time at home in her room with the door closed. During meals, or while riding in the car together, she never spoke. We realized some withdrawal from family is normal for teenagers. However, we assumed that as she dealt with the grief and guilt she felt, the normal adolescent tendencies were intensified. Eventually, she cut off all nonessential communication. We knew it was selfish of us to feel hurt by her withdrawal because we were thinking only of our own needs, but it was still very difficult for us because we needed her so much.

I know we were somewhat to blame for the lack of communication. We should have tried harder to meet her where she was in her mind. If we had done a better job of showing our approval of her interests and relating to her through them, we could have communicated more. For example, as a teenager Becky was an avid fan of the musical rock groups. She could name the members of every current group and tell you their personal histories. Karen and I on the other hand could not tolerate rock music and therefore we didn't think we could relate to Becky through that avenue. However, we should have at least tried to get familiar with her music, even if we didn't enjoy it, and use the music as a point of communication with her.

Karen and I were sure Becky was trying to cope with Beth's loss through those years, but we were never able to get her to talk to us about it. At times, it was difficult to keep from feeling anger toward her because it seemed she was rejecting us personally. We wondered at times if she even cared about us. When we would occasionally try to discuss our feelings with her, we were met with silence, or at most, a minimal response. She didn't come across as hostile; just distant and indifferent to us. We understood she needed space but it was especially difficult for her mother to be isolated from what was now her youngest child. After years of caring for Rachel, and then Beth, now Karen felt she was not needed or wanted. Her youngest child seemed to be rejecting her.

Here is what Becky had to say recently about her teenage years after Beth died. "I withdrew, but I don't know that I withdrew more than any other introverted teen. Other than the pain of what had happened, I wasn't unhappy at all. I enjoyed school, the youth group at church and my friends and consider that I had a good experience of being a teenager. Vicki always talked a lot when she was home, so I didn't have to. Counselling would have probably been a good idea, but I wouldn't have liked it."

It didn't occur to us at the time to seek counseling for Becky. We were fairly self sufficient ourselves and reasoned we knew enough about how to deal with grief to handle Beth's death. How wrong we were. Becky's problems went beyond just the grief of losing her sister. She had to deal with the fact that Beth was in her care when the accident happened. She had to come to grips with the guilt she was hiding inside. We knew it was there, even though we continued to try to assure her by our love and support that it was not her fault. In the end analysis, however, she had to convince herself of that.

Even in the face of discouragement, God always sends a ray of hope. We knew Becky maintained her relationship with God because much of the time while she was locked in her room she was reading her Bible. Our daughters grew up in church, and at the age of seven Becky asked if she could be baptized. When I asked her why she wanted to, she responded with no prompting that she loved Jesus and had asked Him into her heart. "And besides," she said, "Christians are supposed to be baptized because Jesus was and he told us we should be too." There was no doubt in my mind that she knew what she was doing. Her life always exhibited the love and character of Jesus, and I'm sure her faith sustained her through the stress and trauma of her sisters' deaths.

Becky was always extremely sensitive. When she was a young girl, a stern look would cause tears to flow. Her compassion and concern for other people's feelings are still dominant traits in her personality. I once scolded her when she was a young teenager for giving her lunch money to the other kids at school. They all knew she was an easy touch, and if she had money any sob story would cause her to part with it quickly. When I fussed with her about it she went to her room and soon came back with her Bible. She stood in front of me and read Matthew 5:42 aloud...*"Give to the one who asks you, and do not turn away from the one that wants to borrow from you."* I had to admire her knowledge of the Bible and her desire to be obedient to her Lord's command as she understood it. Nevertheless, I still advised her to be more discerning and not let people take advantage of her tender heart.

Becky's tender spirit made her more vulnerable to serious emotional problems when her sister died while in her care. Only the grace of God could have kept her and protected her. And, when the time was right, He delivered her, even from the guilt that weighted her down.

Becky was and is a strong, independent young lady. We admire her spirit and we love her with all of our hearts. We were so thankful to God when he finally worked a healing miracle in her life. It wasn't until she was a senior in college, seven years after Beth died, that she finally found release from the unnecessary burden of guilt she carried for so long. It was interesting how God provided that release. Becky went off to England during her senior year for a short term of study at Oxford. We never imagined that what she would learn there would turn out to be much more profound than English literature.

When Becky arrived at Oxford they housed her, along with three other American girls, in Wycliffe House. It just so happened that the Anglican church also operated a seminary in Wycliffe House for the evangelical arm of the church. The girls had a basement apartment together, but took their meals with the seminarians in the dining room. The girls also shared the common facilities like the television and game rooms with the seminarians. Becky has always been an Anglophile, meaning she loves everything English. Her major was in English and many of the pop music groups she enjoyed were of English origin. Becky quickly took to the English men and women who lived in Wycliffe hall and was subsequently influenced by them in profound ways.

The evangelical movement within the Anglican Church is "mildly charismatic," as Becky expressed it, and as such, the seminarians regularly practiced prayer for healing. Becky later related to us how one of the men named John was sympathizing with her one evening because she was suffering from a sore and stiff neck. He volunteered to pray over her and place hands on her for healing. He did so, but while he was praying for her physical healing, something very unexpected happened. Becky said while the young man was praying over her, she began to think about Beth's accident and brought up all those repressed memories. John asked her what she was feeling so she began to tell him about the incident with Beth.

He then continued to pray for her and suddenly all of the grief and guilt she had carried over Beth's accident for seven years came into focus. Then her emotions overwhelmed her as she felt released from the giant burden of guilt that had weighted down her very soul. She knew she had received full grace and pardon in her soul, not only from God, but from herself. For the first time in seven years she experienced freedom from the burden of Beth's accident.

We knew something profound had happened when Becky shared this experience with us upon her return from England. She had obviously changed and began openly communicating with us. She explained to us how God had moved in her life and she felt she had found God's will for her life. Somehow, God wanted to use her life in His service. However, it wasn't until later that we learned how she felt God was leading her to realize the call she had received.

Don's Answer

"Though he slay me, yet will I hope in Him... Indeed, this will turn out for my deliverance" Job 13:15-16

It is so like God to lead us individually to him by the path that works uniquely for us. With me, it was through the ancient book of Job, written over three thousand years ago. The book of Job was especially meaningful to me after Beth died. I read it not just once, but over and over again. It helped me because I could see how my pain was reflected in Job's experience and in his words. I could relate to Job's confusion and consternation after his multiple losses. But more importantly, I could see how God could be working in our situation to accomplish the same objective.

The Bible tells us Satan received permission from God to afflict Job and to strip him of all his property and riches. The Lord even allowed Satan to take Job's children, and eventually, his health. Surprisingly, it appears Job's suffering was God's idea. Notice in Chapter 1 that it was God who brought up Job's name in the conversation with Satan. God knew he could trust Job to bear up under the trials and even while suffering, to give a strong testimony. And indeed he did.

For thirty-five chapters, Job and his so-called friends debated God's role in Job's sufferings. Job protested that he didn't deserve all the loss and misery that had been inflicted on him by God, but he didn't rebel and curse God as his wife suggested. Job's friends, on the other hand, argued that God wouldn't have let all these bad things happen to him unless he deserved it. They insisted that Job had committed some pretty heinous sins for him to be punished so severely. Job didn't appreciate their accusations, and told them, *"Miserable comforters are you all. Will your long-winded speeches never end?" Job 16:2*

Job's ultimate conclusion after much agonizing over his fate, was to say, *"Though he slay me, yet will I trust him." Job 13:15(KJV).* Job's testimony has glorified God down through the ages and ministered to me in the present age. Job's enduring faith was a defeat for Satan and a resounding victory for the kingdom of God. But it took extreme suffering on Job's part to bring it to pass.

I wouldn't presume to compare myself with Job. Our family hasn't been through the tribulation fires to the extent Job was. However, the theme of Job's book and the lessons learned apply to our situation, and more broadly, to the suffering of all God's people. Job's losses led him to cry out to God all the more. There was no doubt in his mind God was there and he was controlling what was happening in Job's life. He just didn't understand why it had to be done that way and why it had to hurt so bad.

As a result of seeing how God used Job to further his kingdom work, I was greatly encouraged. Just as Satan had to get permission from God to afflict Job, I know he also had to get permission from God before he could afflict and test us. Perhaps God would also use our suffering to glorify himself and further his kingdom's work. If this was all part of God's plan, then it would be worth all of the pain and suffering. Therefore, following Job's example, we too will trust God to the end, no matter what happens.

God spoke to me through Job's cries for help as well as through his testimony of faith. I can see from Job's experience that it's all right to tell God how I feel, even if I feel angry or betrayed. He understands and can accept that and minister healing to me in the process. Even so, I must be careful not to accuse God of acting deceitfully or in bad faith for that would be to accuse him of sin. Unfortunately, Job crossed that line and had to be admonished by God. However, Job's questioning and God's responses demonstrated to us that it is O.K. to ask the hard questions.

What are some of those questions? Well, why do sickness and afflictions have to come? Why do our innocent children have seizures and why do they catch meningitis? And why do they die? Doesn't God care? Is he really in control? Does he intentionally cause these things to happen? Is the Evil One able to penetrate God's defenses and afflict God's people as he pleases?

People have asked these questions down through the ages and God has allowed them to be recorded in his Word. The Psalms, as well as the book of Job, are replete with them. God is not afraid of these questions. I am sure he expects them from us. The only problem is, they are the wrong questions! As Job told his wife, *"You are talking like a foolish woman. Shall we accept good from God and not trouble?" Job 2:10*

These questions seem reasonable from the human point of view, believing as we do in a God of love and justice. The problem is, the human viewpoint is very limited and cannot comprehend nor appreciate the infinite. God sees things in an eternal context and he controls them to bring about the greatest good for now and for eternity. What may now seem very hard and heartless may be necessary for God to accomplish a greater eternal purpose. As radio preacher Woodrow Kroll says, "Instead of asking *why*, it is better to ask *what now?*"

God Speaks From The Whirlwind

"Where were you when I laid the earth's foundation? Tell me if you understand." Job 38:4

Job's eventual enlightenment became my guiding thought. God finally spoke after Job's friends had repeatedly accused Job of sin and after Job had exhausted his questions and accusations against God. Yes, God finally responded, but the answer was not what Job was looking for. God didn't answer Job's questions or accusations directly. God did not enter into the debate. He just allowed Job and his friends to glimpse a tiny bit of his glory and greatness. The message from the whirlwind was simply that God is absolutely powerful, sovereign and in control. No mortal man can comprehend God's greatness, and therefore it is inappropriate for him to question what God is doing. In the later chapters of Job, God's greatness is poetically extolled through the recitation of many of his great acts. God begins by asking Job where he was while God was busy creating the universe. After addressing the wonders of the cosmos briefly, he then proceeds to describe many of the beautiful and impressive forms of life which he created on the land and in the sea. It almost seems as if God was more pleased with the life forms he had created than he was with the rest of the universe. Maybe he actually is, because life seems to be the greatest miracle of all. It is a complete mystery to even the most educated and trained scientists. I've worked in that area for a time, so you can take my word for it. God said in essence to Job, "Are you going to question my judgment when you think about who I am and what I have done?"

I felt that the answer God gave Job was my answer also. I could live with that. I had no right to question God about his motives and his work in my family's life. His greatness is so far above me and he has already shown me that he is a God of love, compassion and generosity. He had given me no reason to question his goodness before now. Therefore, I must fall at his feet in submission and let him have his will in my life. I must accept his will in the loss of our children, trusting him to do the best for my family and me.

However, not everyone may be able to accept this answer as readily as I have. Perhaps some may need more from God than just this offhand pronouncement that he is too far above us for us to be able to question him. For that reason, I would like to take the opportunity now to explore in greater depth the greatness of God and his creation, realizing that we will never be able to approach a beginning knowledge of his infinite goodness and grace. But, perhaps a better appreciation of his greatness will help others come to the point of realization that it is unreasonable to question his goodness and purpose when dealing with their personal tragedies.

The Anthropic Principle

"Oh, how I love all you've revealed; I reverently ponder it all the day long." Psalm 119:97 (The Message Bible)

I have had a passion for astronomy since grade school. I may have even become an astronomer if my 8th grade science teacher had not discouraged me with one simple comment. When I asked her about astronomy as a career, she replied with a shrug, "Oh that takes way too much math." At that point in my life I wasn't enjoying math very much (because of the math teachers I had) so I thought to myself, "So much for astronomy." In high school I turned that interest into a passion for science fiction, especially stories dealing with space travel and other worlds. A few years later I was walking across the Naval shipyard in Yokosuka Japan, nearing the end of my tour of duty in the Navy, Sputnik flew over our heads and the real space race began. Because of my interest in astronomy and space, after we moved to California, Kaen and I visited the Griffith Observatory in Los Angeles and Mount Palomar in the mountains east of San Diego where the world's largest optical telescope is located.

It was my passion for space that led to my study of physics and engineering, and throughout all those years the study of the cosmos has continued to intrigue me. So, going back to God's words to Job, allow me to explain in contemporary cosmic terms how I interpret the picturesque language of Job's encounter with God.

When we simply look out into the universe on a clear dark night when the stars are clearly visible, the immensity of the night sky can quickly overwhelm us. Unfortunately, most of us in the cities never get that chance because of the polution of the air and the constant presence of man made ground lights. My most impressive experience of star gazing was on the 10,000 foot dormant volcano, Haleakala, on the island of Maui, a couple of hours before sunrise. That's the closest I'll ever get to being out in space. It was as if we were alone in outer space with the stars so thick and so close it seemed we could reach out and touch them. I hope that sometime you do find yourself in a dark place at night with a clear moonless sky, and if you do, take a while to soak up the vastness of the universe. It is so far beyond our ability to comprehend. The nearest star to us is Alpha Centauri. It is about 4 light years away. That doesn't sound so far until you stop to think that in earthly terms that is 23 trillion miles (23 followed by 12 zeros).

Can you grasp that large a number or that great a distance? Of course not. Our minds can't begin to comprehend such vastness. And yet, that's just the closest star. It's right next door in comparison with the far reaches of outer space. The Hubble Space Telescope can see light coming from the edge of the universe and even now is telling us that *billions of light years* away, in a far corner of the universe, galaxies are colliding. There are *hundreds of billions* of galaxies, and each galaxy contains *hundreds of billions of stars*. If the distance to the edge of the known universe is about eleven billion light years and if our nearest star is just 4 light years or 23 trillion miles away, that means that those distant galaxies are billions of times more than that! I gave up trying to comprehend those distances back with Alpha Centauri.

Our minds quickly become numb when we try to grapple with such dimensions. We can see no limits to the time and space that God has created, both seeming to go on forever. The concepts of infinity and eternity just don't compute in our little minds. And if we can't comprehend them, we certainly can't explain them. Yet, God is his greatness not only runs this universe, he created it from nothing!

We sometimes get the idea we are just not quite able to grasp the greatness of God. His majesty is just out of our reach. But I have news for you. His greatness is not just barely beyond our comprehension. Rather, it is orders and orders of magnitude beyond us. We can't even begin to comprehend how little of the universe we can comprehend. We can't fathom how small our minds are compared with the greatness of God.

There has been another development in recent years that may assist us in accepting the greatness and goodness of God. It may seem a little far afield from our family's story, but I think you will find this subject to be of interest to you if you want to learn more about the greatness of God and the related current debate over the issue of God's role in the creation of the universe.

The greatness of God and his role in the creation of the universe is at the crux of the debate about the "Anthropic Principle" [3]. Most of the literature on the subject is fairly deep technically, however much of the essence of the principle is distilled in Lee Strobel's excellent book entitled "The Case for A Creator" [4]. I think this book should be read by everyone, sceptic and believer alike. It is a very readable and an accurate summation of many of the aspects of the Anthropic Principle. Most of the popular debate concerning intelligent design still centers on the decades old 'Creation vs. Evolution' controversy, while the Anthropic Principle hasn't been discussed much in the popular press. Still, it is at the heart of the Intelligent Design movement in the U.S. If you're interested in learning more about this principle, you can find plenty of information on the internet by simply typing "Anthropic Principle" into your search engine.

To oversimplify, the Anthropic Principle states that all creation is filled with incredible "coincidences," all of which work together to make life possible. Dozens of physical conditions and properties of matter throughout the universe must be exactly as they are for human life to exist. Included are the specific values of the gravitational constant, nuclear binding forces, chemical valences, and on and on.

I read an article in the London Times reporting that Stephen Hawking, the noted atheistic cosmologist, has counted as many as 80 physical constants and parameters that must be exactly what they are for the universe and life to exist. Yet, he refuses to accept intelligent design. Rather, he posits a theoretical existence of multiple universes. He says that we just happen to be in the one that worked for us. Pretty incredible theorizing. That desparate hypothesis seems to me to require much more faith than would be needed to believe in a creator. There is a mountain of evidence for a Creator, but absolutely no evidence for parallel universes.

Here is a definition I took from Wikipedia on the internet about the origin and essence of the Anthropic Principle.

"The Anthropic Principle was first suggested in a 1973 paper, by the astrophysicist and cosmologist Brandon Carter from Cambridge University, at a conference held in Poland to celebrate the 500th birthday of the father of modern

astronomy, Nicolaus Copernicus. The Anthropic Principle is an attempt to explain the observed fact that the fundamental constants of physics and chemistry are just right or fine-tuned to allow the universe and life as we know it to exist. The Anthropic Principle says that the seemingly arbitrary and unrelated constants in physics have one strange thing in common—these are precisely the values you need if you want to have a universe capable of producing life. The universe gives the appearance that it was designed to support life on earth...."

Within our own solar system, there are dozens of examples of this principle. The size and age of the sun (and therefore its temperature) and the distance of the earth from the sun, put us in the perfect thermal conditions for life to exist. The size, mass and composition of the earth allow it to hold a breathable atmosphere through its own gravity. The abundance of water and oxygen are unique to the earth, although desparate scientists hopefully search the solar system for other planets or moons that may harbor these life-giving elements. The magnetic field around the earth screens out life-threatening radiation from outer space. The chemical compostion of the earth provides the carbon-based building blocks of life. The list goes on and on to provide what is surely the largest imaginable collection of "circumstantial evidence" for the existence of God and his part in the creation of the universe.

I don't want to bore you with a lot of scientific mumbo jumbo, but let me just include a few brief quotes from prominent scientists about the Anthropic Principle. One of the most famous and popular astronomers of the present age was the late Sir Frederick Hoyle. Following the Anthropic Principle logic, he predicted an unknown resonance in the carbon nucleus that would have to exist if life were to evolve in the universe. His prediction was proven to be accurate by laboratory tests after he published his theory. Following is a famous quote from the formerly atheistic Sir Frederick:

Would you not say to yourself, "Some super-calculating intellect must have designed the properties of the carbon atom, otherwise the chance of my finding such an atom through the blind forces of nature would be utterly minuscule." Of course you would . . . A common sense interpretation of the facts suggests that a superintellect has monkeyed with physics, as well as with chemistry and biology, and that there are no blind forces worth speaking about in nature. The numbers one calculates from the facts (the odds) seem to me so overwhelming as to put this conclusion almost beyond question. [5]

Here are just a few more quotes to support the argument.

"A life-giving factor lies at the centre of the whole machinery and design of the world." John Wheeler

"Everything about the universe tends toward humans, toward making life possible and sustaining it"

Hugh Ross

"... the Anthropic Principle says that the seemingly arbitrary and unrelated constants in physics have one strange thing in common—these are precisely the values you need if you want to have a universe capable of producing life."

Patrick Glynn

And, finally, The noted physicist, cosmologist and author Paul Davies notes in the preface to his book, "God and the New Physics" [6],

'It may seem bizarre, but in my opinion science offers a surer path to God than religion."

I'm not sure that many theologians would agree with Professor Davies, but Cambridge astrophysicist, John Polkinghorne, who helped discover the quark, resigned from his professorship to embrace theology. He is now an Anglican priest and one of the most reknowned apologists on the planet. Our son in law, Paul, studied in his department at Cambridge. Polkinghorne sees no conflict between science and religion, and has published a number of books addressing their compatibility.

I'm sure these intellectual debates will go on for as long as the Lord tarries in His return. But, as you can see, many intellectuals accept the logic that there must be some kind of intelligent, great force that created the universe. They would be called Deists, people who accept on purely rational grounds that there must be a creator. But, having gone that far, many refuse to take the next step, acknowledging that this great Creator could make himself known to humankind. They feel they must deny that spiritual dimension because they cannot measure it with their instruments. But, consider how ridiculous that position is. On the one hand they grant the existence of an infinitly powerful creator, but then turn right around and try to put limits on what he can or cannot do. They simply do not want to accept the possibility that this Creator could inject himself into human history by coming to Earth as a baby and living a perfect life amongst men. If they were to accept that concept, it would make them responsible for their actions and they don't want a moral law constraining them.

It seems perfectly logical to me that the Creator would find a way to communicate with his creation. Coming into the human experience, and then preserving his communications in a book (the Bible) seems like a logical way to make himself known to his people, whom he created in his image. Even Job, from his ancient perspective, had the insight to suspect God was going to do more than remain a mysterious Force out in the cosmos somewhere. During one of his monologues about his need to meet God face to face to argue his case, he said in Chapter 9, verses 32-34, *"If there was only someone to arbitrate between us, to lay his hand upon us both, someone to remove God's rod from me so that his terror would frighten me no more. Then I would speak up without fear of him, but as it now stands with me, I cannot."* Job recognized the need for an arbitrator, which is one of the primary roles of our Savior, Jesus Christ, God's Son. Then in Chapter 19:25-27, Job cries out with conviction, *"And as for me, I know that my Redeemer lives, and that in the end he will stand upon the earth. And after my skin has been destroyed, yet in my flesh I will see God; I myself will see him with my own eyes- I, and not another. How my heart yearns within me!"*

Here's my point. For any human to demand of God that he be accoutable to man must be the most extreme hubris. But people do it all the time by demanding that God conform to their ideas of how he should run his universe. They may not put it to God as a demand, but they are essentially saying that if he doesn't conform to their wishes, they won't have anything to do with him. So, to require anything of God is to set oneself up as a master of all of the mysteries of creation, when in reality we are all nothing more than flyspecks in the universe. Only through God's infinite grace are we able even to relate to our Creator. Thank God he made us so.

I like these words from the introduction to the book of Leviticus in the Message Bible. *"One of the stubbornly enduring habits of the human race is to insist on domesticating God. We are determined to tame him. We figure out ways to harness God to our projects. We try to reduce God to a size that conveniently fits our plans and ambitions and tastes. But our Scriptures are even more stubborn in telling us that we can't do it. God cannot be fit into our plans, we must fit into his."*

The Apostle Paul puts it this way:

"Where is the wise man? Where is the scholar? Where is the philosopher of this age? Has not God made foolish the wisdom of the world?... For the foolishness of God is wiser than man's wisdom, and the weakness of God is stronger than man's strength." 1 Corinthians 1:20,25.

We mortal beings need to recognize we are extremely limited in our ability to comprehend and understand the mysteries of God's great universe. It is only through our spirits we can get hold of God, and it is there that God is quick to reveal himself to us. To me, that's the secret to having any hope at all in light of our insignificance in the universe. God is spirit and he has created us with our own spirit within us. In the spiritual dimension, we are right there with God. He meets us willingly and openly, requiring only that we open ourselves up to him and accept his supremacy in our lives. Amazingly, he gives us the freedom to decide for ourselves if we want to do that. If we decide we can't or won't accept him, he leaves us alone. But, then we are on our own and we forfeit all the blessing he has for us.

When we have been impertinent to God and have questioned his moving in our lives, or even his very existence, we must be like Job after he saw a little of God's greatness. We must throw ourselves at his feet in repentance and cry out for mercy and grace because of our impudence and arrogance.

I adore the story of the aged theologian, Carl Barth, who had spent his life studying philosophy and teaching the deep truths of Christianity. Near the end of his life he was asked if he could summarize the most profound truth he had learned over the long years of his scholarship. He responded, "Yes I can, and it is this. Jesus loves me. This I know, for the Bible tells me so."

We must all come to God as children and trust him in childlike faith. That is the only answer to all of the difficult questions of life. That is the only answer I could come to as I grieved over the loss of our beautiful children. His ways are beyond my understanding, but I know that God is love, and that he loves me and has promised never to forsake me. So, I leave it in his hands and trust him to comfort me and my family, and to use our children's death to somehow glorify himself and further his kingdom.

CHAPTER 9

THE WORK OF GRIEF

The Beatitude

"Blessed are those who mourn, for they will be comforted"
Matthew 5:4

Through all of our experiences, I have come to the conclusion that along with love, grief is surely the deepest and most profound of all human emotions. In a real sense, grief is the flip side of love. The two are closely intertwined because without love there would be no grief. The fact we allowed ourselves to love someone makes the work of grief necessary when we lose them. The greater the love, the deeper the sorrow, and the longer it will take to work through it. As Joy says in "C. S. Lewis Through the Shadowlands" [7], "That's the deal!"

We were created by a loving God who knows exactly how we are made and how badly we hurt when we lose a loved one. Among the wonderful beatitudes of Jesus in Matthew 5 is verse 4 which says *"Blessed are those who mourn, for they shall be comforted."* The accepted theological explanation of this beatitude says we should spiritualize this beatitude, indicating that it means when we mourn for our sins, we will be comforted by God's forgiveness. That is fine, and it is surely true. However, I think Jesus' words can be taken literally also. Because grief is perhaps the most profound experience of life, he makes this blessing available to God's children who are in sorrow, those who have lost loved ones. The promise in itself is a great comfort to those of us in grief because it reminds us that God knows the human spirit and he cares. He knows that all of us will have to eventually face the experience of mourning and grief. Therefore, in his great wisdom and compassion he has made provision for us to be comforted.

We can get another insight into God's working in our grief situation through a paraphrase of the 'Sufficient Grace' passage in 2 Corinthians 12:7-10. Equating the pain of our loss of a loved one for the pain Paul experienced with his 'Thorn in the flesh,' the Message Bible addresses our grief situation this way. *"Satan's angel did his best to get me down; what he in fact did was push me to my knees. No danger then of walking around high and mighty! At first I didn't think of it as a gift, and begged God to remove it. Three times I did that, and then he told me, My grace is enough; it's all you need. My strength comes into its own in your weakness. Once I heard that, I was glad to let it happen. I quit focusing on the handicap and began appreciating the gift. It was a case of Christ's strength moving in on my weakness. Now I take limitations in stride, and with good cheer, these limitations that cut me down to size ....I just let Christ take over! And so the weaker I get, the stronger I become."*

How can we know the Lord feels our pain? The clearest indication of that is in the life and ministry of Jesus Christ. Jesus modeled for us the very character of God. Jesus said, *"If you have seen me, you have seen the Father" John 14:9.* By observing the compassion of Jesus, we see the compassion of the Father.

In John, Chapter 11, Jesus tarried when the news of his friend Lazarus' illness reached him. By the time he arrived at the home of Mary and Martha, Lazarus had been dead for four days. Martha, I'm sure, felt betrayed by the Lord. She said, *"Lord if you had been here, my brother would not have died."* She was blaming God for her brother's death, and she was probably right. If the Lord had been there, he most likely would have healed Lazarus, rather than just letting him die in his presence. However, Jesus had a purpose for letting his friend die at that particular time, just as I'm sure he had a purpose for taking our children when and how he did. In our minds there is never a good time for a loved one to die, and that goes for ourselves as well. However, death will visit all of us somewhere along life's path. It's just a matter of when. In the case of Lazarus, we get to see the reason why he died when he did.

Before Jesus revealed his plan to Martha and Mary, he saw the intense pain and grief in their hearts. He understood the confusion and feelings of betrayal they were experiencing. His heart grieved for them to the point that he personally groaned repeatedly in his own Spirit. And then ... *"Jesus wept."* Why? He groaned because he knew and felt the pain in their hearts, and his compassion for these loved ones caused him to weep and grieve with them, even though he knew he would soon restore their brother to them. The Lord knew that in just a few moments they would be experiencing great joy. Still, he wept, feeling with them the sorrow in their hearts.

I can relate this reaction of our Lord to my own experience. Each time a friend or family member came to be with us after one of our children had died, there would always be a new round of tears as we embraced and shared our sorrow. Even as I stood by and watched as someone came in and embraced Karen and they cried together, I would feel my own emotions swell again, and I would weep with them. The sharing of sorrow in this way is a very normal and very healthy thing to do and I think Jesus in his humanity felt the same emotions.

Then Jesus performed what was perhaps his most remarkable miracle as he called loudly into the tomb, *"Lazarus, come forth."* Jesus raised Lazarus from the dead. Yes, Jesus even revealed the reason for Lazarus' death as he prayed to the Father audibly *"...that the people may believe that you sent me."* I know Jesus feels our pain too, and he weeps for us in our sorrow, even though he knows the future will be better than the present, through the working of his Holy Spirit.

While Rachel was fighting for her life in the intensive care ward after contracting meningitis, we met a remarkable person in the hospital waiting room. Ellen Sullivan was a young mother, probably in her early thities, with five small children. Her husband was in a coma as a result of an automobile racing accident and he was not expected to live. Ellen was an attractive and articulate woman, amazing in many ways. As we waited the long night out together in the hospital, the lives of our loved ones hung in the balance. We talked throughout the night, sharing our concerns and our anxieties. Ellen said something very profound that night. When we asked her what she would do if her husband died, she replied with confidence, "You know, the human spirit is very strong. The loss of a loved one can be very painful, but God has made us so we can handle it. We will survive, and we will be all right."

Ellen taught us an important lesson. She helped us realize God created us to be remarkably resilient beings. As a ship is made to be seaworthy, God made us "lifeworthy," or able to cope and endure whatever comes our way. Ellen was sure people could survive and recover from almost anything, given time and faith in God. Even though the death of a child or a spouse seems to us to be more than we can bear, we can survive. And not just survive, but recover! We will heal and we will be able to enjoy life again. God has made us so we can. Ellen used the term "resilient," but as you know, I like to say God has made us "lifeworthy."

Death and dying truly are integral parts of our lives. God created us to live and function in a world where people die. He has equipped us to be able to cope with the death of loved ones, and to go on living. In our minds we can imagine nothing worse than a loved one dying, and perhaps there is nothing more sorrowful. When it happens, however, we survive. With God's help we cope. We go on living and we recover. We may not feel we want to at times, but we do what we have to do. The pain of grief is severe and God knows that, but the pain is also transient. It passes with time. God brings healing in time, and strength and comfort in the meantime. We will find happiness, joy and meaning again in our lives.

I don't know how Ellen came to have so much wisdom for such a young lady. I have always suspected she was an angel in disguise, sent to minister to us. While we were talking to Ellen, her husband's doctor came into the waiting room and announced to her that her husband had just expired. We wept with her and then she gathered her things and walked out of our lives as abruptly as she entered. While we never saw her again, we did keep track of her for a few years through mutual friends we learned of during our vigils. We learned her strength and faith did indeed see her through that crisis.

Her life stabilized again and a few years later she remarried. Her five children had a father again. She was right. We mortal human beings, created in the image of God, can with faith and determination recover from almost anything.

Without a relationship with God, however, recovery must be much more difficult. Unfortunately, even some Christians do not find the peace God has provided in their time of sorrow. Even though the Holy Spirit is there to provide strength, courage, comfort and even a deep wellspring of joy that seems completely out of place, they do not allow him to work in their lives. They seem to prefer to suffer, but that is not God's plan for us. We are not left alone to cope with this most deep and profound emotion. How I pity those who must undergo this process without God in their lives, and without close family and friends to support them.

Expressing Our Grief

"When Jesus saw her weeping, and the Jews who had come along with her also weeping, he was deeply moved in spirit..." John 11:33

We all feel tremendous emotions in the time of grief and we have to express them to find release and healing. It is actually harmful to try to hold your emotions in, for whatever reason. Repressed grief finds its way out eventually, and it can be manifested in unpleasant ways. I am not a psychologist so I can only tell you what I have experienced personally. Even though I tried to deal with my grief outwardly and apparently did some things right, there was still some repressed emotion. You know how men are. We feel we have to be a rock for the family and demonstrate our strength to others around us. I did some of that, I'm sure. But for a long time afterward, months and maybe even a year or two, I would find myself feeling uneasy without any apparent reason. I would tense up and maybe even lose my temper, which is very unusual for me. I've always been an easy going guy and felt blessed that I didn't get upset as much as other men I knew. Each time I prayed about this problem, I got a subtle reminder that what we had been through with the children wasn't going to go away quickly. I needed to talk it out with Karen and the girls, and even close friends I could confide in. Karen told me she was experiencing the same kind of thing, feeling "up tight" and uneasy with no apparent reason. If we were all experiencing the same thing, apparently it was an indication that our psyches were not completely healed yet.

It is good for tears to flow freely as broken hearts express their agony in the language of sorrow and grief. Besides crying, that may mean talking to people about what has happened and what we are feeling. That is the necessary process that leads to healing and recovery. Everyone needs to find that expression. Many people have found grief support groups to be very helpful. They can be located through hospital chaplains and through some churches.

In our family's case, the pain of our grief has been made more intense by the cumulative effect of our losses and those losses changed us in profound ways. When I was younger I was very emotional, and that nature was manifested in my spiritual life. Great music or preaching could easily lift me to the heights of ecstasy. My prayer life was intense and full of feeling, and new insights into Scripture easily excited me during my quiet times. By the time Beth died, however, I had lost much of that capacity. I couldn't even cry when Beth died, even though my heart was broken and I was in great pain.

For years, the only thing that would touch my emotions was peaceful Christian music. I could relax and let the music flow over my soul, and it was as if the Holy Spirit was stroking me gently and reassuring me of his presence. It would give me peace, although it was all receiving. I could give nothing. My prayer life became very different also. I felt as though I was in the presence of the Lord, but my only prayer was, "I love you Lord and I trust you. Please help me and my family through this loss. Thy will be done."

Part of the problem was that I was in the process of learning more of the way God works. I didn't realize it, but I was learning that in his sovereignty God may take some of his children deeper by letting us see the true nature of the work of his kingdom. We generally think and teach that the Christian life is pretty simple. Just accept Christ, obey God's rules for living and take time to study the Bible and pray. That's good policy and for most people that approach will lead to a happy and fulfilled life. You can't go wrong basing your life on those principles.

However, it seems that God needs some individuals to go beyond those simple principles and sample a little of the sacrifice God himself suffered when he gave his Son, Jesus, to experience the agony of the cross for all of us. When God takes us through the deep valleys, he doesn't expect us to happily skip through life as on a lark. I assume that before taking us through extended suffering, he will first know that our faith will stand the test, and he may prepare us ahead of time through various experiences, both spiritual and physical. By taking us through the pain of his suffering, we may become more useful to him in his kingdom's work.

I think that may have something to do with what has happened in our family's lives, but the deep things of God are not easy for us to comprehend. One thing I am sure of is that no matter what pain we may undergo, the comforting words of Jesus are always there. He said *"Come unto me, all ye that labor and are heavy laden, and I will give you rest. Take my yoke upon you and learn from me, for I am gentle and humble in heart, and you will find rest for your souls. For my yoke is easy and my burden is light." Matthew 11:28-30.* One might question whether the burden is easy and light when we are suffering loss, but that's where his miraculous grace manifests itself.

I realized later that when we are in the midst of sorrow, it is enough to just maintain that "love relationship" with the Lord. Just trust him to take care of you, one moment at a time. Don't worry about tomorrow or the next day. Don't think about all of the plans you had made with your loved one and all you were looking forward to together. Don't worry about how hard it will be in the future. Just love Jesus and trust him to take care of you right now. That is the most important thing. It is the essential thing. God will allow us to heal before he asks more of us. Remember, Jesus said, *"Peace I leave with you. My peace I give you.... Do not let your hearts be troubled and do not be afraid" (John 14:27).*

One expert on grief has suggested it takes seven years to get over the death of someone very close. I think I can confirm that assessment in my own life. For several years after we lost Beth, I thought I would never be able to feel deep emotion again. Experiences which before had brought tears to my eyes or excitement to my soul were now bland and plain. But after a few more years I was surprised one day to find a lump in my throat and tears in my eyes after a beautiful worship service. Since that day, I have found myself returning more and more to a full emotional life. I was even surprised recently to find myself tearing up during a goofy love movie. Yes, joy does come in the morning. Life can be beautiful again.

The term "bittersweet" is often used to describe the feeling of grief. It was appropriate for us because the acute pain of grief was mixed with the loving memories of joy and happiness each of our children brought into our lives. We wanted to think about them constantly and remember the love and joy they brought into our lives. That is the sweet part. And yet every thought brought pain and heartache because they were lost to us and that's what made the experience bitter. But, the good thing is that the bitter part fades with time while the sweet part stays with us for life.

The Sin of Self Pity

"Rachel is weeping for her children and she cannot be comforted, for they are gone. But the Lord says; "Don't cry any longer, for I have heard your prayers and you will see them again." Jeremiah 31:15-16 (KJV)

The loss of a loved one is surely one of the most difficult things in life to endure. We know God provides his Holy Spirit, the great Comforter, to minister to us in our grief. If we allow him to, the Lord will move us through the grief process in a reasonable length of time. Even so, it is never easy. It hurts. It hurts terribly. Grieving is hard work, and it is often messy. We may blubber all over ourselves and it makes us say and do things that are inappropriate. But, as I stated earlier, the fact we allowed ourselves to love someone makes the task necessary. It is an arduous task but not an impossible one. We need to recognize and accept the fact it is going to be a difficult job. Then we need to face it like any hard job and tackle it head on.

God has equipped us to handle the job and he will be there to help us through it. As I mentioned earlier, in 1 Corinthians 10:13, the apostle Paul writes,

"No temptation has seized you except what is common to man. And God is faithful; he will not let you be tried beyond what you can bear. But when you are tried, he will also provide a way out so that you can stand up under it."

The word for trial is usually translated as temptation. The message is that God will not put more on a person than he can take, and (this is a very important *and*) he will provide all the necessary help to ensure you can make it through. This verse isn't just talking about resisting temptations to sin. It also applies to the trial of sorrow. God will not put more on you than you can endure.

There is a powerful temptation to sin associated with the grief situation. That temptation is to become immersed in our sorrow and never recover. We can easily begin feeling sorry for ourselves and let the devil gain the victory. Our judgment can become clouded and we can become irrational in our behavior. That in turn can transition into clinical depression, and depression can end up in thoughts of suicide. King David illustrated how this behavior can affect even the best of us. When his son Absalom was killed, he continued to mourn for him incessantly, crying *"O my son Absalom! My son, my son Absalom! If only I had died instead of you - O Absalom, my son, my son!"* 2 Samuel18:33.

Joab, the general of his army, had to come to him and essentially slap him around in order to bring him to his senses. He needed to see his ceaseless mourning was communicating to his troops that they didn't matter. Only his evil son Absalom mattered. God sometimes says to us, it is time to stop mourning, or rise above it, and get on with your life. There is more work for you to do. But, he never says that until he knows we are ready and the time is right. We may never feel the time is right if it were left up to us, but if we keep our eyes focused on the Lord, he will bring us out of it and set us on our feet again.

There is another interesting example from the Old Testament. The prophet Samuel was mourning for King Saul when God said to him *"How long will you mourn for Saul, since I have rejected him as king over Israel? Fill your horn with oil and be on your way..." 1 Samuel 16:1.* God has work for us to do and does not intend for us to spend the rest of our lives grieving. He will sustain us and give us new energy and enthusiasm for life as we trust him and look to him daily for strength and guidance.

Jesus himself identified self-pity as originating with Satan when he admonished Peter for tempting Him to put his own feelings above his mission. He said, *"Get behind me Satan. You are a stumbling block to me; you do not have in mind the things of God but the things of men. Mattthew 16:23*

Grief As Spiritual Warfare

"Therefore put on the full armor of God, so that when the day of evil comes, you may be able to stand your ground." Ephesians 6:13

In Jesus' "High Priestly Prayer" in John 17, Jesus petitioned the Father to protect his followers from "the evil," or some translate it, from "the Evil One." Also, in the model prayer Jesus instructed us to pray *"deliver us from evil."* How can we interpret the death of our loved ones in the light of this prayer of our Savior? If the Father ever heard and answered a prayer, it must have been this prayer of the Son of God. Does evil triumph when a loved one is taken from us suddenly? Did the Evil One have his way when Beth had her accident? Did God lose control?

My answer is no! As God gave Satan permission to afflict Job, God allowed these things to happen to our children within his purpose and in his will. Again, we can't answer the "why" questions, but God is in control. His permissive will sometimes allows earthly life to end early in difficult ways. However, God is still triumphant. The child or the older Christian may join the Father in heaven a few years earlier than we expected, and for them that is wonderful. He eternally multiplies their joy with him. We who are left behind suffer the pain of the loss. But, as I have discussed before, God will use our suffering to personally strengthen us and to accomplish his will in his kingdom's work. We have the love and support of family and friends to help us through. We can come through this time of pain and grief with our faith intact and, as my family learned, even strengthened.

There is a strong parallel between resisting temptation to sin, and withstanding the trials and testing of grief and bereavement. In both cases, the Lord has provided the means for us to withstand. That doesn't mean he will automatically fight our battles for us. He expects us to be involved in fighting our own battles, using the training and equipment which he has provided for us. Yet, even so, he promised us *"Never will I leave you; never will I forsake you."* (Hebrews 13:5). He will see us through.

In Ephesians 3:16 Paul prays for us that *"He may strengthen you with power through His Spirit in your inner being, so that Christ may dwell in your hearts through faith. And... that you, being rooted and established in love, may have power... to grasp how wide and long and high and deep is the love of Christ."* Later in Ephesians, Paul explains to us the fact we are in spiritual warfare. *"For our struggle is not against flesh and blood, but against the rulers, against the authorities, against the powers of this dark world and against the spiritual forces of evil in the heavenly realms."* *Ephesians 6:12* Then he lists some of the provisions God has made available to us to help us in that warfare. He says *"Therefore, put on the full armor of God, so that when the day of evil comes, you may be able to stand your ground."* *Ephesians 6:13* Again, he says to be equipped *"so when the day of evil comes, you may be able to stand your ground."*

To some degree at least, I think these words are the answer to Jesus' high priestly prayer for the Father to *"protect them from the evil."* God provides us with protection by strengthening us in our inner person with his Spirit as we spend time with him in his Word, in prayer, and in service, building our "spiritual muscles." Then, he goes on to equip us for battle with the "Armor of God." Paul lists the pieces of God's armor. He describes the helmet of salvation, the breastplate of righteousness, the belt of truth, and the shoes of peace. In addition, he says, "*... take up the shield of faith with which you can extinguish all the flaming arrows of the evil one. Take... the sword of the Spirit, which is the Word of God, and pray in the Spirit on all occasions." Ephesians 6:16*

I hope you can see as clearly as I do how this teaching applies to the grief situation. Again, I had always thought of this passage in relation to fighting the desires of the flesh, and had never thought of it as applying to the grief problem. While the situations are quite different, there are also many similarities. The Evil One will attack us whenever and wherever he can find an opening. He has no mercy. The fact that we are hurting and devastated with grief doesn't deter him from the attack. He delights to kick us when we're down and vulnerable. We see that clearly in the case of Job. Actually, I think Satan feels he has a better chance for victory when we are down than at any other time. He always attacks the weakest area of our lives, the chink in our armor, at the most opportune time for him. That is logically the worst time for us.

It is true that tragic losses do indeed turn some people away from God. It seems that people either turn to God for strength and comfort, or else they blame him and become bitter and estranged from him. If the Evil One can't turn us against God, he will try to steal our joy by leading us to wallow in self pity or guilt, delaying our recovery as long as possible. Some even give up and waste away in their sorrow until their own lives are gone. In those cases, the evil one does win a victory. It isn't because God didn't answer Jesus' prayer for us, however. It's because people fail to avail themselves of the ample provisions the Father has made for us so "*when the day of evil*" comes, we will be ready.

I know it doesn't seem fair that a person who is crushed with grief should have to stand up and fight the evil one in his or her day of greatest need. In a sense they don't have to if they are properly prepared. Paul prayed for us to be strengthened in our inner person, and to put on the full armor of God, so that *when* the day of the evil comes, we may be able to withstand. So, if we are spiritually prepared ahead of time, we will be able to stand when that day comes, even in our weakened condition.

The message here is not to wait until the day of testing and trial comes to begin preparing for it. We shouldn't wait until the house is on fire to begin reading the instructions for operating the fire extinguisher. Get ready now! Develop your spiritual muscles, and put on the whole armor of God now. Don't let the Evil One catch you unprepared. Unless you die first, you will eventually experience the loss of one of your closest loved ones. Will you be ready? Have you made preparation? Are you strengthened in your "inner man?" Are you equipped with the full armor of God?

You can be sure that the devil won't give up easily though. Manly Beasley, the late evangelist, frequently taught 'if the devil can't defeat you directly, he will try to defeat someone close to you whose defeat will defeat you.' In the case of a family losing a child, that can happen if one of the parents isn't able to bear up. One of the parents may have been able to survive the loss but the defeat of the other could bring them both down. This situation seems to have prevailed with friends of ours who lost a three year old son when he was struck by a car in front of their house. The mother grieved and began to recover from the loss but the father couldn't get through it. He blamed his wife for not watching the child and carried anger in his heart for years. Their marriage eventually failed, but the seeds were planted in his failure to resolve the grief issues properly. But, we can still defeat the enemy if we stay rooted in Christ. I quoted earlier the book of James where it tells us if we resist the devil, he will flee from us. I say now, based on what I believe God told me, if you resist Satan with the Word of God, he will crawl away from you, face down in the dirt.

So, my premise is, the devil can use the grief situation to attack God's children and try to turn us from our faith in God. My advice is that we should expect the attacks and be prepared to repel them. While I have said God expects us to fight our own battles with the provisions he has given us, I didn't say he would abandon us in our battles. No, he is there strengthening us and encouraging us. he will provide peace and understanding if we will let him. He knows we are hurting and not as able to fight as we normally are. He feels our pain and he understands. He will not leave us, nor forsake us.

Some Practical Helps

*"Finally brothers, whatever is true, whatever is noble, what-
ever is right, whatever is pure, whatever is lovely, whatever
is admirable — if anything is excellent or praiseworthy —
think about such things... And the God of peace will be with
you." Philippians 4:8-9*

In a practical sense we can help ourselves through the grief
process by changing many of the habits we developed with the loved
one who is gone. If we always went to certain places or did favorite
things together, those places and things are always going to be painful
in the future. We can work through those experiences in a brute force
manner by continuing to do the same things and go the same places
without the loved one. Eventually the painful association will fade.
Alternatively, we can find new places to go and different things to
do with other people. That may be the more healthy approach, but
it depends on your particular circumstances. You may not have the
option if your circumstances are too restrictive.

Some of the most difficult times are the special days like Christmas
and birthdays. Each special day without them will be very difficult
the first time. For many years those special days will continue to be
hard. To a degree, we simply have to "tough it out" and get through
them. However, we can help ourselves by meeting each special day
head on with a strategy. Karen and I tried to make plans that would
surround us with friends and family, or would otherwise keep us too
busy to dwell on the absence of our missing one. Since Beth died in
February, every year around that time we try to take a special vaca
tion, usually in Hawaii. We indulge ourselves a little but we enjoy
ourselves and keep our minds occupied with enjoyable activities. It
really helps.

Once we have experienced each one of those special days in
a different way without the missing one there, then the next time
it will be a little easier. Even so, the special days and anniversa-
ries will always be somewhat difficult. However, our loved ones
would certainly prefer for us to observe those days with positive and

constructive activities. They wouldn't want us to suffer unnecessarily by spending that day grieving and crying.

Clearly, one of the greatest difficulties in moving on is the emotional attachment to the loved one who is gone. This is where the passage I used to introduce this section can help us. When we find ourselves sinking in depression, that is the time to heed the Apostle's words and discipline our minds to think about other things. Things that are beautiful and healthy. We might began with positive thoughts about the blessings God has given us and build on them. Think about the love of God and his promises to keep us in his care. Tell him how you are feeling and ask for his help. I might suggest reading the book of Philippians where Paul dwells on the joy we have in the Lord. Resist the devil and rely on God.

Even when we feel we are making progress in our grief, we may find ourselves not wanting to let go of their memory or anything that belonged to them. We feel we are being unfaithful to the one we have lost if we do anything to take our focus off their memory. That can be manifested by such things as refusing to clean out their closets and drawers or change anything in their room. However, at some point, we have to let go. It is extremely difficult to do it, but we must.

I remember when we cleaned out Rachel's bureau drawers. We had waited a few weeks to do this heartbreaking task. Just seeing each of the little outfits she wore as we put her things away brought tears and aching hearts. But until we take those actions we can't move on with our lives. Those difficult and emotional tasks will always be there waiting for us until we get them done. Certainly, the one who is gone would not want us to waste our lives away by focusing constantly on their memory, trying to hang on to what is gone. The good memories will still be there to be called up on occasions when it is appropriate. I know we will never forget our children and the cherished memories of them if we live to be 100.

Of all the practical advice we can give regarding the grief process, I think the most important is to just lean on God and hold on. Spend time in God's Word, seeking out his many promises to us and taking strength from them. God ministers to us through his Word. We spent hours and hours in the Bible after Beth's death, and God strengthened us and brought us comfort and understanding through that time with him.

Don't be bashful about seeking out friends or family members to talk to or be with. If they don't come to you then you go to them. Most people want to help but many times they don't know how. If you just get in touch with them to talk, you may find you both end up deciding to go out to dinner or a show. You need to get out and attend social functions at church or other social circles where you are comfortable. That may be hard for you to do if you always did those things together before. But, you really need to get out in some way and not sit at home moping.

It is good to have friends and family who look after you and spend time with you. But, there are also times when you need to be alone. In Martha Whitmore Hickman's book, "I Will Not Leave You Desolate"[8], she writes "We should find some balance between solitude and socializing, both of which we need. People will urge socializing upon us. 'You need to get out,' they will say. We do need to get out in order to re-establish ourselves as persons who belong to life and to current relationships. But we also need time alone, to face our demons, to put down our plumbline and to take our soundings. We will probably cry and feel sad. We will also feel alive and enriched and less tense because we have looked our grief in the face, allowed our feelings to speak their authentic word. And when we move out again into the social world, it may be with a sense of having laid some burden down."

No matter how resolved you are to make it through this personal loss, to some degree you are going to have to just "tough it out" and do the work of grief. It will get better in time. Our knowledge of God's sufficient grace gives us assurance throughout the ordeal that we will survive and there will be better days ahead. Not just by the intellectual knowledge that His grace is sufficient, but by the actual experiencing of that grace.

Karen, the girls and I could each feel the assurance and support of our heavenly Father as He carried us through those dark valleys. That grace continues to this day because His faithfulness to His children is eternal. Although we could not understand why we had to lose three children, we knew God was and is in control. We also know His will can never lead us where His grace will not keep us. That motto hangs on the wall in our home. We know it and believe it in our hearts and in our experience.

The will of God will never lead you
where the grace of God cannot keep you

CHAPTER 10

GRIEF MINISTRIES

Expressions Of Christian Love - Our Responsibility

"And many Jews had come to Martha and Mary to comfort them in the loss of their brother." John 11:19

The role of the Christian brother and sister in the grief situation is essential. I believe that there is no greater Christian service than to minister to the grieving brother or sister in Christ who has lost a loved one. Unfortunately, not all of us are always up to that ministry. I've heard people say, "We don't know what to say to someone in a situation like that, so we just don't go by." Or, "It makes me uncomfortable to be around someone when something has happened like that." A short time after Rachel's death I heard a young seminary student say those very words. Believe me, I gave him some stern brotherly advice. You don't have to worry about what to say. You don't have to say a word. You can handle the discomfort. Just be there! I wonder how our excuses will sound in heaven when the Lord asks why we failed to go to a brother or sister in grief and comfort them? I'm afraid the excuse "I was afraid I might be uncomfortable" will not be received too well.

One of my friends at church, a man named Bill, came to me after Rachel's memorial service. He was not a man given to outward displays of emotion or flowery words, and for a moment he just stood there and looked at me. Then he gave me a big bear hug, never saying a word, and then walked away. Many years after Rachel's memorial

175

service, I attended Bill's memorial service. He died a young man, a victim of cancer. I knew Bill well and we shared many experiences over those intervening years. However, at his memorial service the experience I remembered him for the most was the time he came to me and comforted me with his love when I needed it most. While we had always been good friends and Christian brothers, after that expression of love he was always a special person in my life.

An embrace of a dear friend brings the greatest comfort. A simple, "I'm sorry" is all that is needed. The words "I love you" help us to know we are not alone in our grief. An exquisite expression of love is the tears that flow from your own wounded heart. Wounded because of the personal loss to you of the one who is gone, and broken because of empathy with the sorrowing soul of the loved one. Remember, Jesus wept for those same reasons. It helps to have someone cry with us as Jesus does. The comfort it brings is deep and profound.

When someone in our close circle of friends or family dies, most of us are moved with compassion and sympathy. We want to do something to help but there is not a lot we can do. The common responses are to take food to the home and send flowers and sympathy cards. We may visit the funeral home and attend the funeral if it is convenient for us. The church and the neighborhood may mobilize to help with the family's physical needs until the funeral is over and things settle down. Then the visiting family members leave, and the folks from the church and the neighborhood go on with their lives. But is that the best we can do? My family's experience has shown us there is indeed more we as a church and as individual Christian brothers and sisters can and should do.

The Immediate Need

"Praise be to the God and Father of our Lord Jesus Christ, the Father of compassion and the God of all comfort, who comforts us in all our troubles, so that we can comfort those in any trouble with the comfort we ourselves have received from God." 2 Corinthians 1:3-4

The first thing we need to be sensitive to is the fact that when someone dies the closest family member or members need someone to be there with them immediately; someone to cling to in their confusion and distress. They hold on tightly, needing the personal contact and security of someone who cares. Usually the pastor or hospital chaplain fills this need. However, depending on your relationship and proximity, it may be your responsibility to be that person. The words we speak are not important. We only need to assure them we will not leave them alone. We need to let them talk and share their feelings, even though their thoughts may be confused and even incoherent. If family members aren't present yet, then we need to stay with them to provide the immediate support needed until close family members arrive.

After our losses I became more sensitive to the need to be there for others. There have been occasions when I was able to provide that ministry to ladies on my deacon list when their husbands died suddenly at home with no other family around. At least twice I arrived before the pastor or medical team was able to arrive. In both cases the ladies were distraught and badly needed someone to hold on to. They both held my hands so tight, as though I might try to get away from them. The raw emotions in those early moments of loss are near panic, often distraught and laced with fear. They need someone to hold on to. Those ladies have both reminded me many times over the years how important it was to them for me to be there. I just tell them the Lord arranged the circumstances so I could be there because with my work schedule, that usually doesn't happen. God surely wants to use us to minister to one another in those times of need.

It often takes a day or two from the time a loved one dies for all of the family members to arrive, especially if some of them live out of the area. During this time we need to ensure that the grieving persons have plenty of support around them before we leave them alone. When family members begin arriving there may be such a crowd that we are unnecessary. We may even get in the way. That's the time for us to slip quietly out of the picture, but not too far away. We will be needed again soon.

Before The Funeral

"And if anyone gives even a cup of cold water to one of these little ones because he is my disciple, I tell you the truth, he will certainly not lose his reward." Matthew 10:42

At the funeral, many well meaning people will say to the family, "Now, if there's anything we can do, be sure to call us." Well, there is something you can do. The hours and days between the death of a family member and the funeral are busy. There is a myriad of things that have to get done and there are many opportunities for ministry. You just need to be sensitive, caring and alert to discover ways you can help. Some people are better at it than others, but I suspect that's simply because they care more. We all need to care more.

We had friends come by and say they were taking the girls for the day while we were busy with funeral arrangements and getting visiting family situated. Others came by and volunteered to be in charge of picking up visiting relatives at the airport. I have known families who could have used help with aging parents or with other transportation needs. When family is visiting from out of town, many times an offer of a spare bedroom for a night or two is a real help. One thoughtful neighbor, knowing the children and adults were getting tired of the food that had been brought in, had enough pizzas delivered one evening to feed the whole crowd. It was a welcome change. Do what you can, but don't expect the grieving family to pick up the phone and call you for help. They won't.

We need to be understanding during those few days between the death and the funeral when the family is very much in a state of shock. Sometimes, those who were closest to the one who died, such as the spouse or parent, do not know and don't even care what is going on around them. They realize that people are coming and going, and they may try to politely respond when people stop by or bring food. However, as one dear friend commented after her husband died, "They just keep coming by, bringing food and wanting me to eat, but I'm not hungry. I threw most of it out." Obviously, if there are many family members who come into town for the funeral, they need something to eat, and the food brought by church groups and neighbors is very helpful in meeting that practical need. However, in terms of ministering to personal grief, the food may not an important factor. But don't get discouraged. Keep bringing the food — just don't stop there.

After The Funeral

"When Jesus saw his mother there, and the disciple whom He loved standing nearby, he said to his mother, 'Dear woman, here is your son,' and to the disciple, 'Here is your mother.' From that time on, this disciple took her into his home."
John 19:26-27

The days leading up to the funeral or memorial service are filled with people and activity. Dozens of family members and friends may have congregated from all over the country. Friends and neighbors are in and out with food and condolences for the immediate family. The frenzy of activity peaks at the time of the funeral. Then as rapidly as they came, the crowds disappear. In a few short hours the circus of activity comes to an abrupt halt and suddenly there is nothing but silence. The remaining spouse or other family members may then collapse from fatigue and may even get some sleep the first night. But when the next morning dawns, the real work of grieving begins.

After the funeral, when the crowds have disappeared, is the time for friends and neighbors, and especially the church to shift into phase 2 of their ministry plan. The work of grief is the most difficult endeavor that any human being will have to undergo. No one should have to do it alone. When my dad died, each of us six sons spoke at the memorial service. At the conclusion of my comments I thanked the church and the community for the outpouring of love and support they had shown our family. Then I asked them for a favor. I reminded them we would all be leaving soon, and we were leaving Mom alone with them. We were trusting her to their care. I asked them to please not forget her in the weeks and months ahead. That's when she would need them most.

If we really care, and if we really want to minister, the real need comes after the funeral and after the crowd disappears. During the weeks and months after the loss, the grieving loved ones will spend countless lonely hours and sleepless nights, wishing desperately for someone to talk to or to be with. That is where I think the Christian community often falls down on the job, sometimes quite badly. Once the funeral is over, we forget the need and get on with our own lives. Somehow, we need to learn how to get organized to minister over the long haul, when it is really needed and will make a difference in people's lives.

A wonderful ministry is to just call or visit often in the weeks and months after the loss. Invite them over for dinner or invite them to go out and eat with you. It's always nice to have company when you eat out. You can talk about anything you like, but don't be hesitant to discuss the loved one who is gone. If you want to share some words of comfort with someone in grief, I suggest you share from your own experience some of the good things you remember about the one who is gone. If the loss is a personal one for you, that is important to share. Recall some specific experiences or incidents that are especially meaningful to you and which illustrate your appreciation of the one who is gone. Share those memories and reminisce together about the good times you had and about the good qualities the loved one had. It is very helpful to hear how others loved your loved one and how they miss him or her too.

When Beth died, many friends came to us and reminisced with us about some of the things they remembered the most about her. Many of the experiences were humorous and that was good. It was therapeutic for us to be able to laugh and remember her in those situations. Many others just shared their own sense of loss by telling us how she was special to them. I'm sure sharing grief makes it easier. Your grief over the loss is not as deep as theirs, certainly, but sharing fond remembrances and your own sense of loss is a comfort to the bereaved. I can't stress enough, however, that the most important thing is to just be there, and keep on being there, especially during the weeks and months after the loss.

Let me share one other word that shouldn't be necessary. After losing three children we began to dread "pat answers" from well-meaning people who wanted to help. Sometimes they thought they had spiritual insight that could help us, but more often it was people repeating clichés they had heard, or they were trying to rationalize the loss for us. I'm not saying we know all of the answers either, but at least we had been through countless hours on our knees in hospital rooms and corridors and had prayed our hearts out to God through the sufferings and deaths of our children. We know there are no simple answers to all of the "Why" questions. It just boiled down in our minds to the fact that God is sovereign and He is going to accomplish His will. We wanted nothing more or nothing less. So don't hesitate to go to your friends who are grieving, but please don't try to rationalize the loss by saying things like, "God needed a baby in heaven." Or worse, "Well, at least you won't have to worry over them anymore." Or, "Well, at least you still have the other children." Better to just express your love and compassion, and don't try to interpret God's working in the matter.

Let me just add a couple of comments about flowers and cards. Flowers are an integral part of the funeral scene and provide a convenient way for friends and family to express their love and concern. Flowers are helpful and comforting, but if there are very many of them, individual plants or arrangements lose their significance to the family. The family is mainly interested in keeping the cards so they can know who sent them. Later they will need them to write thank you notes. Deciding what to do with all the flowers is another task the family must do. Some of the nicer ones may be taken home by family members, but we have watched after a funeral as the staff trashed hundreds, or even thousands of dollars worth of flowers in the dumpster. We always look for alternate ways to express our sentiments.

Families often wish after the fact they had set up a memorial fund at their church or other charity to allow friends and family to donate to a good cause. In that way the gifts will have a lasting and practical benefit. A notice about the memorial fund can even be included in the obituary prepared by the funeral home if the family is quick enough to get it included. How the fund will be used doesn't have to be decided until much later.

Sympathy cards have a definite role to play in the ministry to the bereaved. The expressions of love and support communicated in cards can be very meaningful. However, the ministry can be greatly enhanced by just taking a moment to write something personal. Looking back over some of the cards we received, I notice most people either simply sign them or they add a short predictable note, saying something like "God bless you in your sorrow" or "We're so sorry about your loss." With just a little more effort your message could be much more meaningful. If you knew the person who died, say something nice about your memories or impressions of them. If you didn't know them personally, then share something more about how you feel for the survivors. If you can honestly share that you are praying for them, do that and then say what it is you are praying for. Those thoughtful notes will always be remembered and appreciated.

Thoughts About Final Arrangements

"Now we know that if the earthly tent we live in is destroyed, we have a building from God, an eternal house in heaven, not built by human hands. We ...would prefer to be away from the body and at home with the Lord." 2 Corinthians 5:1,8

I mentioned earlier the encounter with Ellen Sullivan in the hospital waiting room during Rachel's meningitis. In addition to helping us see the resilience and strength of the human spirit, Ellen helped us in a very practical way by helping us to see we aren't required to follow the traditional ceremonial patterns laid out for us by our society when we lose a loved one. She had some very interesting ideas about how she was going to handle her husband's arrangements when he died.

When our son Mike died, we experienced 'the routine' for the first time. We didn't know what to do about arrangements so we followed tradition. We were told we could handle it however we wanted to, but usually people do it the traditional way. So, we played by the rules of tradition for the post-death process laid out for us. That routine included visitation at the funeral home, a funeral service at the mortuary or church, and a brief graveside service.

With the experience of Mike's funeral in our background, we were able to see the wisdom of Ellen's suggestions. As a result, we took a different approach ourselves with the arrangements for Rachel's service. That approach primarily involved having the graveside burial service first, and then having a celebrative memorial service afterwards at the church. Having the memorial service after the burial allowed us to complete the process on a positive note, rather than winding up the affair at the cemetery.

When Rachel died we had a beautiful memorial service for her at church after the burial. We were surrounded by our church family as we sang hymns of praise and worshipped the loving God who had blessed us with our little angel. We found that having the burial service first brought closure to the most painful part of the proceedings and then allowed us to experience the celebration of the memorial service as the final event.

When Beth died, we changed a few other things we had found to be unnecessarily painful. We didn't feel a need for the conventional 'visitation' at the funeral home. We certainly didn't want to stand around in front of the casket for hours while people stood in line to see us, or sat around and visited. We could only talk to a few people at a time and the rest of them would be discussing baseball and barbecues while trying to ignore the fact there was a dead body on display there in the front of the room.

However, at the urging of some of our close friends, we agreed to let them put Beth's body out for viewing in the funeral home so those who felt the need to do so could go by and pay their respects. In the meantime, we informed the church we would be having an open house and would be happy to receive folks at our home if they wanted to come by. Many, many friends came by and shared their love and their common sorrow with us. As we all sat around in the living room, there was opportunity for group discussion that couldn't happen in a single file waiting line. We appreciated everyone coming. We were very comfortable in our own home, and were able to welcome people in a relaxed atmosphere. Some of our friends also acted as hosts, both at the funeral home and at our house so we didn't have to worry over our guests.

There was a brief graveside service, which we intended to be very low key. However, the word got out and a crowd showed up even though it was a wet and rainy day. We had Beth's memorial service that Sunday night and the crowd filled the large church to capacity. It was a service of worship and celebration for Beth's release from her seizures and her new joy in God's paradise. The congregation sang hymns of praise and we were blessed again by my brother Jim's song he had written entitled "My Grace Is Sufficient For Thee, My Child." Darryl Pursley, our close friend and Minister of Music sang the song for us. Karen's pastor brother, Craig Atherton, spoke personal words for the family and our Pastor brought a message from the Bible and his own experiences with Beth. The service was positive and uplifting and ended with an altar call. One young girl came and gave her life to Jesus. Nothing could have been more fitting.

When my father passed away recently, Mom asked Karen and me to help plan the arrangements and the memorial service since we were "experienced." We followed the same pattern with the graveside service first, followed later that day by the memorial service. This time the memorial service celebrated the life of a dear saint of God who had ministered and influenced hundreds of people for the kingdom of heaven over the duration of his life on earth. Pop's six sons conducted the service, each one of us sharing our fondest memories and strongest impressions of our father, interspersing our testimonies with hymns and songs of praise and heaven. We knew it would be hard to talk without crying, but we agreed before hand to go ahead and cry if we needed to. We would just take the time when necessary to stop and get our voice under control again, and go on.

Pop's memorial service blessed us all and many people commented that it was the most uplifting "funeral" service they had ever experienced. It was so much better than just having a minister give his stock funeral sermon with a few personal comments added. It was our service for Pop and we think it honored him. It blessed our mother and gave her something to treasure for the rest of her life.

The advice of our family to yours is this: if your loved one was a Christian, then the funeral should not be a time of sadness and gloom, but a celebration and praise service honoring the life of the loved one who is gone. As one of the dear ladies of our church said through her tears when her husband died recently, "Break out the tambourines and dancers. We're going to have a service of celebration." And that's exactly what we did. If at all possible, someone in the family, or close to the family should share at the memorial service those intimate personal remembrances that honor the loved one who is gone. Then the minister can give his remarks and close the service. Those personal touches minister and bring comfort to people hurting with the pain of grief and sorrow. If the family are members of a church, it is certainly better to experience the memorial in the warm and familiar surroundings of the church house with the church family present, than in an unfamiliar mortuary.

The Lord Jesus told the Pharisees when they accused him and his disciples of breaking the Sabbath tradition, *"The Sabbath was made for man, not man for the Sabbath." Mark 2:27*. In the same way, funerals were made for people, not people for funerals. You don't have to be ruled by tradition. You can decide for yourself how you will observe the passing of your loved one. It is an opportunity to witness to all those around you of your faith and trust in God as you celebrate your loved one's entrance to glory.

As pastors, chaplains and personal counselors we may have an opportunity to help individuals understand they aren't required to follow tradition to the letter. Perhaps we can just observe that some people have been blessed by different approaches and arrangements that have met their needs better. In the end analysis, however, whatever ministers to the family is what should be done.

Beth's body is buried within a couple of miles of our home. However, as with the graves of Mike and Rachel in Wichita, we never visit the cemetary. The remains there hold no attraction for us. We have other ways of demonstrating our remembrances than visiting the graves. I must admit, however, that Beth's body is buried on a hillside overlooking the interstate highway, and I usually glance up that way when I drive by. Our remembrances of all of our children, however, will always be of their beautiful countenances, laughing and smiling, hugging and kissing, sharing their love so freely. Our wonderful gifts from God are now with Him, but one day again we will be with them. On that day we will have a glorious reunion with our entire family and will together worship our lovely Savior in glory.

CHAPTER 11

SPIRITUAL DILEMMAS

For the foolishness of God is wiser than men, and the weakness of God is stronger than men." 1Corinthians 1:25

As my family and I wrestled with God through our spiritual searchings, we had to come to grips with some issues addressed frequently in Scripture, but largely ignored in our pulpits. As we came to understand these issues more fully, the things that happened to us began to make a lot more sense. Hopefully, others who have had to undergo great difficulties and hardships in life will be helped if we talk about these things. Some of these concepts may seem strange, but understanding them will assist us in making more sense of what has happened in our lives and in the lives of others close to us.

As I try to communicate where we have come in our deliberations, both in this section and the remainder of this chapter, I would like to borrow a quote from C. S. Lewis in the preface to his book, "The Problem With Pain" [9] because it says what I would like to say, but in a superior fashion. Lewis says in his preface, "If any real theologian reads these pages he will very easily see that they are the work of a layman and an amateur. If any parts of the book are "original," in the sense of being novel or unorthodox, they are so against my will and as a result of my ignorance...I have tried to assume nothing that is not professed by all baptised and communicating Christians."

Does God Want Us To Suffer?

"Dear friends, do not be surprised at the painful trial you are suffering, as though something strange was happening to you. But rejoice that you participate in the sufferings of Christ so that you may be overjoyed when his glory is revealed." 1 Peter 4:12-13

The first topic I want to look at in this chapter is the question, "Does God want us to suffer?" In some ways what I have to say may at times seem like a paraphrase of the deep truths that C.S. Lewis discusses in his books, but they all come from my family's experiences and my own simple ruminations. This question did come up in Lewis' "The Problem with Pain" but only after much preliminary discussion. Lewis succinctly stated the paradox all Christians face. In Chapter 2, concerning Divine Omnipotence, he writes, "If God were good, He would wish to make His creatures perfectly happy, and if God were almighty He would be able to do what He wished. But the creatures are not happy. Therefore God lacks either godness, or power, or both." Lewis goes on to say, "The possibility of answering (the paradox) depends on showing that the terms 'good' and 'almighty,' and perhaps also the term 'happy' are equivocal" He then goes on for several chapters discussing the deep meanings of those words.

I would like to tackle the question from more of a Biblical point of view than a philosophical one. But, the starting point is the same. It apparently seems to some that God must get some kind of sadistic pleasure from watching his children suffer, and therefore, God must not be as good as advertised. In support of that position, one might argue that the Bible says Satan received permission from God to afflict Job and to strip him of all his property, riches and even his health. The Lord even allowed Satan to take Job's children, and eventually bring him to the point of death.

Yes, as I said before, it appears surprisingly that Job's suffering was God's idea. It sounds as if God actually wanted Job to suffer although Job was a beloved, faithful and dedicated servant of God. What reason could there be for God to bring this suffering into Job's life? Must we conclude that God does want us to suffer? Or was he just pressured by Satan to let the devil have his way with Job? The answer to both questions is clearly, No! I don't believe God is pleased to see his children suffer, certainly not just because he enjoys seeing us in pain. No, as I have said before, we may not always know God's mind, but we always know his heart. He loves us and wants the best for us personally, and if we are ready and willing he may even use our suffering to further his kingdom, as he did with Job. However, in order to get to the best for us and for the kingdom, God knows it may be necessary for us to go through some difficulties in order to reach that eventual goal.

When we couple the profound truth of God's unquestionable sovereignty with the New Testament revelation that *"God is Love,"* it convinces us we can not only trust him to accomplish his perfect will in our lives, but that 'His Will' will be the very best thing for us. But, you can write it down. Sometimes there will be pain. Sometimes it will hurt. God will allow pain to come into our lives for any number of very good reasons which we usually cannot discern.

Here's another quote form C.S. Lewis' "The Problem With Pain." "The problem of reconciling human suffering with the existence of a God who loves, is only insoluble so long as we attach a trivial meaning to the word "love," and look on things as if man were the centre of them. Man is not the centre. God does not exist for the sake of man. Man does not exist for his own sake."

God's love is not trivial. It is profoundly deep and it is a giving love. *"God so loved the world that he gave his only begotten son."* We understand the popular term "Tough Love" and recognize that it is sometimes necessary to exercise tough love with our children, or perhaps with a person close to us who is an addict. We need to love them enough to withhold things from them which could hurt them or lead to more pain. We wouldn't let a small child play with a sharp knife or help an addict obtain his desired substance, just because they desired to have those things. In much the same way, God loves us enough to withhold something harmful from us, or to lead us through some dark valley, in order to bring us to a fulfilling reward.

A general perception seems to exist in today's Christian churches. Anytime something painful or unpleasant happens to us, we think it must be the result of a failure in the divine system somewhere. If our conscience is clear and we are sure we haven't sinned and brought the consequences down upon ourselves, then either God doesn't really love us as he says, or somehow God has slipped up and Satan has gotten through and attacked us. We are quick to say God cannot be the author of our problems, even though we know he promised to *"Work all things together for good" (Romans 8:28)* for his children. Some may accept that God "allowed" something bad to happen to us, but most people are not even comfortable with that concept.

Jesus said of painful calamities that will befall us, *"Such things must happen." (Mark 13:7)* There is abundant Scriptural authority for a position that God himself may intentionally bring painful or unpleasant experiences into the lives of believers to accomplish his divine will. As normal human beings it is natural for us to make provisions to ensure that we avoid pain. We don't like pain. It hurts. It seems, however, that in God's plan, pain is sometimes necessary to accomplish something very worthwhile. The "No pain, no gain." principle seems to hold in the spiritual realm as well as the physical.

It is a foreign thought to most Christians that God would purposely bring something painful or unpleasant into a Christian's life. But, why is that necessarily so? I have already quoted many verses from Paul's writings which indicate it may be necessary for Christians to suffer for Christ's sake. Paul suffered horribly at the hands of the Romans and the Jews. For his faith he was imprisoned, flogged, shipwrecked, and denied basic needs like food, shelter, sleep, and clothing. Even though he described himself as being "in weaknesses, in insults, in hardships, in persecutions," he said he took great delight in these things because they happened for the sake of his Lord and Savior, Jesus Christ. When Paul was weak, Christ was strong through him.

Our Lord himself suffered more than any of us because that was the task the Father put upon him. Isaiah 53:5-10 says *"Yet it pleased the Lord to bruise him; He has put him to grief."* God claimed responsibility for his Son's death. But, in his wisdom there was a tremendous payoff; the salvation of the world. Our payoff won't be so grand, but in the Father's wisdom, it will accomplish his purpose, whatever that may be.

God never promised in his Word that life would be free of all pain and discomfort. Not even the Christian life. To the contrary, Jesus advised us to count the cost and cautioned us to be willing to sacrifice everything to follow him. In Luke 9:23 Jesus said something rather startling. He said *"If anyone would come after me, he must deny himself and take up his cross daily and follow me. For whoever wants to save his life will lose it, but whoever loses his life for me will save it."* The apostle Paul made it very clear that the Christian life will not be all laughter and light. He said in Phillipians 1:29, *"For it has been granted to you, on behalf of Christ not only to believe on him, but also to suffer for him."* Then again, in Phillipians 3:10, Paul passionately expressed his desire to know Christ in the most complete and intimate way, even to a degree that may startle us. Paul said, *"I want to know Christ and the power of his resurrection and the fellowship of sharing in his sufferings, becoming like him in his death."*

To know Christ; that was Paul's greatest desire; to have a personal, intimate, experiential knowledge of our Lord, to the point of participating in his power and in his sufferings. Most of us would have no problem participating in his power, but in his sufferings? That is more than most of us would ever be willing to ask the Father for. But that is just what Paul asked Timothy to do when he wrote in 2Timothy 2:3 *"Endure hardship with us as a good soldier of Jesus Christ."* Jesus himself modeled the proper response for us in John 12:27-28 when he said *"Now my heart is troubled, and what shall I say? 'Father, save me from this hour?' No, it was for this very reason I came to this hour. Father, glorify your name!"*

In the case of our family, it is entirely possible that it was for this very reason that our family came to our hours of suffering. Should we say, Father, save us from this pain? Should we forfeit whatever worthy purpose God has for bringing us through these experiences? We say no. Father glorify your name.

The church would have never experienced the explosive growth in the early years if hadn't been for the suffering and martyrdom of many of the early saints of the church. I'm sure their experiences were not something they would have wished for. But Christian martyrdom is not just something from the early church age. Today, an organization called The Voice of the Martyrs can be accessed on the internet. They claim more people have been martyred in recent years for their Christain faith that all the martyrs of the past centuries combined. Most of the suffering for the Christian faith is taking place today in the middle and far east where Christians are vilified, persecuted and even killed. But, the church is growing in those regions faster than it is in places like Europe where Christians are left in peace.

A better known modern day example of the role of the martyrs is the story of Jim Eliot and his missionary friends who died at the hands of the Auca indians in the Columbian jungle. Jim Eliot was a hero of my brother, Jim Clifford, and they reminded me so much of each other. What good could possibly come out of the missionaries' senseless killings? As a result of their death, untold numbers of young missionaries have given their lives to the ministy of the Gospel to lost tribes in South America and elsewhere around the globe. Their story played a role in my brother Jim surrendering to the ministry. The Auca indians themselves have become missionaries to the outside world. The missionaries' sacrifices led to furthering the kingdom of God much more than their work with the indians probably would have. Their story is told in Elizabeth Eliot's book, "Through Gates of Splendor"[10].

The late evangelist Manly Beasley coined the term "Heavenly Sandpaper" to describe the painful works of God in our lives that are not pleasant to experience. He cited Romans 8:29 which says, *"For those God foreknew, he also predestined to be conformed to the likeness of His Son."* Beasley reckoned that to be conformed to the likeness of Jesus meant anything in our lives that didn't look like Jesus had to be removed. Like surgery, we have to endure pain to realize the benefit of God's pruning process. The end product, however, is a thing of beauty fit for God's use.

As we saw in Job, even when it is within God's divine plan to bring difficult moments into our lives, it may be Satan who is the agent who directly afflicts us, though never without the Father's permission. I cited the passage in Luke 22 previously in Karen's story, where Jesus told Peter *"Satan has asked to sift you like wheat."* Then Jesus assured Peter, *"But I have prayed for you Simon that your faith may not fail. And when you have turned back, strengthen your brothers" Luke 22:31-32.*

Note again that Jesus did not pray for Peter to be spared from Satan's attack. He was apparently willing for it to happen and for Peter to suffer the pain. But, he also wanted Peter to learn from his failure, and then come back and help his brothers. Jesus prayed Peter's faith would not fail. In other words, Satan apparently got the permission he requested to sift Peter, but the Lord promised to sustain him through the affliction. Peter was indeed sifted like wheat. He denied the Lord three times before the morning of Jesus' crucifixion. When he realized what he had done, he was repulsed by his own failure and he grieved heavily, tormented in his soul. However, even though Peter suffered great agony as a result of his triple denial of Jesus, his faith did not fail. The Lord restored him to full fellowship and used him mightily after that experience. The help Peter brought to his brothers, and to the whole world through his role in the gospel story, easily justifies the pain that Peter had to endure to learn that lesson. That admonition to Peter to return from his trial and strengthen his brothers is one of the motivating factors behind us making our story known to you.

This concept of keeping the faith is so important for us to understand. Our family can identify with the reality of being "sifted like wheat by Satan," but the important thing is, God did not allow our faith to fail. I know in my heart our Lord was there at the Father's side, interceding for us through it all, so that our faith would not fail. That's what hardships and tragedies in life are all about. God wants us to keep our trust in him through those hard times. He will accomplish his purpose through our afflictions and we will be even more useful to him afterwards if our faith does not fail.

Sometimes the difficulties may seem horrendous, but God will never allow us to suffer more than we are able to withstand. The Apostle Paul makes this extremely clear in the well known passage we cited earlier in 1 Corinthians. *"And God is faithful; he will not let you be tempted (tried) beyond what you can bear. But when you are tempted (tried), he will also provide a way out so that you can stand up under it." (1 Corinthians 10:13).* God prepares us spiritually and then he moves in our lives to empower and enable us to love and trust him through those difficulties. His Holy Spirit dwells within us, ministering to our grief and helping us see beyond the immediate pain to his eternal love. He loves completely, he knows completely, and he works to do his will completely in all things with his children, "... *who have been called according to his purpose*" (*Romans 8:28*).

So, through all of the temptations to feel persecuted and to feel sorry for ourselves when tragedy befell us, God has given my family the grace to trust him completely. It hasn't been easy and we have still had to endure the pain of grief and sorrow. However, he helped us know this truth, the best of all possible courses of action is for his will to be done. He loves us more than we can understand, just as he loved our children more even than we did. Moreover, his compassion for us moves him to minister to us in our grief. We always knew there would be a brighter tomorrow because God is faithful and his grace is indeed sufficient, whether we go through the valley three times or thirty times. His grace will always be sufficient.

Is This Really God's Will?

"We do not know what we ought to pray for, but the Spirit himself intercedes for us with groans that words cannot express. And he who searches our hearts knows the mind of the Spirit because the Spirit intercedes for the saints in accordance with God's will." (Romans 8:26-27)

In the early weeks and months of Rachel's illness, we were sure God must have wanted to heal our baby and restore her to full vitality. Since that was what we wanted, it seemed logical that it must have been what God wanted. We felt God had an obligation to answer our prayers just the way we wanted them answered. Generally, all of us want and pray for God's will to be done in our individual situations, but there's usually not much doubt in our mind as to what the best solution is. We know what we want and we are certain what the best thing would be for us. That was certainly the case with our children. We knew of no reason that it wouldn't be God's will for Rachel to be healed. However, just because we think something should be God's will doesn't mean it is. The fact is, if our minds are already made up about a situation, it will be very difficult for us to discern God's will in it.

The Lord used a very special book to help us in this regard during our spiritual journey. Hanna Whitehall Smith wrote in her classic work, "The Christian's Secret of a Happy Life" [11] "If there is any reserve of will upon any point, it becomes almost impossible to find out the mind of God in reference to that point." In other words, if we have any desire in a matter, we will not be able to discern God's will in that matter, period. This is a very important point and one I think few Christians, let alone the general public, realize. Mrs. Smith addresses this issue at length in her book, but the essence of the matter is that we cannot assume that what we want is what God wants for us. This principle applies in cases where we are asking God for leadership in decisions we need to make. We want his will to be done, but we frequently have our own feelings about the best solution. This happens especially when matters of the heart are involved, or where a desired course of action is based on improving our situation. As long as we want that thing, Hanna Smith says we will not be able to discern God's will in our prayers.

The question then becomes, how can we free ourselves from self will in regard to a point or issue that is very dear to us. That is not a trivial concept and I have learned that it is only accomplished with much prayer and surrender. From our limited perspective, only our present "instant gratification" seems relevant to us. Therefore, we assume what we want must be what God wants for us. Some people seem so quick to make that assumption. How many times have you heard someone way, "God told me I should…, or God told me to do ….." The thing they say God told them to do is often something they wanted or wished to do anyway. It's pretty hard to refute that kind of assertion because who can say whether God spoke to them or not. But how many of those people have really prayed through their situation to the point of being able to give it up if that's not what God wants for them.

This issue became important to us as we sought God's will for our children. We prayed for Rachel's healing, but how could we be sure of what God really wanted to do in her situation? There's no question that it would have been very difficult for me to pray about her healing without any self will in the matter. I cared so deeply, I only wanted her to be healed. But to really know God's will meant having to come to the place where I could surrender her to God, trusting him to care for her and do the best for her.

I have sometimes had to deal with that principle in other situations... ridding my life of self will in order to find God's will in a matter. When I want something very badly, I am very good at rationalizing and "reasoning" with God about the issue. I can point out to him that answering my prayer would be a good thing for all concerned, and good for his kingdom as well. However, I am arguing from my own deep-seated desire to see that event happen the way I want it to happen. I have found first-hand that it is very difficult to bring myself to the point of having no self-will in a matter that is important to me. It takes much prayer and soul searching to come to the point where I can say "I don't really care what happens here, as long as it is God's perfect will." When and if I come to that point, I have accomplished what Hannah Smith was talking about. I have no reserve of self will in that matter.

Admittedly, it is an arduous task to rid oneself of a strong desire and I suspect that few of us get there without strong help from the Holy Spirit. I was never able to come to that point when praying for our children, but I don't really think God needed that from us at that time. We were sure he was taking care of us, we were in his will and we knew his will was good. The bottom line is, we must be willing, even desirous, to see God's will done above all else, even if that means our loved one is not healed.

Faith Healing Vs Faith Healers

"The prayer offered in faith will make the sick person well; the Lord will raise him up." James 5:15

During Rachel's years of lingering, there were times we were grasping for any ray of hope. We prayed regularly for Rachel to be healed and made whole. We also prayed endlessly for Mike and Beth to be healed of their seizures. We even went through the process of seeking out "faith healers" and searching for the correct "formula" for praying for healing. We listened to people who told us if we would just have enough faith and pray, believing God would heal our children, then surely he would. They would ask, "Isn't that what the Scriptures say? *By his stripes we are healed?*" When we responded by mail to television ministers' offers to pray for Rachel's healing, we received in return requests for money. They had to have "Seed Money" before they would pray for her. From some speakers we were told that we had to use the right words in our prayers to ensure God would answer. But when Karen and I prayed about our confusion, there was a clear leading from the Lord that we should not try to manipulate Him through some "formula" of prayer.

Through our experiences and our Bible study, we have come to our personal theology of healing. I know this is a controversial area and I don't want to offend anyone who feels they can pray for anyone at any time and expect to see them healed. The Scriptures do say the prayer of faith will heal the sick. But, what is meant by the "prayer of faith?" I believe the Lord has impressed us that the prayer of faith is not something we can conjure up by straining our spiritual muscles. Otherwise, all of our children would have been healed and this book would not have been written. God knows that we spent untold hours praying for our children. But God is Sovereign. He does things his way, and his ways are good. The question is; is the prayer of faith a prayer any believer can pray anytime, for anyone, or is it a prayer God gives us when he pleases to do so. I tend to think it is the latter as I will explain in a moment. If it really is a prayer God gives us, Karen and I had not received that prayer for Rachel, but we had received his grace to live well and be happy in the circumstances as they were.

It's easy to pray for health, peace and prosperity. I think that's why so many of the TV and Revival Faith healers have such a booming business. But God is looking for people who are willing to surrender their creature comforts to be used of him. He wants us to surrender everything to him, trusting his love, his compassion, his wisdom and his omnipotence to do the very best thing, both for his eternal kingdom, and for us personally. If we can just get our eyes off our immediate gratification and let God work, he will do great and mighty things, and the benefits will be eternal.

There is no question in my mind that God has power to heal and that God still works healing miracles. However, I don't feel I can dictate to him whom, when or how he must heal. I certainly have the right and privilege as a child of God to bring my petitions to him, but then I must allow him to be sovereign. I must trust him to answer my prayers in his knowledge of what is best for me and those I am concerned about. Most of the time I don't even know what exactly to pray for because I cannot foresee what the consequences will be if my prayers are answered. I would much rather leave myself in his omniscient and omnipotent hands than try to specify to him how to take care of me.

We knew a family who believed God promised to deliver them from all adversity. They didn't think God ever wanted them to get sick or die, or to have any serious problem. They thought the only requirement was for them to believe and trust God enough to get him to give them whatever they wanted. They really had to work at their theology when they had a baby born with a defective liver. Karen and I were not even allowed to come and visit at the hospital because we weren't of their charismatic denomination and their pastor didn't think we had enough faith to believe God would heal the baby. So, this family and their church friends held all night prayer vigils for the baby, believing sincerely God would heal him. Unfortunately, the baby didn't survive and neither did the emotional stability of the parents. They felt they had failed by not having enough faith. They had followed their formula for praying for healing and believed it with all of their hearts. Then they were distressed and their faith was nearly destroyed because God had not done what they wanted him to do. The mother gave signs of an emotional breakdown and refused for weeks to believe that her baby was dead. The pain of losing the baby was bad enough, but it was greatly amplified because of their certainty that the baby would be healed if they followed the prescribed course of action. I'm sure God didn't want that extra pain for the parents, but they were basing their faith on what they had been taught. Any teaching which tells us to insist that God answer our prayers just doesn't seem to fit the Scriptures I know.

So what does it take to get God to heal if such intense believing prayer doesn't do it? Our son in law, Paul, has regular healing services at his church, which is somewhat charismatic, and they believe they have seen people healed frequently. I have no problem with that and praise the Lord with them when someone receives healing. I've already told you about the healing experience our daughter Becky had when she was in England the first time. We thank the Lord for that very real, emotional healing she experienced.

But, I wonder if God intends for all who are hurting to be healed. There are plenty of examples in Scripture where God doesn't heal people when he has a chance to. The Apostle Paul prayed three times for God to remove his thorn in the flesh. God said no, just rely on me. When Jesus healed the crippled man at the Pool of Bethesda, he ignored the multitude of other crippled people lying about the pools. And it certainly wasn't because of the crippled man's faith because he didn't seek out Jesus. Instead, Jesus picked him out of the crowd. It seems to me that the reason he picked out that particular cripple was because he knew how the man would react when he told him to pick up his bed and walk. His healing provoked an encounter with the Jewish leaders over Jesus healing on the Sabbath. That confrontation was what Jesus apparently had in mind when he picked out that man for healing.

I think most of the healings performed by Jesus and his followers were done for the purpose of validating Jesus' ministry and calling. They were to prove that Jesus was indeed the Son of God. For as Nicodemus said in John 3:2, *"Rabbi, we know you are a teacher who has come from God. For no-one could perform the miraculous signs you are doing if God were not with him."* Then in John 14:11 Jesus says to his disciples, *"Believe me when I say that I am in the Father and the Father is in me; or at least believe on the evidence of the miracles themselves."*

I don't mean to say that Jesus never healed anyone simply because he had compassion on him or her. I'm sure he did. That would be completely within his character because he is the epitome of compassion. But he stated many times that his works were generally for the purpose of proving who he was and validating his ministry and his calling. He may still heal individuals for the purpose of bringing glory to God, but that's his decision. He may have other ends in mind, so we can't assume he wants to do the same for us.

It seems to me that when we ask God to heal everyone in the church that has an ache or pain, we are trying to manipulate God into doing what we want him to do. Instead, I feel we need to seek the will of God and join him in what he wants to do. If that is to heal, that's great. If it is not to heal, then that has to be just as wonderful because it is God's will. Do we trust him enough to believe God is able to bring greater benefit and happiness in the long run by doing things his way, rather than ours?

Perhaps the churches that have healing services can reason that since we don't know who will be healed and who won't, it makes sense to pray for everyone who has a problem and then let God sort out whom he will heal. My only problem with that approach is it would seem to leave many people feeling rejected if they are not healed, or feeling that their faith isn't adequate to the task. This again seems to be contrary to the way God normally works. But, I am not a trained theologian and there may be other provisions or Scripture passages I am unaware of.

I have witnessed a few healing services and I can attest that there can be a tremendous amount of emotional and spiritual energy focused on the person being prayed for. Usually a number of people gather around the subject of the prayers and lay hands on them or touch them in some way. I've heard people testify that nothing may happen at first, but after continuing prayer with everyone beseeching God fervently, eventually something starts to happen. Healing may come gradually but persistence seems to pay off and some, but not all, of the persons feel relief from whatever was ailing them. I'm sure all that energy directed at the person is going to have some emotional impact, and perhaps along with their spiritual faith, changes take place in the body. Medical science tells us a huge percentage of physical ailments have emotional causes. It is wonderful if the prayers for healing can release some of that physical stress and bring relief to the individuals being prayed for.

But for me, the concept of the 'prayer of faith' is a prayer God gives us for specific situations. That approach to healing was one of the main themes of Rees Howells' ministry. Howells lived during the great Welch Revival in the early part of the twentieth century. His ministry of intercession was popularized through the book by Norman Grubb entitled "Rees Howells, Intercessor" [12]. That book had a tremendous impact of my spiritual life in a number of areas, but especially in the area of healing. Howells gained the reputation of being able to pray successfully for healing, but only after failing when he prayed for a woman suffering from tuberculosis. He had to learn that praying for healing was not a simple process. He prayed for the woman and wrestled with God extensively until the Lord impressed on him that Howells was going to be required to actually take the woman's tuberculosis on himself in order for her to be healed. He had to be willing to become sick with the disease himself before he could ask God to heal her. His walk with God was so intimate and personal that he eventually was able to trust God to take care of him if that happened, even though the end result of tuberculosis in those days was usually death. He actually assumed he would die so the woman could live, but he was sure in his spirit that the woman would be healed. When she died he felt the Lord was telling him to walk the road as a failure, surrendering the woman's case to him as the first fruits of his intercessory ministry.

God used that first experience to bring Rees Howells through additional spiritual struggles until he came to the place where he could discern God's will in healing. However, he found that what God was trying to teach him was that "Intercession so identifies the intercessor with the sufferer that it gives him a prevailing place with God." Mr. Howells would often speak of the "gained position of intercession" which could only be attained by the inner wrestlings and groanings of the spirit. Howells said "The price is paid, the obedience is fulfilled, the inner wrestlings and groanings take their full course, and then 'the word of the Lord comes.' The weak channel is clothed with authority by the Holy Ghost and can speak the word of deliverance."

He was later able to pray successfully for healing for other people, but he could only be assured of their healing if he received "the Word of the Lord" to that effect. I think that "Word" is what we are calling the "Prayer of Faith." People brought family members and friends to Rees and asked him to pray for them, knowing he had successfully prayed for healing in other cases. But Rees couldn't just blindly pray for their healing without spending much time with them and in prayer seeking God's will for that individual. Only when he had paid that price could he come to the position of intercession, and then only for a specific person or situation. Rees reported, "Even though an intercession may have been gained, the Lord's will must be revealed in each case."

Most of the time when a sick person was brought to his attention, if he didn't receive a word from the Lord, he would simply pray for their general well being and for God's will to be done in their life. But, in other cases when he was impressed by the Spirit, he prayed through for them and usually saw the individual healed of their infirmity.

Several years ago I had the privilege of traveling to Wales with my preacher brother Jim to do some personal research into Rees Howells background. Jim was living in England at the time as a missionary and church planter and I stopped by for a visit after a business trip to France. We drove to Wales and with some difficulty we were directed to the old homestead of the Howells family in Brynamman. The difficulty arose because we could scarcely understand the Welch people with their thick brogues. But, we not only found the house but several other sites mentioned in the book, including the Bible College started by Howells in Swansea. We had the privilege of meeting his grandson there, Steven Howells, who autographed several copies of the book for us to take back for our family and friends.

Unfortunately, we were not able to find anyone who remembered anything about the famous Welch Revival in the early 1900s.

The kind of intercession practiced by Rees Howells is a far cry from what we normally see with "faith healers" on TV or in some of our churches. If their messages were true, and I don't see from the Scriptures that they are accurate, then no one should ever die. Either that, or no one has enough faith to move God to do what they claim he said he would do. That would indicate a pernicious God who teases his children by promising something he never planned to deliver.

I believe I have experienced God giving me a prayer of faith for healing, but it wasn't for any of our children. In our church there was a young couple who had a baby daughter who had been born with a defective heart. The doctors said there was no hope for her survival, so the parents had lost all hope and had gone so far as to buy a burial plot and make the funeral arrangements. But during a deacons meeting two or three of us felt impressed by God not to give up on the baby. We testified that we felt the Holy Spirit speaking to us, saying not to give up hope for this child. The deacons began to pray for the baby. We brought the matter before the church and the entire church began to pray for her healing. I remind you this was in a Southern Baptist Church.

I believe God came through because he put it into our hearts to pray for that baby. He brought a miraculous healing through a last desparate surgery. The doctor wrote the family telling them that he felt he had witnessed a miracle because he was certain there was no chance for the baby to survive. But before God moved in our hearts, we had given up too. It was his moving in us to involve us in his healing ministry that led us to pray the prayer of faith. Now when we see that little girl running and playing, the whole church is able to praise God and glorify him to the world.

So again then, how are we to pray when someone close to us is sick or even dying? If God hasn't given us the prayer of faith for healing in our hearts, what can we pray? We can still ask God for healing and he may be gracious and bring healing. But if he does, it is what Rees Howells called a "gift of faith." We are not guaranteed a positive result unless we have received that word from God. For myself, I pray the prayer that God gives me to pray. In most cases that is a prayer for peace and assurance of God's presence and care. Above all, it is a prayer for God's perfect will to be done. We also pray for God to use the problem to work in the lives of everyone affected to bring something good and to glorify him in it all. *"God works for the good for those who love him, who have been called according to his purpose." (Romans 8:28)* But if God speaks to us in our spirit to pray for healing, we can rejoice and pray, believing God is going to heal the person for his glory.

In summary, I think it is clear that God can and does heal people miraculously. He does it every day. He wants us to be a part of his healing ministry, but I don't think he wants us to dictate to him when and where he should act. He has a plan for every believer's life and we don't know what that is. Our responsibility is to always be in close fellowship with him so he can use us to minister and pray according to his will. Above all, he wants us to trust him and believe he really knows what is best for us, much better than we know for ourselves. If it wasn't God's will to heal our children, then he must have had something better in mind. We were content to wait on him and trust him. We could say, 'His Grace is Sufficient,' and therefore, 'It is Well.'

Surprising Joy

"If anyone would come after me, he must deny himself and take up his cross daily and follow me. For whoever wants to save his life will lose it, but whoever loses his life for me will save it." Luke 9:23-24

While Karen and I were praying about having another baby after Rachel died, I remember clearly praying for God to show us his will, and to lead us in our decision. We felt that God was saying yes. When Karen became pregnant, we dedicated the baby to God, surrendering it to God, fervently praying for God to use this new life in a special way. We prayed that the baby would be sanctified, and that God would further his kingdom through this child. I remember praying that God would fill our child with the Holy Spirit from the womb even as John the Baptist was. And I felt God was saying he would honor those prayers. In my spirit God assured me he was going to use the child in a special way. Our surrender of Beth to the Lord was complete before she was conceived and before she was born. As we had learned with Rachel, however, to surrender someone or something to God means to be willing for him to take the ownership from you and do his will with that person or thing.

I remember back to the time when the reality and the consequences of total surrender to God first came to me while Beth was still with us. I had a sort of dream-vision. I don't know how to better describe it. In this vision I held in my hands a box full of my most prized possessions. Symbolically, all of the important things in my life were in that box. My wife and children, my friends, my job, my possessions, everything was there. God spoke to me in this dream-vision and asked me to surrender the things in my box to him. In obedience, I began handing my prized possessions to the Lord, one at a time, surrendering them to him.

As the Lord took them from me, I wonder if he somehow endued them with a holy glow as he placed them in a special place of sanctification; a place where he could use them for his own purpose. I continued to hand over my treasures to him until finally, my box was empty. But the Lord was saying that there was something else; one more thing he wanted. I said, "But Lord, I've given you everything. The box is empty." Then the Lord said, "I want the box." The realization came then that the box was me, and he didn't just want the people and things in my life, he wanted me. Whatever that meant, I said "Yes, Lord. Take the box. Take me."

The surprising thing about the full surrender of our lives to God is that it is a wonderfully joyous experience. Many of us harbor concepts of God as a kill-joy. We're sure we will end up as missionaries in a muddy village in Africa, or at least in abject poverty if he has his way with us. But Jesus said in John 14 and 15 he will give us his love and peace and our joy will be complete if he has his way with us. He also said he would give us life abundantly. What better definition of happiness could there be than an abundant life full of peace, love and joy? That sounds like heaven to me, and that's exactly what God has given to our family; life abundant saturated with his love, his peace and his joy.

So when Karen and I surrendered our unborn baby to the Lord, there were no qualms about it. We knew God loved that baby even then, more than we would ever be able to love her. I know also that as he accepted her, he sanctified her. So, I wondered how God would use this new baby. Would it be a boy who would grow up to be a great preacher, thrilling crowds with his sermons? Maybe he would become a missionary evangelizing parts of the world never reached before. How would God further his kingdom through this child?

But all the time, in my spirit I knew it might not be in a way that was exciting and glamorous. It could be through pain, suffering or loss, on the child's part or on ours. When the baby was born a girl, I thought, 'Well, so much for the great preacher idea.' But the dedication and commitment of Beth to the Lord was solid in our minds, and she was always the Lord's child.

When Beth began to manifest her seizure disorder, again I felt the path of her service and glorification of God would not be other than through the valley of suffering. I wanted to think her service might be like the blind man whom Jesus healed, that God might be glorified in the healing. While Karen and I were certainly willing for God to do that, and while we frequently prayed, "*Father, if it can be thy will, please let this cup pass from us,*" we could not pray specifically for God to deliver her from the seizures as the deepest desire of our hearts. The reason we couldn't pray that prayer is because the deepest desire of our hearts was for God's perfect will to be done. We had surrendered her to him and we had no way of knowing what that perfect will was. Unless God specifically gave us a word that He wanted to physically heal her, we couldn't pray that prayer. We never received that word.

To pray only for Beth's healing or delivery from the seizures would be to take her back after I had surrendered her to God. I would risk refusing God's will for her life and ours. It would mean rejecting the witness in my spirit that God was in control of her life, just as we had asked him to be from the beginning. I even felt if I prayed for God to spare her from the seizures, we would be forfeiting the greater things God had in store for her, and ultimately for his kingdom. If we would just trust him, he would be faithful to answer our prayers in his way and in his time.

I still believe today God has done just that. Beth is perfectly healed in heaven and is enjoying the glories of that glorious place. We will join her before long, because this life is short. Our time on earth is insignificant compared with eternity and the glories that await us there. If we can just get our eyes off our immediate gratification and let God work, he will take care of us and grant us great and mighty things with benefits for eternity.

It Will Be Worth It All

"I consider that our present sufferings are not worth comparing with the glory that will be revealed in us."Romans 8:18

I don't believe any suffering the Father brings into our lives will be wasted. Nevertheless, God is not obligated to reveal to us how he will use our sufferings. Sometimes he does, but often he does not. He wants us to trust him completely. If we demand to see how our sufferings are used, we are expressing a selfish desire to gratify our own lusts. Yes, we even have to surrender that satisfaction to him.

How can God use our trials for his glory? One possible way is described in the book of 2 Corinthians. *"The God of all comfort.... comforts us in all our troubles so that we can comfort those in any trouble with the comfort we ourselves have received from God. For just as the sufferings of Christ flow over into our lives, so also through Christ our comfort overflows." 2 Corinthians 1:3-4*

Our earnest prayer is that God can somehow use the sufferings of our family to allow us to minister to others. We have sought to allow him to use us in such cases, trying to be sensitive to the needs of others in difficult situations where our experience might allow us to minister.

Another way God might use our sufferings is by allowing our faithfulness in difficult circumstances to draw someone else to Christ and eternal salvation. We may never realize until heaven if God used our testimony to such an end. But make no mistake, people are watching to see how you and I will handle the difficult situations.Without the painful circumstances in your life, some person or persons might never be brought to eternal salvation. Since we are unable to see the consequences of our suffering from an eternal perspective, we must continue to have faith in God's perfect goodness and trust him to do all things well. Be assured that he will.

Joni Erickson Tada was a happy, healthy young lady in 1967, just before she dove into shallow water and broke her neck. She became a quadraplegic, confined to a wheelchair with no use of her hands. She spent long weeks and months grieving over her loss and questioning why God let that happen to her. But, God did a marvellous work in her life by giving her the ability to speak and write of her love for Jesus, and even to paint beautiful pictures using a brush held in her teeth. I'm sure that she and thousands of others prayed earnestly for her healing, but God had a better plan. She founded "Joni and Friends," a wonderful ministry that included radio broadcasts and other ministries to disabled people and their families. God was able to use her obedience to bless untold numbers of people, whether disabled or whole, and bring many to Christ. Was it worth it? You be the judge. But, I've heard Joni give thanks that God has allowed her to be who and what she is.

Another very real possibility is that God brings trials into our lives in order to eliminate our character defects and bring us to maturity, for our own good and for his good as he molds us into useful servants of his. In the book of James, Chapter 1, verses 2 to 4, James tell us, *"Consider it a great joy, my brothers, whenever you experience various trials, knowing that the testing of your faith produces endurance. But endurance must do its complete work, so that you may be mature and complete, lacking nothing."* So, we are instructed to accept our trials joyfully, knowing that God is going to use them to our benefit, molding us into mature, useful citizens and servants of God.

In summary, what is the payoff for our suffering? Is it just God working in our lives to bring something better to fruition? Well, it might be. But, it may be something much more grandiose than that. It may be that God is giving us the privilege of suffering for him. It may not be for everyone to be selected by God for this privilege...that is, as the Apostle Paul put it, *"to share in his sufferings."* It may be that God calls out individuals whom he loves and has endowed with enough faith (as he did Job) to allow us to contribute to the futherance of his Kindom by our sufferings. Wouldn't that be a tremendous privilege? In the process, we may end up giving more glory to God than could be accomplished any other way. After all, our major purpose in life is to glorify God and to work to advance his Kingdom.

The Apostle Paul apparently didn't know how God would use his suffering either, but he put his money where his mouth was, so to speak. In Acts 21 Paul was on his way back to Jerusalem, although all his friends and followers warned him not to do it. The Jewish leaders were furious with him and couldn't wait to get their hands on him. But Paul was adamant and said to them, *"Why all this hysteria? Why do you insist on making a scene and making it even harder for me? You're looking at this backward. The issue in Jerusalem is not what they do to me, whether arrest or murder, but what the Master Jesus does through my obedience. Can't you see that"* Acts 21:14-15, The Message Bible. That translation hits the nail on the head. What can the Master Jesus do through our obedience? It's up to him, but I know he will do something great for his glory and for his kingdom.

I don't want to leave the impression that I feel that myself or my family are in any way special to God. I just believe that in his sovereignty God calls different individuals to different missons or tasks, according to how he has gifted and prepared them. Our losses and our faithfulness through them may be the mission God has called us to.

I also do not want to imply that God can be heartless or unkind. God is very compassionate and I know from Scripture that he receives joy from our happiness and well being. It is God's nature to be generous and giving. It says in Ephesians 1:7-8 that he *"Lavishes the riches of his grace upon us."* But it also says a few pages later in Philippians 1:29 *"It has been granted for Christ's sake, not only to believe in Him, but also to suffer for His sake, experiencing the same conflict which you saw in me, and now hear to be in me."*

So when disaster befalls us and people ask, "Has the Evil One gotten his way with God's children in opposition to God's plan?" My answer is the same as the apostle Paul's, *"God forbid that it could be so."* God is in complete control. As the song writers said, "We may not know God's mind, but we always know his heart." I do know God's heart. He is true and merciful. He is kind, loving, tender-hearted and forgiving. His actions with his children are more compassionate than an earthly father's could ever be. His Spirit witnesses to my spirit that it is so. When tragic and painful things happen in our lives, it is not because God doesn't love us, or he doesn't care. To the contrary, it is because he does love us and wants the best for us eternally. Moreover, he has promised to reward our faithfulness. Every Christian who has suffered a God-ordained loss can look forward to the glories waiting for them in heaven.

It will indeed be worth it all, when we see Jesus. It is impossible for us to be able to see how it will be worth it all while it is happening to us, but it is possible for us to observe other situations and see how God has worked the pain and grief of others to his glory and the futherance of his kingdom. Here is one of many such cases from church history.

It Is Well With My Soul
Horatio G. Spafford - 1873

I know all people are different and some of us are wired differently that others. However, I know many people are like me and are ministered to by Christian music and by books which speak to our emotions during the time of sorrow. A very helpful ministry to those suffering loss might be to give them gifts of music or written material that can be of help to them. When my dad died, Mom depended on tapes of favorite hymns and other gospel music to comfort her to sleep. In my grief I also was comforted by music which seemed to come straight from the heart of God.

Of all the music that ministered to us during our dark days, one ministered to us more than all the others. Perhaps it was because it was (and is) so popular that we hear it more often. But even though it is so well known, I came to know it even more intimately because I began to research the origin of the words of the song. While we wept for Beth, we were strengthened by the hymn we all know as "It is Well With My Soul." The occasion for the writing of the hymn, whose actual title is "When Peace Like a River Attendeth My Way" [13] is fairly well known. In 1870 Horatio Spafford, the author of the hymn, was a successful lawyer and business man in Chicago. He was also a dedicated and active Christian layman who enjoyed a close friendship with Moody, Sankey, and numerous other evangelistic leaders of his day. In the great Chicago fire of 1871, all of Spafford's real estate holdings on the shore of Lake Michigan were wiped out. Shortly afterward, upon the advice of their family physician, he planned a European vacation for the benefit of his wife's health. An unexpected last minute business development required him to remain in Chicago for a few days, so he sent his wife and four daughters ahead on the ship S.S. *Ville du Havre*.

On November 22, 1873 in calm seas the ill-fated ship collided with another ship in the North Atlantic and in only twelve minutes it sank. Mrs. Spafford was saved, but all four of their daughters perished. When Mrs. Spafford landed with the other survivors in Cardiff, Wales, she cabled her husband a two word message, "Saved alone." Spafford immediately left by ship to be with his wife, and on the high seas, near the scene of the tragedy, he wrote the words to the great hymn.

In seeking to know more about the man who wrote this moving and profound hymn, I read the book written by his daughter born after the tragedy at sea. Bertha Spafford Vester's book is entitled "Our Jerusalem" [14]. In that book, Bertha Vester recalls her mother's graphic account of the tragedy at sea. She wrote that Anna Spafford stood on the deck of the sinking ship with her two year old daughter Tanetta in her arms and the other three girls, Annie, Maggie and Bessie clutching at her skirts. As the ship sank beneath the waves, Vester wrote "Maggie lifted her dark eyes and said... 'Mama, God will take care of us." Then 10 year old Annie, the oldest of the girls, said, 'Don't be afraid. The sea is His and He made it."

Bertha went on to write "The sea rushed over the afterdeck as a watery canyon opened to receive the vast ruin of the *Ville du Havre*. The little group went down together, with all on that crowded deck and all those trapped below into blackness whose depth stretched many miles, into a whirlpool created by suction of bodies, wreckage, and savage water. As Mother was pulled down she felt her baby torn violently from her arms. She reached out through the water and caught Tanetta's little gown. For a moment she held her again, then the cloth was wrenched from her hand"

"Only twelve minutes after the *Ville du Havre* was struck it sank with all on board. The sea had just annihilated one of the largest steamers afloat, and engulfed, as if in play, two hundred and twenty-six lives"

The account continues, "The splash of an oar brought her to consciousness. She was lying in a boat, bruised from head to foot and sick with sea water....She knew, with no need of being told, that her children were gone. They estimated that Mother had been in the sea for an hour. She had been rolled under and down, and as she rose unconscious to the surface a plank floated under her, saving her life. Mother told me, long after, that when she came back to consciousness in the boat and knew she had been recalled to life, that her first realization was complete despair. How could she face life without her children? Horrible as was her physical suffering, her mental anguish was worse. Her life had been bound up in her little girls. What was life worth now, and what could it ever be without them?"

"Then, she told me, it was as if a voice spoke to her. *'You are spared for a purpose. You have work to do."* In that moment of returning consciousness she lifted her soul to God in an agony of despair and humbly dedicated her life to His service."

God did indeed have more work for Anna Spafford to do. The plank that had miraculously taken her unconscious body to the surface of the sea and floated her for an hour before the rescuers found her was no less a miracle than Jonah's fish. As God had a mission for Jonah, so did he have a vital mission for Anna Spafford.

A few years after the shipwreck the couple had another daughter and a son. Both children contracted scarlet fever and the boy died at the age of four. The religious community, instead of supporting the family in their renewed sorrow, intensified their suffering by accusing them of sinning before God. Like Job, their friends could not believe God would allow His children to suffer such great loss unless it was as punishment for sin in their lives.

Finding no solace from the church community in Chicago, Horatio and Anna left Chicago, and with a group of loyal friends they moved to Jerusalem to establish the American Colony. That colony became an integral part of the Jerusalem scene and over the next half century played a key role in the events of that eternal city. Untold thousands of Jews and Arabs have been helped through the ministry of the mission and many were brought to Christ spiritually through their work.

The daughter who survived the scarlet fever grew up to become Bertha Spafford Vester. She carried on the work of the American Colony and became the author of the book which finally told the story of this exceptional family. Karen and I had an opportunity to visit the American Colony during our visit to the Holy Land in 1998. An enclosed frame in the lobby of the main building held the hand written original manuscript of Spafford's verses which became the verses of the famous hymn.

The pain and grief that came to us with the loss of Beth was the most difficult challenge to our faith of all our losses. We were so convinced God would not let anything happen to her. The beautiful hymn has blessed countless thousands of believers over the years and has brought them closer to God, as well as providing comfort and inspiration. God has used the sorrow of the Spaffords to glorify his name and advance the kingdom in a major way. The profound faith of Horatio Spafford and his wife while in the depths of their sorrow also inspired and comforted us, as it has others familiar with their story. Just before he penned the words to the great hymn while he was at sea, Spafford wrote these words in a letter. "On Thursday we passed over the spot where she went down, in mid-ocean, the water three miles deep. But I do not think of our dear ones there. They are safe, folded, the dear lambs, and there, before very long, shall we be too. In the meantime, thanks to God, we have an opportunity to serve and praise Him for His love and mercy to us and ours. 'I will praise Him while I have my being.' May we each one arise, leave all, and follow Him."

When Peace Like A River Attendeth My Way

When peace like a river attendeth my way,
When sorrows like sea billows roll,
Whatever my lot, thou has taught me to say,
It is well, It is well with my soul.

213

Though Satan should buffet, tho trials should come,
Let this blest assurance control;
That Christ has regarded my helpless estate
And hath shed His own blood for my soul.

My sin - Oh the bliss of this glorious tho't ;
My sin, not in part, but the whole,
Is nailed to the cross, and I bear it no more.
Praise the Lord, praise the Lord, Oh my soul

And Lord, haste the day when the faith shall be sight,
The clouds be rolled back as a scroll.
The trump shall resound and the Lord shall descend.
Even so, it is well with my soul.
It is well ....With my soul.
It is well, it is well, with my soul.

There is more to Horatio Spafford's story that bears on our family's story. In addition to the hymn "It Is Well With My Soul," he wrote other verses that would challenge any believer. His hymns and poems reveal that Spafford and his wife came to know Christ in a way beyond what most of us experience. They reached a level of understanding and surrender to God's plan that few achieve. That understanding is expressed in the words of a later hymn Spafford wrote after becoming even more acquainted with sorrow. It is quoted on page 54 of his daughter's book "Our Jerusalem" .

A Song In The Night
Long time I dared not say to Thee
O Lord, work Thou thy will with me,
But now so plain Thy love I see
I shrink no more from sorrow.

So true, true and faithful is He,
Kind is my Savior;
Alike in gladness and in woe,
I thank Him who hast loved me so.

I could not say with Spafford, "I shrink no more from sorrow." My faith has to grow more before I can voice that prayer to God. But I do want to know Christ, for as Paul also said, *"For me to live is Christ, and to die is gain," Phillipians 1:21.* To completely know Christ must be to live life to the fullest extent possible. I think my family has experienced some of that gain for we have come to know Christ in a more intimate way through our losses than we could have any other way.

I can only say Amen. Thank you Lord for ministering to your children by inspiring some of them to write music and words such as these which minister to us in our deepest sorrow. We know above all else *"God is Love" , 1 John 4:16 .* Thank you Lord for demonstrating through others of your children that their tragedies have been used by you in your great love to accomplish your will in your creation. Perhaps, somehow, you will be able to use our testimony also in some small way to glorify your name.

CHAPTER 12

JESUS LOVES THE LITTLE CHILDREN

"For I tell you that their angels in heaven always see the face of my Father in heaven." Matthew 18:1

There is a nagging question that often lingers in the minds of many parents who have lost small children. Karen and I have discussed this question at length. The question is, "Is my child (or in our case, our children) safe in heaven?." Some churches teach that as long as the child was baptized as an infant, it is safe in the Father's care. However, most evangelical churches do not practice child baptism and teach (by implication if not directly) that children are eternally lost until they reach the "age of accountability" and accept Jesus as their Savior. This teaching springs from the doctrine of 'Original Sin,' stated first by the church father Augustine, that everyone is born a sinner as the result of Adam's sin. No sinner can enter Heaven except by accepting Jesus Christ as their personal Savior. Since small children who die do not have a chance to accept or reject Christ, this doctrine reasons they must be eternally lost. This doctrine led to the practice of baptizing infants in the Catholic Church and has carried over to some Protestant churches in the present age.

The idea that babies are lost and cannot go to heaven is a very difficult concept for grieving parents to accept, yet the traditional doctrine seems to leave no way out. Apparently it is such an unpleasant concept that preachers shy away from it. In addition, relatively few families lose small children, so for most people it is not a pressing question. However for the parents of the little ones that die, it is a question of paramount importance. The evangelical Christian parents I know who have lost small children generally refuse to accept that teaching. They assume that somehow, their children are secure in the Father's care and they will see them again in heaven. It just intuitively makes sense. But when I have questioned them about the scriptural basis of their belief, their response seems to be based more on their feelings than any specific teaching in the Bible.

I looked for something already published that would tell us what the Bible has to say about the eternal destiny of our little ones. Nothing I found treated the subject to my satisfaction so I began to do my own search of the Scriptures. I understand that I was searching in hopes of finding the answer I was looking for. I was looking for assurance for Karen and me that our children were safe with the Lord in heaven. However, I really tried to be objective even though that was a difficult thing to do.

It turned out I didn't have to worry about being too subjective in my search. I was gratified to find that there are many, many passages that speak of God's love for the little children and of their security with him. I will let you know before I get into the specifics that my conclusion is that God somehow makes special provision for the little ones, and takes it upon himself to cover them with the blood of Christ, to cleanse them of their original sin if that is indeed what is necessary. I hope this study will help and comfort grieving parents as it has helped Karen, my girls and myself.

I'll begin with some passages from the Old Testament that teach us about God's attitude toward little children and his feelings toward them. Remember first, King David, a man after God's own heart. His story is told in 2 Samuel 12:23. His baby son was near death, and after David prayed and fasted many days for his son, the boy died. David's words were, *"I will go to him, but he will not return to me."* If one believed that David held no hope for life after death, he might interpret this verse as saying that David would also go to the grave, but the child would not come back to life. The only problem with that interpretation is, David did believe in eternal life after death. This is the same man who gave us the 23rd Psalm, which ends with the glorious words, *"...and I will dwell in the house of the Lord forever."* So I'm sure David believed that he would see his son again in eternity. So also do we believe that we will see Mike, Rachel and Beth again in eternity.

In Psalm 139:13 and following, the Psalmist writes *"For you created my inmost being; you knit me together in my mother's womb. I praise you because I am fearfully and wonderfully made; your works are wonderful, I know that full well. My frame was not hidden from you when I was made in the secret place. When I was woven together in the depths of the earth, your eyes saw my unformed body. All the days ordained for me were written in your book before one of them came to be."*

How could we have a clearer statement about our children's eternal destiny than this, that God has ordained all of the days of their existence before even one of them came to be? I think these verses apply equally to the child who never sees the light of her first day and to one who is taken from his earthly parents after birth. The theme is the same. God is in control of the lives of our children from conception and he will keep them in his care.

God's attitude toward the children is displayed clearly in the stern pronouncement of God told by the prophet Ezekiel in chapter 16 of his book. God says to the nation Israel, *"You took your sons and daughters whom you **bore to me** and sacrificed them as food to the idols....You slaughtered **my children** and sacrificed them to the idols." Ezekiel 16:20-21.* (My emphases)

Notice that God refers to the children as *"My Children.. the children you bore to me."* God here takes ownership of the little ones. The one sin in the Old Testament that God condemned most intensely was the pagan practice of child sacrifice. In the depths of their depravity, even the children of Israel resorted to sacrificing their children by fire to the pagan gods. God expressed his utter contempt of this sin in some of the strongest words in the Bible. For example, he said in Jeremiah 19:4-6,

"For they have forsaken me and made this a place of foreign gods; they have burned sacrifices in it to gods that neither they nor their fathers nor the kings of Judah ever knew, and they have filled this place with the blood of the innocent.

They have built the high places of Baal to burn their sons in the fire as offerings to Baal — something I did not command or mention, nor did it enter my mind. So beware, the days are coming, declares the Lord, when people will no longer call this place Topheth or the Valley of Ben Hinnom, but the Valley of slaughter."

This place of sacrifice outside Jerusalem known as the valley of Hinnom in the Old Testament became known in the Greek New Testament as Gehenna. In Jesus' time it was the location of the city dump where fires smoldered and the stench of rotting garbage filled the air. God cursed this historic place of child sacrifice so that its very name became a synonym for hell. Whenever the name Gehenna appears in the New Testament, it is translated into English as "Hell." Rather than indicating that children might suffer the punishment of hell, God curses the very place where children were burned by fire.

In Psalm 8:2 the Psalmist sings *"O Lord, our Lord, how majestic is your name in all the earth! You have set your glory above the heavens. From the lips of children and infants you have ordained praise."* Somehow, God has ordained praise from the lips of his children and infants. Jesus even quoted this Psalm when the Jewish leaders accosted him and complained about the children waving palm branches in the temple and shouting *"Hosannah to the Son of David."* It may be impossible for us to grasp how God could ordain praise from the lips of infants unless it is just that their very existence is a miracle; a miracle that glorifies God. Whatever the case, they are a living testimony to him, giving him glory, and praising his name. I think there is even more to it than that, however. Our children have a very special place in the heart of God and if he wishes for them to leave this earth early, he has clearly ordained for them a place with him in heaven where they can praise him eternally.

Now let's look at another setting in the New Testament. The familiar children's stories from Matthew Chapters 18 and 19 tell about Jesus and the children who were brought to him by their parents. The disciples refused to allow the parents to bother the Master, but Jesus said, *"Let the little children come to me, and do not hinder them, for the kingdom of heaven belongs to such as these."*

Matthew 19:14. Now, let's associate this story with other teachings of Jesus where he repeatedly taught that he did nothing on his own, but only did what he saw the Father in heaven doing. For example, in John 5:19 and following Jesus said *"I tell you the truth, the Son can do nothing by himself; he can only do what he sees his Father doing, because whatever the Father does the Son also does. For the Father loves the Son and shows him all he does."*

When Jesus told the disciples to let the little children come to him, I believe that he first looked into heaven and saw the Father doing that very thing. Jesus saw the heavenly Father gathering to himself the innocent little children, saying *"Forbid them not to come unto me."* A paraphrase of this passage from the "Message" Bible puts it this way. *"Jesus called (the children) back, saying 'Let these children alone. Don't get between them and me. These children are the kingdom's pride and joy."* Luke 18:16-17. I like this paraphrase because I believe it communicates what Jesus was saying to his disciples; "Don't get between me and my children."

Looking at another passage, in 1 Corinthians 7 the apostle Paul teaches about the sanctity of marriage and the responsibilities of husbands and wives to one another. In verse 14 he makes a very interesting statement about the children of a believing Christian. He says that *"For the unbelieving husband has been sanctified through his wife, and the unbelieving wife has been sanctified through her believing husband. Otherwise your children would be unclean, but as it is, they are holy."* The word 'holy' is also translated 'sanctified,' a word meaning 'set aside for God.' I don't pretend to understand all of what Paul is teaching here about the unbelieving spouse, but clearly the proof of his argument is that *"...otherwise your children would be unclean, but as it is they are holy."*

Paul says in this inspired text that the children of believing parents are sanctified to God; they are holy! They are children of God's covenant. Radio pastor John MacArthur has dubbed them "Covenant Children." God's constant message regarding children in the Word is that God loves children; he wants them to come to him, and they are holy to him. There is no indication anywhere in Scripture that small children will be cast into hell or into a "limbo" nonexistence. Rather, the heavenly Father welcomes the innocent children into his presence just as Jesus welcomed them into his arms so freely.

Remember also that in Matthew 18:1-5, Jesus responded to a question from the disciples about *"Who is the greatest in the kingdom of heaven?"* Jesus called a little child and stood him among them. *"And he said, I tell you the truth, unless you change and become like little children, you will never enter the kingdom of heaven. Therefore, whoever humbles himself like this child is the greatest in the kingdom of heaven. And whoever welcomes a little child like this in my name welcomes me."* Then in verse 10 Jesus said, *"See that you do not look down on one of these little ones. For I tell you that their angels in heaven always see the face of my Father in heaven."* Their status with the Father is unquestioned. He has his angels watching over each one of them personally. When Mike died in his crib, his own personal angel was there to carry him gently to the Father in Heaven. Likewise, Rachel and Beth had their angels accompanying them and caring for them. Even our unborn children had angels assigned to them from conception.

It is clear from Jesus' teaching that we should be trying to become more like children rather than trying to make the children be more like us. Finally, Jesus stated very clearly in verse 14, *"...your Father in heaven is not willing that any of these little ones should be lost."* What could be clearer? If it is not God's will that any of them be lost, then they won't be lost.

These passages and many others have brought great comfort to my family. Our assurance is complete and we know with certainty that our children are with God, and that he has welcomed them with open, loving arms. In our family, not just Michael, Rachel and Beth are with God, but also the two who didn't make it through the pregnancies. I don't understand much about how they will appear and how we will know and recognize them when we get to heaven, but I won't be surprised if we see them there.

It seems the Catholic Church has recently come to the same conclusion that I have. In an Associated Press release dated April, 2007, Vatican City issued a statement noting that Pope Benedict XVI has reversed centuries of traditional Roman Catholic teaching on limbo. He approved a report that says "there were 'serious grounds' to hope that children who die without being baptized can go to heaven. ...We can say we have many reasons to hope that there is salvation for these babies." I wonder if they did the same Bible study I did? A Jesuit spokesman for the committee that released the report stessed that there was no certainty, just hope.

I feel we can go beyond hope, based on the teaching in Scripture concerning God's tender concern for our little ones. In Randy Alcorn's recent, wonderful book about Heaven, entitled simply, "Heaven"([15]) the author speculates, "Perhaps in Heaven many people will meet their children who were aborted or who died in miscarrages... Many parents will be reunited with children who died at an early age. Perhaps these children will grab our hands and show us around the present Heaven. Then one day, after the final resurrection, we'll enjoy each other's company on the New Earth and experience its wonders together." Randy goes on to speculate that perhaps we will meet our children in heaven as they were when we knew them, and then have the joy of watching them grow to adulthood there in heaven. I like that idea. But, we'll have to wait a little while to see how that all works out.

The bottom line is that we will be reunited with all believing loved ones in Heaven. God's love for his little ones is inscribed indelibly throughout the Holy Scriptures, and in our hearts. We are looking forward to that great reunion. Come quickly, Lord Jesus.

CHAPTER 13

GRIEF LESSONS LEARNED

"Consider it pure joy, my brothers, whenever you face trials of many kinds, because you know that the testing of your faith develops perseverance. Perseverance must finish its work so that you may be mature and complete, not lacking anything." James 1:2-4

God taught our family lessons through our children's sicknesses and deaths that we would never have learned otherwise. Most of them are discussed in other sections of the book, but I would like to summarize many of them here in a single listing, similar to the wisdom sayings in the book of Proverbs. These are not spiritual proverbs, but they are constructed like the time-proven book of Proverbs. These are the things we have learned and believe with all our hearts are true. I hope as you examine them you see some truth in them for yourself. Here they are.

1. Living with death is a part of life. God has created and made us lifeworthy to cope with the death of ones close to us.
2. Faith in God provides the power to go on through all trials, no matter how difficult. "I can do all things through him who strengthens me."
3. The Word of God is our rudder, pointing the way for us through life's trials. "His word is a light unto my path and a lamp unto my feet."

4. Total and complete surrender of our wills and our lives to God makes us usable to him. What can he do with our obedience?

5. Our grief can be used by God to strengthen us and prepare us for future service which will be profitable not only to us, but also to God's Kingdom and Glory.

6. The way we handle our grief can be a strong testimony. People are watching.

7. Grief is most tolerable when we trust God completely and allow his goodness to comfort and guide us. He is the Great Comforter.

8. When in sorrow, we must live in the present moment. We must not let ourselves dwell on what might have been...or what it will be like without our loved one. God is always taking care of us at the present moment.

9. Grieving is hard work. It is a difficult job but we can do it.

10. God does not leave us alone to cope with this most deep and profound emotion in our own strength. He will never leave us nor forsake us.

11. People deal with grief differently. Everyone has to cope with grief in their own way.

12. Writing down your thoughts during a time of sorrow is therapeutic. Start a Journal.

13. Although we may feel we are being unfaithful to the one we have lost, at some point we have to let go of them (and their things) and get on with our lives. They would want us to.

14. A dramatic change of routine is very helpful in accelerating the healing process. Filling the mind with new and different experiences helps displace the recent memories of the loss.

15. We can help ourselves get through holidays and other special days by meeting each special day head on with a strategy. Plan ahead.

16. Comfort is ministered best through close personal relationships. Cultivate them now while you have a chance.

17. God wants us to support his children who are in grief. It is his intent that we be there, sharing our love and concern. We are his representatives.

18. Those in grief are comforted when we express our own love and grief for the one who is gone. Go ahead and cry with them.
19. Don't just ask what you can do to help. Take the initiative and do whatever you can without having to be asked.
20. The real need comes after the funeral when the crowd disappears. That is the lonliest time of the entire experience.
21. You can minister most effectively by staying in frequent contact during the weeks and months after the loss. Call regularly and stop by to talk when you can.
22. Don't try to rationalize the loss by offering some possible explanation for what happened. You are not God.
23. God may intentionally bring difficult and painful situations into our lives for his own purposes. We need to be able to accept that fact gladly.
24. How we respond to the situations is what concerns our Lord. Jesus prayed that Peter's faith would not fail, not that he would be spared from Satan's sifting.
25. We may be called to suffer as Christians for the purpose of leading others to a saving knowledge of Jesus Christ.
26. God rewards faithfulness. He will restore completely if we trust him completely.
27. Don't tell God how to solve your problem (or anyone elses). Just share your concern with him and let him fix the problem his way.
28. Never pray for a specific course of action unless you are convinced God is leading you to pray for it.
29. God is good. His compassion for us knows no bounds and he is in control.
30. We can be the happiest in the worst circumstances when we let God have complete control. God can actually bring joy in the midst of sorrow.
31. Death is a form of healing. We are all perfect in heaven.
32. Feelings of love, peace and joy are what bring quality to life, and those things depend only on our fellowship with God.
33. Material things have little bearing on true joy. Money can't buy peace and happiness.

34. More faith is required to trust God through difficulties than to pray for their removal. It's easy to pray for health, peace and prosperity.
35. Our babies and young children who die are safe with God in heaven. They are dear to his heart.
36. The devil always attacks us at our weakest point. He has night-vison goggles to spot the chink in our armor.
37. The devil will take advantage of our emotional exhaustion to attack us. He has no mercy.
38. If the devil can't defeat us directly, he will try to defeat someone close to us whose fall will defeat us.
39. Don't let the evil one catch you unprepared. Begin now to prepare for your own experience with grief. Develop your spiritual muscles and put on the whole armor of God.
40. Do not to give place to the devil by allowing habitual sin in your life. We give the devil a foothold in our lives when we sin willingly.
41. God is looking for people who are willing to surrender every-thing to him, trusting him to use your obedience both for his kingdom and for you.
42. When we know God is in control, then regardless of the circumstances, "It is well."

EPILOGUE

Job's Restoration

"The Lord blessed the latter part of Job's life more than the first." Job 42:12

As God restored Job when the time of testing was over, in the same way God has restored our family. When the sorrow of losing our three sweet children receded to the point that our lives began to stabilize, God began showering us with blessings at every turn. He graced us with blessings we would never have thought to ask for. I can only share a few of the wonderful ways God has blessed us.

First of all I think of the spiritual blessings which the Apostle Paul enumerates for us in the book of Ephesians, Chapter 1. Just to be chosen to be a member of God's family is the greatest blessing of all because it has eternal benefits which we will be able to enjoy forever. As a part of that blessing, I am thankful for our Lord Jesus Christ who left the glories of heaven and paid the price for my salvation. The blessings of a clear conscience, knowing that Christ has paid the price for my sins and cleansed my soul, leaves me full of humility as I bow at the feet of my Savior. Then, there is the gift of the Holy Spirit living in us as God's presence, serving as a deposit on God's promise of heaven.

All of these spiritual blessings enable us to have and enjoy the blessings of health, family, friends, church family and others around us. These are the special people blessings we usually think of first.

Next I praise and thank God for the beautiful world he has given us to live in, from our neighborhoods to the ends of the earth, and beyond. We have travelled around the world and I never cease to be amazed at the beauty of the world, so full of fantastic vistas no artist could conceive of. I also thank him for the blessings of government with the protections and benefits provided. Then, finally, I thank God for the material blessings which he so generously bestows upon us. And, I don't want to forget the bonus blessings which he just gives us because it pleases him to do so. Those bonuses add fun and spice to our lives.

In every one of these categories, my family has been blessed abundantly. As Paul writes in that Ephesians passage, *God lavishes his blessing upon us*. Now, in the context of our story, I want first of all to thank him because he has given Karen and me to each other through all of our sorrows, keeping our bond strong and vital. I cannot overstate how important that has been to us. We know that the survival and strengthening of our marriage has been by the grace of God. It is truly "A God Thing," assured by his bringing us together in the first place as he promised me while I was still in the Navy, then when he gave us that special spiritual bonding on our first anniversary. As I mentioned before, the emotional stress that comes with the death of a child is frequently devastating to the marriage. A very large per centage of families experience serious trouble when just one child dies. Thankfully, God spared us from that tragedy. Instead, each one of our losses drew Karen and me even closer together as we held on to each other for support.

God has been so gracious to give us Vicki and Becky, and to watch over them through all of these trials. God has also given us extended family and friends to support us. Our church family stood by us faithfully during Rachel and Beth's situations. And now we have grandchildren who add joy and fulfillment to our lives. In addition to these people blessings, God has given us so much more. He has blessed us materially and he has given us opportunities for ministry and fulfillment that make life interesting and worthwhile. On top of all these things, he has given us bonus blessings of happiness and enjoyment beyond measure. Indeed, he has blessed us in ways we would not have the audacity to ask for. But, the greatest of these personal blessings has been our daughters and our grandchildren. Vicki and Becky also lived through the deaths of our other children, so their lives were also greatly impacted. Let me share a little more of their stories with you.

Faithful Vicki

"Where you go I will go, and where you stay I will stay. Your people will be my people and your God my God." Ruth 1:16

Our oldest daughter, Vicki Lynette Clifford, was born during my college years in Kansas, her mother was only 18 years old. In a sense, we have grown up together with Vicki because we were so very young ourselves when she was born. Vicki's devotion to her mother and her faithfulness to our family values reminds me of Ruth and Naomi in the Old Testament. Our people are her people and our God is her God. Vicki has been our rock through all of the hard times. It was Vicki who was there for us to love and focus our affections on after Mike died. It was Vicki who learned to take care of herself and her mom when Karen was laid up with pregnancy problems and the eventual miscarriages. Vicki baby sat with Rachel when no one else could or would because of Rachel's special problem. It was Vicki also who helped us take care of Beth when she had her problems.

Our oldest daughter has been a welcome constant in our life of change. She has been with us through it all. She has suffered the same losses as Karen and I have, but from a different perspective. She was less than four years old when Mike died and a freshman in college when we lost Beth.

In concert with the grief experiences, Vicki went through the normal adolescent stages where she had to test her boundaries and express her independence. Through all of that, however, she was never rebellious against us or her God. Many children would have had major emotional problems dealing with the deaths of their sisters, but our daughter handled it all and maintained a steady course. That is, of course, a testimony of God's unfailing grace manifested in her life.

Our oldest daughter made her decision for Christ when she was around 7 years old. Vicki was a regular in the Children's Worship services that I led in our church during her early grade school years. She demonstrated her grounding in the Bible when our Children's Worship group challenged the adult department, where many of their parents attended, to a Bible contest. We had learned an outline of the book of Genesis, including the memorization of several key verses. Vicki was able to summarize the entire book and quote the passages from memory. As I mentioned, Vicki made her public profession of faith while she was quite young, but many years later she confided to me she felt God had spoken to her in a special way during a youth retreat, and she had recommitted her life to the Lord.

Vicki lived at home while attending Missouri Baptist College where she majored in Administration of Justice and met her future husband, Scott. She graduated in just three years. She had some prep courses in high school and went straight through the summer sessions in order to graduate early. She did all that while working several part time jobs and cheer leading during basketball season. After graduation, she went to work for a local legal firm as a paralegal, where she worked full time until her babies came.

Vicki has always been there when we needed her. She has always been close by, and has stayed in close contact with us. After her marriage, she and Scott moved into an adjoining community not far from us. Vicki is a model of stability and organization. She has given us three grandsons and a granddaughter, about whom I will write more later. Since she and her family were active members of our church during our troubled years, we are able to see them there and worship with them regularly. Karen and I count Vicki and her family among the greatest blessings of our lives.

Vicki's husband, Scott, is a fine Christian man who loves the Lord and loves his family. Scott and Vicki are both very active in their church. Scott has taught youth and young singles in Sunday School, and has served in many areas of responsibility in the church. When the church asked him to serve as a deacon, we couldn't have been prouder. We love him as if he were our own son.

Becky, The Vicar's Wife

"Those who sow in tears will reap with songs of joy. He who goes out weeping, carrying seed to sow, will return with songs of joy, carrying sheaves with him." Psalms 126:5-6

I have already shared the story of Becky's release in Chapter 8. In her younger years, Rebecca Dawn was always a happy, bubbly kid who enjoyed life to the fullest. As she began to mature we noted an interesting side of her personality emerging. She had always been a very sensitive, very compassionate young girl, but we began to see a tougher side of her as well. She was exhibiting some of her mother's toughness and showing us that she had a pretty strong will. I think God was working in her life all along, preparing her also for what was to come. She would need that toughness to survive the trials to come.

After high school Becky wanted to attend William Jewell College in Liberty, Missouri. She wasn't able to matriculate there her first year, but did eventually graduate from there after her short but pivotal time in England. She was an honor student majoring in English Literature, which bolstered her infatuation with all things English. The profound moving of God in her life during the time she spent in England went beyond her emotional healing we discussed earlier. She felt a calling to ministry, related in some way to her international experience. Later it turned out there was another factor involved in her calling. It was a young man. One of the English seminarians she had met during her stay had become very special to her. In fact, a few weeks after her return, it became clear that they were very serious about each other.

We had met Paul Harcourt briefly when we visited Becky at Wycliffe Hall in Oxford, and our first impressions of each other were not favorable. Being the conservative Midwesterners we are, his long straight hair distressed us and what we mistakenly saw then as his British arrogance offended us. His impression of us was not much better. When we learned later that Becky had fallen in love with this long-haired person who looked to us like a refugee from an English rock group, our lives were thrown into turmoil again.

We had fully expected Becky to meet and marry a good Baptist boy from the Midwest. In fact, she had become very close to a young man she met at William Jewell College before she went to England and we thought the relationship held promise. However, all of those thoughts and expectations were dashed when she met Paul and found her destiny across the sea.

After all of our experiences and the lessons we had learned, how did we handle this news? Not very well, I'm afraid. We were upset and very concerned. We worried about the ramifications of having our little girl marry an Englishman and live across the sea. To her mom, it seemed like rejection of us, her country, her culture and even her religion. We desperately worried about the difficulties awaiting her and the high potential for failure in their relationship. We wondered, how could a Baptist girl from Missouri find happiness as the wife of an Anglican Vicar across the sea?

For Becky it was true love and a surrender to God's call to the foreign mission field, all in one. As we got to know Paul, we found our misgivings of the young man were unfounded and quickly came to love him and appreciate him. To be honest, he made that easier for us when he cut his hair short at graduation time. He suddenly turned into a fine looking young preacher boy. I especially respect his intellect and his devotion to the Lord. He was an honor graduate from Cambridge in mathematics and had felt a call to the ministry before his graduation. He then went on to seminary at Oxford. When he graduated from Oxford, he became part of a select group of people who have graduated with honors from both Oxford and Cambridge. He especially impressed me when he became the first person I knew who could beat me (sometimes) at the game of Bible Trivial Pursuit. Most importantly, however, we saw that he loved Becky as he loved the Lord, and as the Lord loved the church. Paul's calling to the ministry was very real and his leadership over the years has confirmed that many times over.

Becky and Paul were married in the chapel of Fee Fee Baptist, her childhood church, in April 1992. Paul's parents were there for the wedding and his father, Robin Harcourt, shared a reading from Scripture in his cultured British accent. After a brief honeymoon in Texas, Becky and Paul returned to Oxford where he completed his seminary training in June of that year. Their friends sponsored a reception for them at Wycliffe Hall when they returned and they were able to repeat some of their vows in a small ceremony at that time. After graduation, they accepted a call to an evangelical Anglican church near Liverpool. It was a ministering, evangelical church full of young families and Becky and Paul fit right in.

So now our youngest daughter is 'living happily ever after with her Prince Charming' and we are happy for her. After a few years at the church in Moreton, Paul was assigned as a Curate (Assistant Pastor) to All Saints Church in the beautiful and affluent suburb of Woodford Green just outside London. After a few years on staff at All Saints, Paul was called as the Vicar (Senior Pastor). He was the youngest Vicar in the history of that church, and when Becky's daughter, Rachel, was born, she was the first child ever born into the Vicarage. (Most vicars of large Anglican churches are well along in age.) If that name Rachel sounds familiar, it should. Becky named her only daughter after her dear departed sister after conferring with Karen and me to make sure we were okay with her decision. Their first child, Joshua Michael (after her brother) was born before Paul became the Vicar. Now they are the parents of two beautiful children; a boy and a girl. With her mother's travel connections, Becky and her family are able to get to the States every year, and we usually manage to make a trip to England once or twice a year. As a result we see them about as much as many parents see their children who don't live in the same city. We talk every week by telephone and are able to video-conference over the internet. God has provided a closeness to Becky and her family we didn't expect, and as a result we are a part of their lives. The children know us and love us and give us great joy. God has shown again that he is in control and if we will just wait on him, he will work all things together for good for his beloved children.

Blessed Grandchildren

"May the Lord bless you from Zion all the days of your life; may you see the prosperity of Jerusalem, and may you live to see your children's children." Psalms 128:5-6

Karen and I now have six lovely grandchildren. I think that's all there will be, but they are sufficient to fill our lives with joy. Vicki and Scott have three healthy, energetic boys who have filled our lives with love and activity. Kevin, Kyle and Korey are all full of energy and spunk. And, now later in life, Vicki and Scott have adopted a girl to go with their team of boys. Vicki says that they adopted Kathy because God told her to. Kathy joined the family at the age of 13, making her the second child in order of age. She has had a lot to overcome, taken from an abusive mother at the age of six, then living in various foster homes for seven years until she joined our family. Now she is one of us, fully integrated, accepted and loved as a part of our family. She has brought with her some challenges, but mostly more love. She is a beautiful blond headed girl with a sweet giving personality. Kathy has added a lot of happiness to all our lives.

Vicki, and her three oldest children have all had a chance to go to England and stay with Becky and Paul for a few days. Becky and Paul's son, Joshua, is autistic and doesn't speak. However, he is a happy boy and seems to enjoy life. He has become more sociable and more loving to his family than he was in the early years. Joshua is now eight years old and is attending the Special School district in London. We continue to pray for Joshua, recognizing that God is able to heal him. We pray that God will work Joshua's handicapped situation together for good, for the family and for their church. We trust him. He will do the best thing for Joshua, for his family, and for their church. And most of all, for his glory and the futherance of his kingdom. Rachel, his five year old sister, is in the gifted program at school and is a beautiful, sweet girl.

God restored Job's family and fortune after his trials and tribulations. So also, God has brought Karen and me healing through our grandchildren. God has blessed us immensely through them. We have been able to feel the emotional healing taking place as we've cuddled and loved each one of them as babies. Then, when they were too old for that kind of foolishness, we've been able to be a part of their lives and feel their expressions of love… and we know God cares. God teaches us so much about his love through our grandchildren. Yes, God has restored us and given us blessing upon blessing through our children, our sons-in-law and our grandchildren. God is truly good.

GOD'S EXTRAVAGANT GENEROSITY

"Give and it will be given to you. A good measure, pressed down, shaken together and running over, will be poured into your lap." Luke 6:38

As we look back now on the experience of our three-fold loss, we have the advantage of several years of healing, and time to see how God has used the experiences in our lives. The most important fact is this: God has been faithful to us every moment. Our testimony is that his grace is always sufficient. He sustained us through our times of loss and grief, providing comfort, peace and strength for each day as well as courage to face the future. After the sorrow and intense memories of the losses had faded and we were able to receive them, he graced us with blessing upon blessings.

Yet, even while we were in the depths of our sorrow, we knew life does go on and God faithfully brings healing. We may never be completely the same as we were before the losses, but we can be restored to health and happiness. The most intense period of pain and grief passes in a few weeks, and after a few months we can begin to see hope for the future. As more time passes, we find ourselves enjoying life again, even though we still have times of sorrow. It may have taken seven years after Beth died before I could again feel the emotions I had felt before. As I write now, the feelings of loss are remote, but they are real and I will never forget the love that was ours in each of our three children. Today, life is truly full and meaningful for each of our family members. The scars have faded, but we can testify there was life in abundance then, and there is life abundant now, long after the deaths of our children. Let me share with you just a few of the ways we have been blessed through God's extravagant generosity.

Travel Blessings

Karen and I have always enjoyed getting out and doing things. We like to travel around the U.S. and when we can we even travel abroad. We enjoy visiting new and different places and mixing with people of different cultures. For many years after Beth died, Karen worked as a travel agent and at points in her career had a clientel that spread across the country. On a given day she might get calls from people in New York, Kentucky, Texas, Colorado and California as well as from her local clients. She viewed her work as a ministry because most of her work involved the Christian community and she always found the lowest fares and ways for her clients to travel. That means she didn't make much money. Even so she enjoyed helping people, even though the travel business itself can be very frustrating at times. Her work gave her a sense of accomplishment and it certainly kept her occupied. She didn't have time to sit around thinking about what might have been.

Some of our personal travel has been with groups we have helped organize, and some has just been alone or with friends. Most of our group tours have been church groups, usually choir tours to foreign mission fields where we are able to stay in the homes of local Christians. While we go there to minister to them, they usually minister to us in greater measure. Sometimes Karen and I are able to take off on a holiday and just enjoy being together, especially during the winter months when memories of our losses always come to mind. Karen is always on the watch for a bargain and is able on occasion to get special rates on cruises, hotels and cars. With my frequent flyer miles on the airlines, and Karen's ability to find good deals, the Lord has enabled us to do quite a bit of traveling without spending a lot of money.

God has given us some great experiences during our travels. Here is one small example of how the Lord sometimes blesses his children more than we could ever have the nerve to ask for. This is one of those "bonus blessings" that spices up our lives. A few years ago Karen found a special airline promotion where we could fly free to anywhere in Europe during the winter months using just a few frequent flyer credits on Northwest Airlines. Within a couple of weeks we were on our way with our friends, Darryl and Shirley Pursley. Since it was winter we flew to the southern-most destination of that airline, which happened to be Frankfurt, Germany. From Frankfurt we rented a car and headed south. After a quick tour of Switzerland and Italy, including three days in Rome, we headed back up to the Bavarian Alps.

There in beautiful Bavaria, we had an amazing experience that the richest man in the world could not buy at any price. We visited Neuschwaunstein Castle, the beautiful structure which Disneyland used as the model for their famous fairyland castle. We arrived in the vicinity after dark and found a Zimmer (German Bed and Breakfast) less than a mile from the castle. We awakened the next morning to a fairyland scene right out of a Disney fantasy. During the winter night a rare frost had coated all of the trees and hills. A glaze of ice covered the frost and when we opened our window and looked out, the bright morning sunlight made the whole world appear to be a field of sparkling diamonds.

Looking down over this breathtaking scene was the fairyland castle perched on the snow covered mountain opposite us, looking over its enchanted kingdom below. We were all breathless at the beautiful sight. The ice lasted late into the morning, giving us time to have breakfast, take pictures and then travel through the sparkling fairyland to the castle. To further enhance the experience, we played cassette tapes of rousing German folk music on the car tape player as we drove through this enchanted land. We couldn't stop praising God for his goodness to us.

The Lord blesses us a lot like that. I could tell dozens of stories of how he has amazed us with his bountiful provisions through our travel experiences. However, I will only summarize briefly a few of the highlights. Our favorite destination is Hawaii. We love everything about the Islands, including the weather, the scenery, the people, the music and the cultural variety. One of our favorite pastimes there is watching the sunsets. Every evening at 6:30 we join hundreds of other tourists and natives on the beach to watch the sun make its daily trip down past the distant clouds to its hiding place beneath the horizon. With the right mix of clouds the sunsets are spectacular displays of God's artistry. But even when the sun sets in a clear sky, there is something about watching the sun set over the ocean that gives perspective to God's careful organization of his creation.

We have watched sunsets from some of the most beautiful places in the world. We have watched from the top of Sugar Loaf Mountain as the lights of Rio de Janeiro came on below us. That breathtaking view competes with the view of the lights of Hong Kong and Kowloon that we have watched with fascination from the top of Victoria mountain. From the charming resort village of Lisan perched high in the mountains of Taiwan, we watched from above the cloud deck as the sun set into the clouds generating a kaleidoscope of colors. The scene reminded us of the sunrises viewed from above the clouds on Haleakala Crater on the island of Maui.

We are just average people, but we have experienced pleasures reserved for the privileged few. We participated in a gala high society wedding in Paraguay where we partook of the most fabulous food and entertainment in South America during a huge party on the lawn of an exclusive estate. Becky was along on that trip; she was a good friend of the groom whom we met on an earlier mission trip to Brazil when Becky was along. On another occasion, we were served a twelve course Chinese meal at the fabulous Grand Hotel in Taipei where we dined with astronauts, famous scientists and national leaders at a state dinner. We were entertained by Chinese opera, dancers, singers, jugglers and acrobats; the top Chinese entertainers in the nation.

We have sunned on the world famous beaches of Copa Cabana, Ipanema and Cabo Frio in Brazil and explored the wonders of magnificent Iguassu Falls in the interior of South America. After eating freshly caught salmon in a fishing village on the North Sea coast of Scotland, we listened to tales of the Loch Ness from an old fisherman who had seen strange things in the Loch. The night before we slept in a Scottish castle dating back to the seventh century and could almost feel the history around us. We have explored the catacombs in Rome and dined on top of the Eiffel Tower in Paris. We distributed Bibles to remote villagers along the Volga River in Russia after witnessing to soldiers in Red Square in Moscow. We marveled at a dozen glaciers flowing into the College Fjord in Alaska and compared the mountains with the Alps of Switzerland where we had viewed glaciers from atop the Schilthorn.

We enjoyed all of these experiences and many more, but the greatest travels have been those where the purpose of the travel was to do the work of ministry for the Lord and for His church. Together, Karen and I were able to help organize and lead groups on mission tours to Scotland, South America, and most recently, to England. Our first mission trip was in 1983, two years after Beth died. We began by going alone with Darryl and Shirley to urban and remote village churches in Brazil where we conducted worship services. I spoke about God's provision through our difficulties (with the help of an interpreter) and Darryl sang. Our wives also sang and played and gave testimonies. In 1985 we took 45 people, including Becky, on a choir tour of Scotland.

I was able to visit Ella Ruth Hutson again in Taiwan, and this time Karen and the Pursleys were along. Ella Ruth told her congregation that she had received only two visitors from the United States during her forty years on the field, and I was both of them. We were able to speak in some of the churches and join the Chinese worshipers in a unique Easter sunrise service.

Taiwan had matured as an independent nation by time of my second visit. We visited the national shrine to Chang Kai Chek in Taipei and the National Museum of Chinese Treasures. The Communist Chinese regime in Peking takes the position that those treasures were stolen from the mainland when Chang and his armies fled to Taiwan in 1949. The tensions between Taiwan and China are still very evident. The mainland Chinese continue to maintain that Taiwan is the property of China and still intend to reclaim it eventually. Stay tuned to your news on this subject.

During our visit this time, we were there when Ella Ruth needed someone to support her. During our visit, she received a letter from her mission board saying she was being retired and they were bringing her home. It was totally unexpected and a severe shock to her. We were able to console her and help her begin working her way through the adjustment. After everything she had meant to us, I was glad we could be there to help her, even in a small way.

Ella Ruth did retire without enthusiasm, but God's grace was sufficient for her too. She returned to her denominational headquarters in Ohio and after serving there where she could, she finally was forced by health concerns to enter the Friends Assisted Living facility where she now lives.

Karen and I returned to the United Kingdom in 1994. We took 40 members of the Fee Fee Baptist Church choir on a tour of several churches in England. The highlight of the tour was our concert at the Anglican church in Moreton where our daughter Becky and her husband Paul were on staff. Paul coordinated our visit there and we had a warm crowd and a great concert.

Christian Radio

"From the rising of the sun to the going down of the same, the name of the Lord is to be praised." Psalm 113:3

Another way God has allowed us to be a part of his kingdom's work is through the ministry of Christian radio. In 1976 we had the opportunity to join a group of four men who wanted to purchase a country western radio station in Wichita, Kansas for the purpose of making it a full time Christian station. I had always been a fan of Christian radio and we felt somehow God was preparing us for something special when this opportunity arose. We scraped together every penny we had and borrowed beyond our limit to join the group. Several months later KSGL was on the air, "Sharing God's Love with South Central Kansas." Now, decades later, Karen and I, along with her family, own and operate the station on our own.

KSGL played an important role in the much publicized 1991 abortion protests in Wichita known as the "Summer of Mercy." Local churches and ministers planned an extensive series of protests against the infamous abortion clinics in Wichita, which are the most notorious in the nation. A national organization known as Operation Rescue came to town to lead the protests during that summer. Our station was on national network news when Keith Tucci, one of the leaders of the protest movement, was arrested while at our control console broadcasting his program. The FBI came in, handcuffed Keith, and took him off to jail while national TV and newspaper reporters filmed the entire event. KSGL was a pivotal force in mobilizing Wichita to action during those important protests. We were gratified God chose to use the station for that service. Dick Bott, owner of a network of Christian stations in the Midwest, came to Wichita and joined forces with us to get the live broadcasts from the abortion scenes broadcast to other stations across the country.

Karen's brother, Terry Atherton is general manager of KSGL, and in 1992 he and his wife Hazel were invited by Broadcaster Rob Linstead to be guests of his broadcast team on a mission trip to Russia. Karen and I somehow managed to join the tour (at our own expense, but with the Lord's provision) which included time in Moscow and St. Petersburg, plus five exciting days on a river cruise on the Volga between the two cities. Over 300 committed Christians took over the entire cruise ship for the purpose of distributing over two million Bibles and tracts, along with food and medicine to this formerly atheistic country, now released from communism.

I will never forget the experience of seeing spiritually starved people reaching and pleading for Bibles. Those people were desparately grabbing up the Bibles as if they were precious stones. I will especially remember one grandmotherly woman pleading for a

Bible with tears in her eyes as the doors of our bus closed in her face as the bus pulled away. We had to leave quickly because the crowds had become unsafe and were rocking the bus demanding more Bibles. The contrast with the United States made me wonder what our country has come to when we can't give a Bible away on the streets of our cities because of indifference and even hostility to the Word and work of God.

Conclusion

I am retired now, but while I was working God was just as busy guiding and directing my paths at work as He was in my private life. My career was enjoyable and fulfilling from my first job out in California, right up to the present. I don't know if most people would agree that a person can be "called" to a secular job, but as far as I am concerned, God prepared me mentally, emotionally and spiritually for my vocation. My job in the aerospace industry was as glamorous and exciting as any job could be. After my job in the nuclear business in California, I spent about 15 years working in the field of atmospheric electricity (lightning), building up the most extensive lightning test facility in the aerospace industry and lecturing around the world about the effects of lightning on aircraft. Later I worked on the space side of the company, designing and loading experiments aboard the space schuttle at the Cape. One of the most interesting projects was working with NASA and biochemists to develop equipment and experiments for use on the Space Station, some of which are still in progress now, long after I have retired. It is a very great blessing to be so happy in your job. It has only happened because God was faithfully leading me even before I had a clue as to what my life's profession should be.

So, in every area God has blessed us wonderfully and has given us lives full of joy, happiness and meaning. I'll say it again, I wouldn't have the audacity to ask God for all of the wonderful blessings he has poured out upon us. He has proven to us indeed, "Joy comes in the morning." As my preacher son in law Paul says, it is God's nature to be generous. And, as it says in Ephesians 1:8, God loves to lavishes his spiritual gifts on his children. His generosity is indeed extravagant. He has proven that to us. God is good. So very, very good.

While all of these amazing blessings have been gratefully received, the greatest and most meaningful blessings are still those of our faith and our family. If you were to ask if we would trade all of the recent blessings we have had for the children we lost, our answer would be, "Yes, of course ....in a heartbeat." The wonder and excitement of external blessings cannot replace the love of family. The very thought of having all of our children with us now is far more attractive than any imaginable fantasy trip or any amount of material blessings. We can only dream about what might have been if Mike, Rachel and Beth had all grown up and had normal lives. How many grandchildren would we have by now if they were here? What would they have become? We can only wonder, but then we remind ourselves that God has chosen a different way, and it is best because it is of him.

Now, God just keeps on blessing us. We don't feel guilty about receiving God's blessings; we're just grateful to him for being so good. I guess you could say we feel perhaps we have paid our dues. We know God is in control of our lives, and just as we accepted the painful events as God's will, so also we accept the blessings as his will. We are humbled by the abundance of blessings, and we seek to remain faithful to him in every thing we do, every day we live. The Lord keeps us very busy with our children and grandchildren, as well as with our churches, our work, our travel, and with our other ministries. We want always to maintain our love relationship with God, and be faithful to follow, wherever he leads.

Our 23rd Psalm

"He restoreth our souls" Psalms 23:4 (KJV)

As I conclude the story of our journey and the lessons we have learned, I want to emphasize one more time how God carried us through it all, but in the context of the 23rd Psalm.

God has been our constant shepherd. We have never lacked for anything we needed. He has led us beside the peaceful still waters and made us to lie down in green pastures of comfort and security. Now he has restored our souls, beautifully and completely. He has led us in the paths of righteousness so we might be in a position to glorify him. He led us three times on our missions through the valley of the shadow of death. We have never feared the evil one, however, for God has always been with us. He has comforted us with his rod of strength and his staff of peace. He has annointed us with holy blessings and our cup of happiness has truly overflowed. Surely, the goodness and mercy of God shall see us through until we dwell with all of our family in the house of the Lord forever.

We long for that day when our children welcome us home and we are a complete family again. As they usher us into the presence of our beautiful Savior, we will be able to worship the Lord together and thank him face to face for all he has given us and for all he has done in our lives. I hope we will see you there too.

What a day, glorious day, that will be. Come quickly Lord Jesus. Amen

THE BENEDICTION

"He will swallow up death in victory; and the Lord God will wipe away tears from all faces." Isaiah 25:8

"Now to him who is able to do immeasurably more than all we ask or imagine, according to his power that is at work within us, to him be glory in the church and in Christ Jesus throughout all generations, for ever and ever! Amen." Ephesians 3:20-21

REFERENCES

1. *My Grace Is Sufficient For Thee* by James E. Clifford, Published by Christian Music Service, Shawnee, Kansas 66218
2. *Trust His Heart,* by Eddie Carswell and Babbie Mason, in the Christmas Musical "From Heaven's Throne," arranged and orchestrated by David T. Clydesdale, created by David T. Clydesdale and Steve Amerson. Distributed by Word Inc.
3. *The Anthropic Cosmological Principle* by John D. Barrow and Frank J. Tipler; Oxford University Press, 1988
4. *The Case for A Creator* by Lee Strobel; Zondervan Copywright 2004
5. *The Universe: Past and Present Reflections,* By Fred Hoyle" in *Annual Review of Astronomy and Astrophysics. 20.* (1982), p. 16.
6. *God and the New Physics* by Paul Davies, Simon and Schuster, Copyright 1983
7. *C.S. Lewis Through the Shadowlands,* by Brian Sibley, Revell Publishers, January 1994
8. *I Will Not Leave You Desolate"* by Martha Whitmore Hickman, Abingdon Press, May 1994
9. *The Problem Of Pain,* by C. S. Lewis, The Centenary Press, London 1940
10. *Through Gates of Splendor,* by Elizabeth Elliot, Tyndale House Publishers, 25th Anniversary Edition, August 2005
11. *The Christians Secret of a Happy Life,* by Hannah Whitehall Smith. A Spire Book, published by Pyramid Publications for the Fleming H. Revell Company, Old Tuppan, New Jersey
12. *Rees Howells, Intecessor,* by Norman Grubb, Lutterworth Press, Guildford and London

13. *When Peace Like a River Attendeth My Way*; article from *Companion To The Baptist Hymnal*, by William J. Reynolds. Broadman Press, Copyright 1976
14. *Our Jerusalem* by Bertha Spafford Vester, Doubleday Press, 1950
15. *Heaven* by Randy Alcorn, Tyndale House Publishers, Carol Stream, Illinois, Copywright 2004

AUTHOR'S BIOGRAPHY

The author, Don Clifford, was at the helm while his family went through the experiences described in this book. Don authored this book, but only with extensive encouragement and support from his wife and two daughters. Mr. Clifford has written extensively in the technical arena, having published over 42 technical papers and journal articles while working as an aerospace engineer and executive in St. Louis. As a lifelong Christian and teacher, he spent 45 years leading Bible studies, including seminary level courses on the origin of the Scriptures, Biblical research and Missions. Mr. Clifford is also the president of Agape Communications, Inc., which operates Christian Radio Station KSGL in Wichita Kansas. Don lives with his wife Karen in St. Charles, Missouri where they are currently involved in planting new churches and enjoying their retirement. Their two surviving daughters, Vicki and Becky are both married to strong Christian leaders and have given Karen and Don six grandchildren. Don and Karen together have coauthored a companion book entitled Heavenly Grief, A Christian Guide to Spiritual and Emotional Healing. We would love to hear from you if this book has touched you or helped you in anyway. Our e-mail address is d.Clifford@sbcglobal.net.

CPSIA information can be obtained at www.ICGtesting.com
Printed in the USA
LVOW07s0010171115

462800LV00001B/185/P